From Babel to AI

From Babel to AI

Idolatry, Transhumanism,
and the Crisis of *Imago Dei*

DAWN LEWIS SUTHERLAND

WIPF & STOCK · Eugene, Oregon

FROM BABEL TO AI
Idolatry, Transhumanism, and the Crisis of *Imago Dei*

Copyright © 2025 Dawn Lewis Sutherland. All rights reserved. Except for brief quotations in critical publications or reviews, no part of this book may be reproduced in any manner without prior written permission from the publisher. Write: Permissions, Wipf and Stock Publishers, 199 W. 8th Ave., Suite 3, Eugene, OR 97401.

Wipf & Stock
An Imprint of Wipf and Stock Publishers
199 W. 8th Ave., Suite 3
Eugene, OR 97401

www.wipfandstock.com

PAPERBACK ISBN: 979-8-3852-4180-4
HARDCOVER ISBN: 979-8-3852-4181-1
EBOOK ISBN: 979-8-3852-4182-8

Permissions for any included excerpts, illustrations, or third-party material have been obtained and are cited where applicable.

All Scripture references are from the New Revised Standard Version, Updated Edition (NRSVUE) unless otherwise noted. Copyright © 2021 National Council of Churches of Christ in the United States of America. Used by permission. All rights reserved worldwide.

To my husband, whose steadfast love and encouragement have been my anchor, and to my family, whose unwavering support has carried me through life's challenges and lifted me in its joys. Your love has been my rock in difficult times, and a gentle breeze, lifting my heart like a feather on God's grace, through life's happiest moments. This work stands as a testament to your sacrifices, patience, and unshakable belief in me. I am endlessly blessed with an incredible husband and the most extraordinary, epic kids.

To Louis, Katie, Ronnie, Selah, and Samuel

In every human face, the image of God resides—a sacred reflection of divine creativity, purpose, and worth. No technology, no ambition, no failure can erase this truth.

Contents

CHAPTER 1: *Why Theology?* | 1

    Theological Frameworks and Scholarly Precedent | 2
    Historical Development of the *Imago Dei* | 5
    Transhumanism's Quest for Immortality | 8
    Ancient Philosophy and Theological Critique | 11
    Moral Agency and Autonomy | 14
    Reflections on Identity and Continuity | 17
    Salvation vs. Technological Enhancement | 21
    Transhumanist Eschatology | 24
    Conclusion: Theology as a Framework | 27
    Case Study #1: Opacity in Healthcare Decision-Making | 29
    Case Study #2: Predictive Policing | 32

CHAPTER 2: *The Imago Dei and the Crisis of Human Identity* | 34

    Exegesis of Genesis 1:26–27 | 35
    Patristic and Medieval Understandings | 46
    Reformation and Modern Interpretations | 49
    The Restorative Aspect of the *Imago Dei* | 54
    Conclusion: The *Imago Dei* and Human Identity | 60
    Case Study #3: Human Enhancement | 61
    Case Study #4: End-of-Life Healthcare Decision-Making | 63

CHAPTER 3: *Idolatry and Technology: Gods of Our Own Making* | 66

    The Biblical Critique of Idolatry | 67
    Anthropomorphizing the Divine | 87
    Conclusion: AI and Theological Boundaries | 92

viii CONTENTS

    Case Study #5: Digital Immortality | 92
    Case Study #6: Employment Discrimination | 95

CHAPTER 4: *Human Hubris and Divine Boundaries* | 97
    Exegesis of Genesis 11:1–9 | 98
    Wisdom of the Crowd and AI | 104
    AI as a New Language and New Tower | 107
    Boundaries for Technological Progress | 113
    Conclusion: Babel, Technology, and the Perils of Hubris | 115
    Case Study #7: An AI-Integrated Smart City | 116
    Case Study #8: Gene Editing | 118

CHAPTER 5: *AI and the New Idolatry* | 121
    AI as Modern Idolatry | 122
    AI as a "New God" | 123
    From Graven Images to Algorithms | 124
    Defining Idolatry in the Context of AI and Biotechnology | 133
    AI's Challenge to the *Imago Dei* | 138
    Ethical and Spiritual Dangers: AI as a Tool of Control | 144
    Practical Responses | 148
    Conclusion: Preserving Human Dignity | 153
    Case Study #9: AI-Driven Worship | 153
    Case Study #10: AI-Generated Organoids | 156

CHAPTER 6: *Transhumanism and the Quest for Immortality* | 159
    Transhumanism as a Modern Movement | 160
    Overcoming Mortality Through Technology | 166
    Death and Immortality in Antiquity | 172
    Christian Theology: Death and Resurrection | 176
    Technological Salvation? | 184
    Conclusion: Transhumanist Salvation vs. Christian Hope | 188
    Case Study #11: Transhumanist Immortality | 189
    Case Study #12: Cybernetic Super Soldiers | 192

CHAPTER 7: *Salvation, Grace, and the Limits of Technology* | 195
    Divine Grace: A Theological Foundation | 198
    Redemption Through Christ | 206
    Human Limitation and Divine Grace | 213
    The Limits of Technology: A Theological Critique | 217
    Grace, Redemption, and Resurrection | 220
    Conclusion: Salvation Beyond the Singularity | 226
    Case Study #13: AI-Augmented Afterlife Experiences | 227
    Case Study #14: Global Governance | 229

CHAPTER 8: *The Future of Humanity* | 232
    Reclaiming the *Imago Dei* | 232
    Ethical Engagement with Technology | 233
    Reimagining Human Flourishing | 234
    Conclusion: A Call to Action | 235

A Prayer for Readers | 237
Bibliography | 239

CHAPTER 1

Why Theology?

As artificial intelligence (AI) and transhumanism continue to reshape human society, fundamental questions about human identity, purpose, and destiny are increasingly urgent. While these technological advancements offer immense potential, they also pose profound ethical and theological dilemmas that challenge the very core of Christian anthropology—particularly the doctrine of the *imago Dei*. This ancient belief, rooted in Scripture, holds that humanity is created in the image of God, endowed with intrinsic dignity, relationality, and moral agency. However, as AI and transhumanism promise to transcend human limitations—through cognitive enhancement, artificial immortality, and the creation of autonomous entities—these movements introduce a modern form of idolatry. They risk distorting the *imago Dei* by prioritizing autonomy, self-deification, and mastery over human frailty.

In contrast, this book asserts that the restoration of the *imago Dei*, fully realized in the deity and humanity of Jesus Christ, provides the key to understanding true human flourishing. Christ, as 100 percent divine and 100 percent human, exemplifies the perfection of the *imago Dei*—both in his divine nature and in his relational, embodied existence. Through his redemptive work, humanity's fractured relationship with God is restored, offering a path to eternal life that no technological innovation can replicate.

This book argues that the doctrine of the *imago Dei*, fully restored and perfected in Jesus Christ, provides the theological foundation for addressing the ethical and spiritual challenges posed by AI and transhumanism. As humanity seeks technological transcendence, it risks distorting its divine identity and repeating the ancient errors of idolatry and self-deification. The restoration of the *imago Dei* through Christ offers a counternarrative to these technological aspirations, calling believers to reclaim their true identity as bearers of God's image. This theological framework not only critiques the ethical overreach of AI and transhumanism but offers a hopeful vision for how humanity can engage with technology without losing sight of divine purpose and identity.

Drawing on theological anthropology, biblical exegesis, and ethical reflection, this book invites readers to navigate the challenges of AI and transhumanism by rooting their understanding of humanity in the redemptive work of Christ. Just as the Tower of Babel represents the ultimate hubris of human self-deification, modern AI-driven ambitions mirror this desire to transcend divinely ordained boundaries. However, through the work of Jesus Christ, humanity is called to rediscover its purpose and dignity, not through technological mastery but through grace and communion with the Creator.

The pages that follow present a detailed examination of how AI and transhumanism confront the very essence of what it means to be human. Yet it is within this confrontation that theology offers the most profound response, one that points back to the image of God, restored through Christ, as the true foundation for human dignity and flourishing in an increasingly technological world. This examination is not made in isolation but is deeply informed by a rich tradition of theological and ethical scholarship, which has long wrestled with the implications of human identity in relation to technology and divine purpose.

THEOLOGICAL FRAMEWORKS AND SCHOLARLY PRECEDENT

There is a robust scholarly precedent for using a theological framework to engage these issues. Noreen Herzfeld, in *In Our Image: Artificial Intelligence and the Human Spirit*, argues that the doctrine of the *imago Dei* is critical for assessing the ethical boundaries of AI and its attempt to replicate human characteristics.[1] Herzfeld's approach underscores that AI cannot fully reflect the divine image imprinted upon humanity, as technology lacks the moral and relational dimensions of the human soul, which are essential to the *imago Dei*. Herzfeld's work is part of a broader

---

1. Noreen Herzfeld, *In Our Image: Artificial Intelligence and the Human Spirit* (Minneapolis: Fortress, 2002), 23–46.

conversation about how morality is inherently tied to theology, a view shared by theologians like Alasdair MacIntyre and Stanley Hauerwas who assert that moral values cannot be separated from their theological roots.[2] This aligns with the concept that technology, by operating outside a divinely informed ethical framework, risks becoming a tool for idolatry and dehumanization.

Similarly, Brent Waters, in *From Human to Posthuman*, argues that Christian theology offers a counternarrative to the transhumanist pursuit of overcoming human limitations.[3] Waters emphasizes that theological anthropology and eschatology provide a robust framework for understanding human destiny, one that is incompatible with the transhumanist vision of technological salvation. Waters's critique is grounded in the idea that Christian theology maintains a distinction between God's sovereignty over life and death and human attempts to control or transcend these boundaries through technology. His work echoes themes found in Reinhold Niebuhr's *Moral Man and Immoral Society*, where Niebuhr warns of human overreach and the dangers of equating technological progress with moral progress.[4] For Waters and Niebuhr, the transhumanist promise of immortality is not just a misguided pursuit but a moral misstep that denies the reality of human finitude and the necessity of divine grace.

In contrast to transhumanism's emphasis on autonomy and individual enhancement, Christian theology centers on relationality as an essential element of human identity. Theological anthropology, particularly the doctrine of the *imago Dei*, holds that human identity is not self-constructed but divinely bestowed, reflecting God's nature and sovereignty. This concept is foundational to understanding human dignity and relationality, affirming that humanity's worth is intrinsic, not conditional upon ability or achievement. Dietrich Bonhoeffer's work further highlights the importance of relationality, emphasizing that the true nature of the human person is found not in isolation but in community, where individuals reflect the *imago Dei* by existing for others.[5] Bonhoef-

---

2. Alasdair MacIntyre, *After Virtue: A Study in Moral Theory*, 3rd ed. (Notre Dame: University of Notre Dame Press, 2007); Stanley Hauerwas, *The Peaceable Kingdom: A Primer in Christian Ethics* (Notre Dame: University of Notre Dame Press, 1983).

3. Brent Waters, *From Human to Posthuman: Christian Theology and Technology in a Postmodern World* (Burlington, VT: Ashgate, 2006), 89–110.

4. Reinhold Niebuhr, *Moral Man and Immoral Society* (New York: Scribner's Sons, 1932), 34–58.

5. Dietrich Bonhoeffer, *Ethics*, trans. Neville Horton Smith (New York: Simon and Schuster, 1995), 246.

fer critiques the isolating tendencies of technological advancements, which often promote individualism over the communal aspects of human existence. For Bonhoeffer, the church plays a critical role in resisting these isolating effects by fostering technology that promotes community-centered relationality rather than cognitive isolation.

John Kilner asserts that the *imago Dei* provides a basis for ethical decision-making, grounding it in humanity's reflection of divine goodness and justice.[6] Kilner's argument is strengthened by the broader theological tradition that connects morality to divine command theory, where moral obligations are grounded in the commands of a good and just God. This framework rejects the notion that moral values can be arbitrarily redefined by human or technological developments, maintaining that moral truths are immutable because they reflect God's unchanging nature.

Jürgen Moltmann, in *The Ethics of Hope*, similarly emphasizes that true human flourishing is found in relationality—both with God and with others.[7] Moltmann warns of the dehumanizing effects of technological systems that prioritize efficiency and autonomy over moral responsibility and human connection. For Moltmann, the relational aspect of the *imago Dei* must be preserved, and the church must stand against technologies that isolate individuals from their communities. In his view, AI and transhumanism pose a significant threat to this relational foundation by encouraging self-reliance and cognitive enhancement over the deeper human need for relationship and interdependence.[8]

Stanley Grenz builds on this by emphasizing that morality flows from humanity's relationship with God, affirming that humans are not merely autonomous agents but reflectors of God's moral nature.[9] This relational understanding of morality draws from Karl Barth's theological ethics, particularly in his rejection of human-centered ethics in favor of a God-centered approach.[10] For Barth and Grenz, true morality is discovered only in relationship with God, and any attempt to define good

---

6. John F. Kilner, *Dignity and Destiny: Humanity in the Image of God* (Grand Rapids: Eerdmans, 2015), 35–58.

7. Jürgen Moltmann, *The Ethics of Hope*, trans. Margaret Kohl (Minneapolis: Fortress, 2012).

8. Moltmann, *Ethics of Hope*.

9. Stanley J. Grenz, *The Social God and the Relational Self: A Trinitarian Theology of the* Imago Dei, Matrix of Christian Theology (Louisville: Westminster John Knox, 2001), 145–64.

10. Karl Barth, *Church Dogmatics*, vol. 3/4, *The Doctrine of Creation*, ed. G. W. Bromiley and T. F. Torrance, trans. A. T. Mackay et al. (Edinburgh: T&T Clark, 1961).

and evil outside of this divine relationship leads to ethical relativism, a danger present in the unbounded promises of AI and transhumanism. By maintaining a focus on relationality, these theologians highlight a key contrast with transhumanist ideals, which prioritize cognitive autonomy and technological enhancement at the expense of community and divine dependence. These theological frameworks are indispensable for addressing the complex ethical dilemmas posed by AI and transhumanism, especially as these technologies begin to blur the lines between human agency, moral responsibility, and divine sovereignty.

HISTORICAL DEVELOPMENT OF THE *IMAGO DEI*

The historical development of the *imago Dei* doctrine further illuminates its relevance to the contemporary debate, particularly when viewed through the lens of the *exitus-reditus* framework, a philosophical and theological concept rooted in Plotinian cosmology and later adopted by Augustine.[11] This framework describes human existence as an exit from the divine source (*exitus*) and a return to it (*reditus*), underscoring that humanity's identity is not self-constructed but a reflection of its divine origin, with the ultimate purpose of returning to that divine source.[12] In simpler terms, Augustine viewed human identity as a reflection of God's nature, with our ultimate goal being to return to God. Augustine's theology of the *imago Dei* was shaped by this framework, portraying human identity as derived from and oriented toward God.[13] In fact, Augustine proposed that human identity is a reflection of God and the divine plan, which exists in a participatory union with its source. In essence, Augustine taught that humanity's divine image represents not just a reflection of God but a participation in God's plan, where humans are called to live

---

11. *Exitus-reditus* refers to a process of departing from and returning to God, representing humanity's orientation toward the divine in Augustine's theology. Augustine, *The City of God*, trans. Henry Bettenson (London: Penguin, 1972), XII.4.

12. Dawn Lewis Sutherland, "God's Narrative of Redemption: Creation, *Imago Dei*, and Water Imagery" (PhD diss., Liberty University, Apr. 2024), 120, https://digitalcommons.liberty.edu/doctoral/5352/.

13. Augustine's understanding of the *imago Dei* has been foundational to Christian anthropology. Despite critiques of his views on original sin, particularly his pessimism regarding human nature post-fall, Augustine's participatory framework of the *imago Dei* as reflecting God's rationality and relationality remains influential. See Gerald Bonner, *St. Augustine of Hippo: Life and Controversies* (Norfolk, UK: Canterbury, 1986), 102–5.

in alignment with their divine source. This idea of the return to divine identity is a central theme that echoes throughout theological history.[14]

Thomas Aquinas emphasized that humans participate in God's nature through intellect and will, but fundamentally, he argued that our purpose is to reflect God's moral and rational nature.[15] For Aquinas, human beings participate in this return through their moral and intellectual faculties, emphasizing that the *imago Dei* encompasses more than mere cognitive abilities.[16] John Calvin added another dimension to this framework by emphasizing that the *imago Dei* reflects humanity's relational capacity to commune with God through faith and obedience.[17] These varied perspectives highlight the comprehensive nature of the divine image in humanity, which includes relationality, moral agency, and rationality.[18]

Through the *exitus-reditus* framework, the doctrine of the *imago Dei* not only presents humanity as a reflection of God but also as intrinsically oriented toward a return to divine likeness. In contrast, transhumanism, with its focus on enhancing autonomy and intelligence through AI, represents a distortion of this return. Herzfeld, in her analysis of AI, points out that technology lacks the moral and relational dimensions necessary to reflect the divine image.[19] Similarly, Waters critiques the transhumanist project, arguing that it undermines theological anthropology by substituting human autonomy for divine grace.[20] In this sense, AI and transhumanism echo the ancient practice of idolatry, in which humanity places its trust in created entities rather than the Creator.

Grenz and Kilner contribute to this critique by emphasizing that the *imago Dei* is not reducible to intelligence or functionality; rather, it encompasses moral agency and relationality. Human beings, as reflections

14. Sutherland, "God's Narrative of Redemption," 121.

15. Aquinas's synthesis of Aristotelian philosophy with Christian doctrine, particularly his views on reason and moral agency as central to the *imago Dei*, has shaped theological discourse for centuries. While some critics find his reliance on natural law too rigid, Aquinas's contributions to the understanding of human participation in the divine order remain significant. See Jean-Pierre Torrell, *Aquinas's Summa: Background, Structure, and Reception* (Washington, DC: Catholic University of America Press, 2005), 112–14.

16. Thomas Aquinas, *Summa Theologiae*, trans. Fathers of the English Dominican Province (New York: Benziger Brothers, 1947), I.93.4.

17. John Calvin, *Institutes of the Christian Religion*, trans. Ford Lewis Battles (Philadelphia: Westminster, 1960), 1.15.1.

18. Sutherland, "God's Narrative of Redemption," 135.

19. Herzfeld, *In Our Image*, 23–46.

20. Waters, *From Human to Posthuman*, 89–110.

of divine goodness, have a moral responsibility to reflect God's justice and ethical order.[21] The pursuit of transcendence through AI and technology, without consideration of these relational and moral dimensions, risks turning technology into a modern form of idolatry. This aligns with Alasdair MacIntyre's critique of moral fragmentation and Reinhold Niebuhr's warnings about human hubris.[22] By focusing on individual enhancement and autonomy, transhumanism distorts the true purpose of human identity, which is to reflect and return to the divine.[23]

The *exitus-reditus* framework becomes crucial in evaluating these technologies through a theological lens. It reminds us that true transcendence is not achieved through human autonomy or technological advancements but through a return to the divine origin.[24] Robert Adams notes that moral obligations are grounded in divine goodness, emphasizing that moral truths are immutable because they are reflections of God's nature.[25] As theologians and ethicists engage with the ethical challenges posed by AI and transhumanism, the *imago Dei* doctrine offers a rich theological framework that affirms human dignity, relationality, and moral responsibility.[26]

In light of these historical perspectives, transhumanism's effort to enhance human intelligence and autonomy through AI falls short of capturing the full essence of the *imago Dei*. This pursuit of autonomy and cognitive enhancement distorts the relational and ethical dimensions of human existence that are intrinsic to the divine image. By attempting to transcend human limitations through technology, transhumanism not only neglects these essential aspects of humanity but also risks redefining human identity in ways that sever the relational bond with the Creator.[27] As Richard Lints suggests, the divine image is intricately connected to worship and honor—humans are called to honor God through their moral and relational existence.[28] Any technological effort that seeks to

---

21. Grenz, *Social God and the Relational Self*, 145–64; Kilner, *Dignity and Destiny*, 35–58.

22. MacIntyre, *After Virtue*, 69–75; Niebuhr, *Moral Man and Immoral Society*, 34–58.

23. Sutherland, "God's Narrative of Redemption," 135.

24. Augustine, *City of God*, trans. Bettenson, XI.28.

25. Robert M. Adams, *Finite and Infinite Goods: A Framework for Ethics* (New York: Oxford University Press, 1999), 23–40.

26. Adams, *Finite and Infinite Goods*, 23–40.

27. Sutherland, "God's Narrative of Redemption," 140.

28. Richard Lints, *Identity and Idolatry: The Image of God and Its Inversion* (Downers

replace or redefine this relationship with autonomy is fundamentally idolatrous.[29]

The doctrine's historical evolution also connects the *imago Dei* to notions of moral responsibility. If human beings are created in the image of God, then their moral agency must reflect divine justice, goodness, and relationality. The pursuit of technological transcendence, which often focuses on autonomy and individual enhancement, may neglect or distort these relational and moral dimensions. As AI and transhumanism challenge traditional notions of human identity and morality, theologians are increasingly drawing on this rich tradition to respond to the ethical challenges of the digital age.[30]

TRANSHUMANISM'S QUEST FOR IMMORTALITY

Transhumanism's quest for immortality brings profound ethical implications into sharp focus, particularly as it engages with the doctrine of the *imago Dei* and the foundational theological view of human finitude. The transhumanist vision, which seeks to transcend death through technologies like consciousness uploading or genetic enhancement, is not merely a scientific ambition but a philosophical and existential challenge to deeply held theological concepts. Central to transhumanist thought is the belief that death is a technical problem, one to be solved through human ingenuity and innovation. Yet this framing stands in direct opposition to the Christian understanding of death, which is seen as an inevitable part of the human condition—one that is bound to the broader narrative of sin, redemption, and divine sovereignty.

In theological terms, death is not an obstacle to be overcome through human effort but a marker of human finitude, serving as a reminder of humanity's dependence on God. As Waters articulates, Christian eschatology offers a radically different perspective on immortality, one that is grounded not in the pursuit of human enhancement but in the promise of divine grace. According to Christian doctrine, the hope for eternal life is not something to be grasped through technological innovation but a gift bestowed through the death and resurrection of Christ.[31] Waters

---

Grove, IL: InterVarsity, 2015), 79–83.

29. Lints, *Identity and Idolatry*, 85.

30. Sutherland, "God's Narrative of Redemption," 150.

31. Waters, *From Human to Posthuman*, 98.

underscores that salvation, as envisioned in Christian theology, cannot be reduced to human efforts to transcend the physical body; rather, it is a spiritual transformation that occurs through God's redemptive work. This theological tension with transhumanism raises ethical questions not just about the nature of life and death but about the limits of human agency in the face of divine sovereignty.

The transhumanist pursuit of immortality is inherently problematic because it assumes that human beings can achieve a god-like control over life and death. Technologies such as CRISPR[32] and AI offer pathways to modify the human genome or extend life indefinitely, yet these advancements carry significant ethical risks. From a theological standpoint, the attempt to circumvent death through technological means bypasses the spiritual and moral significance of mortality as understood in Christian doctrine. Irenaeus of Lyons, for example, emphasized that true human perfection is not achieved through escaping bodily limitations but through the transformative power of Christ's resurrection.[33] In Irenaeus's view, human beings are not meant to transcend their nature but to be restored and perfected through divine grace.

Furthermore, the ethical concerns surrounding transhumanism's vision of immortality extend to questions of human nature and identity. Kilner argues that attempts to alter or enhance the human body through genetic modification or consciousness uploading risk undermining the intrinsic value of human beings as bearers of the *imago Dei*. Kilner points out that human dignity is not conditional upon physical or cognitive abilities but is inherent in humanity's creation in God's image.[34] Therefore,

---

32. CRISPR, which stands for Clustered Regularly Interspaced Short Palindromic Repeats, is a revolutionary gene-editing technology that allows scientists to precisely modify DNA sequences within living organisms. Originally discovered as a bacterial defense mechanism against viruses, CRISPR technology utilizes the Cas9 protein to target and cut specific DNA strands, enabling genetic modifications. This technology has opened unprecedented possibilities for treating genetic disorders, enhancing human capabilities, and even extending lifespan. However, its potential for germline editing—altering genes that can be inherited by future generations—raises significant ethical concerns regarding human identity, moral responsibility, and the manipulation of life itself. For further discussion, see Arthur L. Caplan, "No Time to Waste—The Ethical Challenges Created by CRISPR," *EMBO Reports* 17:10 (2016) 1401–6; Françoise Baylis, *Altered Inheritance: CRISPR and the Ethics of Human Genome Editing* (Cambridge, MA: Harvard University Press, 2019); and S. Matthew Liao, "Designing Humans: A Human Rights Approach," *Bioethics* 33:1 (2019) 98–104.

33. Irenaeus, *Against Heresies*, trans. Alexander Roberts and William Rambaut (Edinburgh: T&T Clark, 1868), 5.2.1.

34. Kilner, *Dignity and Destiny*, 50.

efforts to modify or "improve" the human body for the sake of achieving immortality can distort the theological understanding of human worth.

In addition to the theological critique, secular scholars have also raised concerns about the ethical implications of transhumanism, particularly with regard to the consequences of human enhancement technologies. Nick Bostrom, one of the leading proponents of transhumanism, acknowledges that the quest for immortality raises difficult ethical questions. Bostrom argues that while the pursuit of life extension and human enhancement can offer potential benefits, it also risks creating new forms of inequality and exacerbating existing social divisions.[35] The prospect of immortality, if only available to a select few, could lead to unprecedented social and ethical dilemmas, including issues of access, justice, and the meaning of life itself. Julian Savulescu, another secular ethicist, adds that the moral permissibility of life extension technologies must be weighed against the potential for harm, particularly when considering the environmental, economic, and societal impacts of a dramatically extended human lifespan.[36]

The ethical debate over transhumanism's quest for immortality is thus multifaceted. On the one hand, transhumanism offers an appealing narrative of progress and liberation from the constraints of human biology. On the other hand, both theological and secular scholars highlight the potential dangers of this vision, which may undermine the fundamental understanding of what it means to be human. From a theological perspective, transhumanism's rejection of death as a meaningful part of the human experience denies the transformative power of suffering and redemption as articulated in the Christian tradition. As Reinhold Niebuhr once remarked, "Man's capacity for justice makes democracy

---

35. Nick Bostrom, "Transhumanist Values," in *Ethical Issues for the Twenty-First Century*, ed. Frederick Adams (Charlottesville, VA: Philosophy Documentation Center, 2005), 3–14. Bostrom argues that while the pursuit of life extension and human enhancement can offer potential benefits, it also risks creating new forms of inequality and exacerbating existing social divisions. He emphasizes that these advancements may disproportionately benefit the wealthy, leading to increased social stratification and ethical dilemmas regarding access and justice.

36. Julian Savulescu, "Procreative Beneficence: Why We Should Select the Best Children," *Bioethics* 15:5–6 (2001) 413–26. Savulescu argues that the moral permissibility of life extension technologies must be weighed against potential harms, particularly the environmental, economic, and societal impacts of an extended human lifespan. He highlights the ethical dilemma of resource distribution, suggesting that life extension may exacerbate existing inequalities and place significant strains on environmental sustainability and social welfare systems.

possible; but man's inclination to injustice makes democracy necessary."[37] In a similar vein, one might argue that humanity's capacity to innovate makes technological progress desirable, but humanity's inclination toward hubris makes ethical reflection on that progress imperative.

In light of these concerns, the Christian narrative of redemption provides a counternarrative to the transhumanist vision of immortality. Where transhumanism seeks to overcome death through technological mastery, Christian theology insists that eternal life is a gift of divine grace, received through participation in God's redemptive plan for creation. This view does not reject technological advancements outright but calls for a careful consideration of their ethical and spiritual implications. As Lints has observed, the quest for immortality, when detached from its theological moorings, risks becoming a form of idolatry, wherein humanity seeks to transcend its creatureliness through its own efforts rather than through communion with the Creator.[38]

In conclusion, transhumanism's quest for immortality represents a profound ethical and theological challenge. While the promise of life extension and human enhancement may appeal to the modern desire for control and autonomy, it raises significant questions about the nature of human identity, dignity, and mortality. Both theological and secular perspectives emphasize the need for a more nuanced understanding of the ethical implications of these technologies, particularly as they relate to the deeper questions of life, death, and the human condition.

ANCIENT PHILOSOPHY AND THEOLOGICAL CRITIQUE

Building upon the previously discussed framework of *exitus-reditus*, ancient philosophy offers a rich source of critique when addressing the ethical challenges posed by AI and transhumanism. Aristotle and Plato were particularly concerned with hubris, the dangerous overreaching of human limits, which serves as a direct parallel to the ambitions of transhumanism. Aristotle defines hubris as an overstepping of natural limits, a violation of the ethical mean.[39] His emphasis on balance and

---

37. Reinhold Niebuhr, *The Children of Light and the Children of Darkness* (Chicago: University of Chicago Press, 1944), 9.

38. Lints, *Identity and Idolatry*, 120.

39. Plato's and Aristotle's philosophical frameworks, particularly their theories on forms, matter, and hylomorphism, have deeply influenced Christian theological thought. While some critiques note tensions between Platonic dualism and biblical

moderation contrasts sharply with transhumanism's drive to transcend the natural boundaries of human life.[40] Aristotle believed that virtuous living required an acknowledgment of one's human limitations, with the ethical mean serving as the guide to flourishing. Transhumanism, by attempting to eradicate finitude, represents a modern form of the classical vice of excess, where technology is used to pursue power over life and death rather than virtue.

Expanding on this, Plato in his dialogues frequently warned against the dangers of pursuing knowledge without wisdom. In the *Republic*, he depicts the philosopher-king as the ideal ruler precisely because of his ability to harmonize knowledge with ethical purpose.[41] Transhumanism's pursuit of knowledge and enhancement, however, often lacks this wisdom, opting instead for technological power without proper moral guidance. Plato's famous allegory of the cave serves as a cautionary tale, illustrating how the pursuit of superficial knowledge—symbolized by shadows on the wall—leads to ignorance and spiritual blindness. The transhumanist vision of immortality can be likened to the prisoners' fixation on shadows, chasing the illusion of god-like power while neglecting the true nature of human existence. In contrast, authentic human existence is rooted in moral and spiritual transformation.

Plotinus's work in Neoplatonism deepens this critique. For Plotinus, human fulfillment is achieved not through manipulation of the material world but through an intellectual and spiritual ascent toward the One, the source of all being.[42] Transhumanism, by promising artificial transcendence through material means, represents a distortion of this metaphysical framework. Rather than seeking true unity with the divine, transhumanism reverts to a form of material idolatry, attempting to achieve spiritual ends through technological means. This pursuit mirrors the hubris critiqued by Plato, where humanity seeks to transcend its nature without acknowledging the moral and metaphysical consequences of such ambition.

---

concepts like bodily resurrection, their ideas provide a critical foundation for understanding the intellectual and rational dimensions of the *imago Dei*. See John M. Rist, *Plato and the Christian Thought* (Cambridge: Cambridge University Press, 1968), 178–80.

40. Aristotle, *Nicomachean Ethics*, trans. Terence Irwin (Indianapolis: Hackett, 1999), 1123b.

41. Plato, *Phaedrus*, trans. Robin Waterfield (Oxford: Oxford University Press, 2002), 265a; *Republic*, trans. G. M. A. Grube (Indianapolis: Hackett, 1992), 595b–598c.

42. Plotinus, *The Enneads*, trans. Stephen MacKenna (London: Penguin, 1991), VI.9.

Beyond the ethical warnings of Plato and Aristotle, Stoic philosophy offers another classical perspective on human ambition and control. Seneca and Epictetus emphasized the importance of accepting fate and living in accordance with nature's laws. For the Stoics, human flourishing was not found in transcending limitations but in embracing them with virtue and wisdom.[43] Transhumanism, in contrast, seeks to rebel against these natural boundaries, portraying human limitations as problems to be solved through technological enhancement. The Stoic insistence on accepting human mortality and finitude stands in stark opposition to transhumanism's hubristic desire to control and extend life indefinitely.

Epicureanism also offers relevant insights into the ethical implications of the transhumanist quest for immortality. Epicurus, while often misunderstood as promoting hedonism, actually advocated for a life of moderation and tranquility, achieved through the proper understanding of life and death. He famously argued that death should not be feared, as it is simply the cessation of sensation.[44] Transhumanism's fixation on overcoming death and extending life represents a fundamental misunderstanding of the human condition, in Epicurean terms, by elevating the fear of death to a central problem that must be conquered at all costs. This obsession with avoiding death distorts the natural flow of life, as understood in both Epicurean and Stoic philosophies, where human flourishing is attained through wisdom, acceptance, and virtuous living.

In the realm of tragedy, Aeschylus's *Prometheus Bound* provides a dramatic example of the consequences of defying divine limits. Prometheus, punished for stealing fire from the gods, symbolizes humanity's hubristic desire to wield god-like powers.[45] Transhumanism, in its quest to manipulate the very building blocks of life, echoes Prometheus's rebellion, seeking to claim powers traditionally reserved for the divine. In both cases, the consequence of overreaching ambition is not only ethical failure but existential suffering, as humanity struggles with the unforeseen outcomes of its defiance.

---

43. Seneca, *Letters from a Stoic*, trans. Robin Campbell (London: Penguin, 2004), 65–66; Epictetus, *The Discourses*, trans. Robert Dobbin (London: Penguin, 2008), 1.1.

44. Epicurus, "Letter to Menoeceus," in *The Essential Epicurus: Letters, Principal Doctrines, Vatican Sayings, and Fragments*, trans. Eugene O'Connor, 51–54 (Buffalo, NY: Prometheus, 1993).

45. Aeschylus, *Prometheus Bound*, trans. David Grene (Chicago: University of Chicago Press, 1991), 12–30.

Classical philosophy thus offers a profound critique of transhumanism's ambitions. The hubristic pursuit of technological mastery over life and death violates the ethical boundaries set by thinkers like Aristotle and Plato, and it undermines the metaphysical principles articulated by Plotinus and the Stoics. The rejection of human finitude in favor of technological control risks leading humanity into a state of moral fragmentation and existential disarray, where the pursuit of power supplants the pursuit of virtue and wisdom.

Hans Jonas and Alasdair MacIntyre build upon these classical critiques in their modern evaluations of technological ethics. Jonas, in *The Imperative of Responsibility*, argues that technology must be constrained by ethical principles that prioritize human dignity and responsibility over power. His critique mirrors Aristotle's insistence on moderation, warning that the unbridled pursuit of technological control can lead to ethical catastrophe.[46] MacIntyre, in *After Virtue*, continues this line of critique by emphasizing that the modern technological ethos reflects a deeper moral and philosophical crisis, where virtue has been supplanted by the desire for control.[47] Both thinkers, drawing on the classical tradition, provide a valuable lens for understanding the ethical dilemmas posed by transhumanism and AI.

Ultimately, the philosophical warnings against hubris, combined with theological concerns, reveal the profound ethical and metaphysical risks of transhumanism. By attempting to transcend human limitations through technological means, transhumanism embodies the ancient critique of hubris—a dangerous overreaching that not only threatens to undermine human identity but also jeopardizes the moral and spiritual foundations of human existence.

MORAL AGENCY AND AUTONOMY

The ethical concerns surrounding AI and transhumanism become increasingly complex when considering their impact on human agency and autonomy. As AI systems evolve and gain autonomy—capable of making decisions independently of human oversight—profound theological and ethical questions emerge. One central question is whether

---

46. Hans Jonas, *The Imperative of Responsibility: In Search of an Ethics for the Technological Age* (Chicago: University of Chicago Press, 1984), 23–30.

47. MacIntyre, *After Virtue*, 91–93.

AI, a machine created by human ingenuity, can ever truly possess moral agency in the same sense as human beings. If AI is capable of making morally significant decisions, what are the implications for theological ethics, particularly in regard to human responsibility? Moreover, as AI becomes further integrated into decision-making processes across sectors like healthcare, governance, and warfare, the concern over the erosion of human autonomy deepens, raising the specter of dehumanization in ethical decision-making.

Proponents of AI, such as Elon Musk, have acknowledged both the potential and the risks of autonomous systems. Musk has famously stated that AI represents "the most significant existential threat to humanity."[48] While AI proponents generally celebrate its capacity to enhance decision-making and efficiency, this statement reflects deeper anxieties about what happens when machines gain control over moral decisions that have historically been the sole province of human beings. For instance, the increasing use of AI in military applications, such as autonomous drones, underscores the ethical dilemma of machines making life-and-death decisions—decisions traditionally reserved for human moral agents. The fear, as expressed by Musk and others, is that AI may eventually become an uncontrollable force, stripping humanity of its autonomy and the moral agency that has long defined it.

From a theological perspective, this raises critical questions about the nature of human freedom and responsibility. Immanuel Kant's philosophy of moral agency, which asserts that true freedom involves acting in accordance with moral law, is particularly relevant in this context. Kant contended that moral agency is inseparable from human autonomy; to be free, one must act under the moral law as a rational being.[49] However, as AI systems increasingly assume roles in decision-making processes, this raises the question: How can moral responsibility be preserved when machines are the ones making decisions? If a machine makes a morally significant choice, who is ultimately accountable—the AI itself, its creator, or the society that allowed such autonomy? This ambiguity threatens to blur the lines of moral responsibility, which is a critical concern in both Christian theology and Kantian ethics.

48. Elon Musk, quoted in Samuel Gibbs, "Elon Musk: Artificial Intelligence Is Our Biggest Existential Threat," *Guardian*, Oct. 27, 2014, https://www.theguardian.com/technology/2014/oct/27/elon-musk-artificial-intelligence-ai-biggest-existential-threat.

49. Immanuel Kant, *Groundwork of the Metaphysics of Morals*, trans. Mary Gregor (Cambridge: Cambridge University Press, 1998), 4:412.

Another important voice in this conversation is Oliver O'Donovan, who in *Resurrection and Moral Order* emphasizes the theological connection between moral responsibility and the order of creation. O'Donovan argues that humans, as moral agents, are called to reflect divine order and justice through their actions, which are grounded in their God-given autonomy.[50] When moral decision-making is delegated to AI, however, this divinely bestowed autonomy is compromised, removing the crucial human element of ethical reflection and accountability. Similarly, Jürgen Moltmann in *The Ethics of Hope* warns of the dehumanization that occurs when technological systems dictate human choices, asserting that moral responsibility must remain firmly within the realm of human agency, not technological determinism.[51] Both O'Donovan and Moltmann emphasize that moral agency is not a transferable quality—it is inherently tied to human beings, as bearers of divine responsibility, who must make ethical decisions that reflect their relationship with God.

Moreover, Stephen Hawking, the celebrated physicist and thinker, warned that "the development of full AI could spell the end of the human race."[52] Hawking's concerns, while directed at the potential for AI to surpass human intelligence, also reflect an existential crisis of moral agency. If AI gains the ability to act autonomously, without the limitations of human morality, it introduces the possibility that machines could make decisions beyond human control, thus rendering human autonomy increasingly irrelevant.

In the realm of governance, the use of AI for predictive policing and surveillance presents serious ethical dilemmas. The idea that algorithms could be used to predict criminal behavior raises concerns about justice, fairness, and human dignity. Jacques Ellul, in *The Technological Society*, argues that modern technology, by imposing its own rationality, erodes human autonomy and moral responsibility. Ellul warns that the rise of autonomous systems risks turning ethical deliberation into a mechanized process, subordinating human values to technological efficiency.[53] This danger is mirrored by Hannah Arendt's critique in *The Human Condition*,

50. Oliver O'Donovan, *Resurrection and Moral Order: An Outline for Evangelical Ethics*, 2nd ed. (Grand Rapids: Eerdmans, 1994), 23–27.

51. Moltmann, *Ethics of Hope*, 92–97.

52. Stephen Hawking, quoted in Rory Cellan-Jones, "Stephen Hawking Warns Artificial Intelligence Could End Mankind," BBC News, Dec. 2, 2014, https://www.bbc.com/news/technology-30290540.

53. Jacques Ellul, *The Technological Society*, trans. John Wilkinson (New York: Vintage Books, 1964), 138–44.

where she warns that the modern obsession with efficiency and predictability leads to the dehumanization of decision-making, reducing actions to mechanistic processes rather than evaluating them based on ethical merits.[54] In contexts like law enforcement and governance, human beings increasingly risk being reduced to mere data points within algorithmic systems, which threatens to undermine the moral agency central to Christian anthropology.

In the context of warfare, AI-driven technologies, such as autonomous drones, further intensify the ethical dilemmas surrounding human autonomy and moral responsibility. The theological implications are profound. If AI is empowered to make life-and-death decisions, it challenges fundamental Christian beliefs in the sanctity of human life and the moral accountability of those who wield lethal power. Ellul's critique resonates here, as he argues that the uncritical embrace of technology leads to a loss of moral deliberation, where decisions are made not based on human ethics but on technical imperatives. The central question remains: Can a machine ever bear the full weight of moral responsibility, or does the use of AI in warfare represent a dangerous abdication of human ethical accountability?

In conclusion, the rise of autonomous AI systems presents profound challenges to human moral agency and autonomy. Both theological and secular ethical perspectives emphasize the need to maintain human responsibility in the face of increasingly sophisticated AI technologies. The risk is that by delegating decision-making power to machines, we dehumanize individuals and undermine the very moral agency that defines us as bearers of the *imago Dei*. As the ethical discourse surrounding AI continues to evolve, it is essential that human autonomy remains at the forefront of these conversations, ensuring that technology serves humanity rather than supplanting it.

REFLECTIONS ON IDENTITY AND CONTINUITY

The transhumanist vision of human enhancement, particularly through AI, challenges traditional theological and philosophical understandings of human identity and continuity. Thinkers like Ray Kurzweil and Nick Bostrom argue that humanity is merely a precursor to a more advanced

---

54. Hannah Arendt, *The Human Condition* (Chicago: University of Chicago Press, 1958), 297–304.

form of intelligence—what Bostrom calls "posthumanity." This future, where biological limitations are transcended, raises profound theological concerns regarding the integrity of human nature and the continuity of personal identity.

Philosophically, the issue of identity continuity is central to these debates. Transhumanism envisions a future where consciousness could be uploaded into machines or radically augmented through AI. This challenges fundamental philosophical understandings of personal identity, especially those outlined by John Locke. Locke's theory of personal identity, particularly in *An Essay Concerning Human Understanding*, posits that identity is tied to the continuity of consciousness rather than the material substance of the soul or body. For Locke, memory plays a crucial role: if a being can remember its past experiences, that continuity of consciousness is sufficient to establish personal identity, even if the body or soul undergoes substantial changes.[55]

Locke's framework, though seemingly adaptable to transhumanist ideas of consciousness being separated from the body, encounters several tensions when applied to the transhumanist project. One such tension involves the limits of memory as the defining criterion for identity. Locke assumed that memory is inherently tied to the biological experience of the individual. If a person's memories were uploaded into an AI or augmented artificially, would that AI or enhanced person still be the "same" individual? Locke's theory offers no clear answer to this, particularly because his philosophy presupposed the indivisibility of memory and human consciousness within the context of a biological framework. The transhumanist aspiration of disembodied memory challenges the Lockean view by questioning whether memory alone is sufficient to maintain personal identity when consciousness is no longer tied to the organic body.

Additionally, Locke's theory assumes that the subject remembering past experiences also shares moral and social responsibilities for those experiences. This premise becomes complicated when considering the moral status of an uploaded consciousness. If AI can replicate a person's memories, does that AI inherit the original person's moral obligations and ethical responsibilities? For Locke, personal identity is not just a question of memory but also of moral accountability, a concept rooted in the biological person who acts in the world. Transhumanist aspirations

---

55. John Locke, *An Essay Concerning Human Understanding*, ed. Peter H. Nidditch (Oxford: Clarendon, 1979), 2.27.9–2.27.23.

to transcend the body would sever this connection, raising significant concerns about the continuity of moral agency.

Further complicating this issue is Locke's notion of "personhood," which involves more than mere memory. For Locke, personhood entails the capacity for rational thought, moral responsibility, and the ability to engage in social and legal relationships. While an AI may be programmed with a person's memories, Locke's emphasis on moral and legal agency remains inseparable from the human body and its embeddedness in social contexts. If transhumanism succeeds in uploading consciousness into machines, the question arises: Can AI truly function as a person, with the same rights, duties, and responsibilities, or does the separation of mind and body strip the uploaded entity of its moral agency? Locke's theory implicitly suggests that personhood, moral agency, and personal identity are not simply cognitive functions but are embedded within a biological, social, and ethical framework that cannot be easily replicated in a machine.

Locke's ideas intersect with theological concerns, particularly in Christian anthropology, which emphasizes the unity of body and soul. Thomas Aquinas, in his *Summa Theologiae*, argued that the soul is incomplete without the body, emphasizing that human identity and moral agency are inherently tied to the physical experience of life.[56] The transhumanist attempt to disembody consciousness, then, not only distorts philosophical understandings of identity but also fundamentally disrupts theological conceptions of the human being as a unified body-soul entity. This separation of mind and body undermines the theological conviction that human moral agency is exercised through embodied existence.

In this light, transhumanism's vision of posthumanity, where consciousness is uploaded into machines, begins to resemble the ancient temptation of idolatry. As I argued in my dissertation, transhumanism is not just a neutral technological ambition; it reflects a form of *idolatria* where humans place their faith in their own creations rather than in divine providence.[57] This idolatry is not simply the worship of technology, but a fundamental shift in how humans perceive their role in creation. The attempt to upload consciousness into machines is a manifestation of humanity's age-old desire to achieve immortality on its own terms, bypassing dependence on God's grace. In the same way that the builders of

---

56. Thomas Aquinas, *Summa Theologiae*, I.75.4.
57. Sutherland, "God's Narrative of Redemption," 43.

Babel sought to construct their own pathway to heaven, transhumanism seeks to bypass divine authority by engineering a future where humanity transcends its God-given limitations.

Theologically, this view contrasts sharply with the Christian understanding of the *imago Dei*, where human beings are seen as reflections of God's moral, relational, and embodied nature. Hans Urs von Balthasar asserts that the divine image is fully expressed only through the unity of body and soul, which allows humans to act morally, create relationships, and fulfill their roles as stewards of creation.[58] The attempt to transcend the body through technology risks severing this reflection of the divine, raising significant ethical and theological concerns about what it means to be human in a posthuman future.

Further expanding the critique of transhumanism's vision of disembodied identity, Charles Taylor's work in *Sources of the Self* highlights how modernity's emphasis on autonomy and control over nature has led to a fragmented understanding of human identity.[59] Taylor argues that the quest for self-determination, particularly through technological control, often leads to alienation from one's true self and the created order. Transhumanism, with its promise of disembodied consciousness and enhanced autonomy, exemplifies this modern alienation. Rather than finding identity and fulfillment through participation in relationships, communities, and the divine order, transhumanism encourages a self-referential identity—one based on individual autonomy and technological mastery.

Taylor's critique aligns with theological concerns that the pursuit of autonomy, particularly through technology, reflects a fundamental misunderstanding of human finitude and dependence on the created order. Christian theology posits that human beings are not autonomous creators of their own identity but are relational beings, created in the image of God and dependent on the natural world for their moral and spiritual development. The transhumanist desire to transcend human limitations and "be like God" echoes the ancient narrative of the Tower of Babel, where human ambition to achieve god-like power leads to alienation from God and the natural order. In this way, transhumanism's vision of

---

58. Hans Urs von Balthasar, *Theo-Drama: Theological Dramatic Theory*, vol. 2, *The Dramatis Personae: Man in God*, trans. Graham Harrison (San Francisco: Ignatius, 1990), 176–77.

59. Charles Taylor, *Sources of the Self: The Making of the Modern Identity* (Cambridge, MA: Harvard University Press, 1989), 3–24.

identity continuity and enhancement reflects not only a philosophical misunderstanding of human nature but also a theological error that fundamentally distorts the divine-human relationship.

In conclusion, transhumanism's vision of human enhancement raises profound philosophical and theological questions regarding personal identity, embodiment, and continuity. While John Locke provides a framework for thinking about identity continuity in an age of AI, his assumptions about memory and moral agency are challenged by the transhumanist desire to transcend the body. Charles Taylor and Christian theology further critique this vision, emphasizing the importance of embodiment, relationality, and moral responsibility as integral to human identity. In seeking to transcend these limitations, transhumanism risks becoming a form of modern idolatry, where humans attempt to supplant their reliance on God with technological mastery.

SALVATION VS. TECHNOLOGICAL ENHANCEMENT

One of the key theological challenges posed by AI and transhumanism is the tension between the promise of technological salvation and the Christian understanding of divine grace. Transhumanism, by promising to overcome human limitations—whether cognitive, physical, or mortal—offers a secularized version of salvation grounded in human effort rather than divine intervention. In this vision, humanity's future is one of limitless enhancement, where technology functions as the means of attaining immortality, knowledge, and perfection. This contrasts sharply with the Christian narrative of salvation, which emphasizes human dependency on God's grace rather than self-sufficiency.

The doctrine of salvation by grace posits that human beings, in their finite and fallen state, cannot achieve eternal life through their own efforts. Ephesians 2:8–9 declares, "For by grace you have been saved through faith, and this is not your own doing; it is the gift of God—not the result of works, so that no one may boast." The core of the Christian faith insists that salvation is not something to be attained through human ingenuity or technological advancement, but rather a divine gift. The promise of resurrection is not the result of human achievement but of divine intervention, where death is overcome through Christ's victory over the grave (1 Cor 15:55–57).

In this sense, the transhumanist pursuit of eternal life through technology is not only misguided but dangerous. It represents a fundamental misunderstanding of human nature and destiny. By seeking to transcend the limits of the body and achieve immortality through technological means, transhumanism risks severing humanity from its relationship with God, the true source of eternal life. The desire to attain perfection and immortality through technology echoes the temptation in the garden of Eden, where humans sought to "be like God" (Gen 3:5) through their own efforts, resulting in their alienation from God and the fall of creation. This transgression leads directly to the distortion of the *imago Dei*, a distortion that is only restored through the redeeming work of Christ.

As I argued in my dissertation, the restoration of the *imago Dei* is central to God's ultimate plan for redemption. The *imago Dei*, distorted in the fall, is not fully restored through human effort but through participation in the redemptive work of Christ. Humanity's true perfection and immortality are found not in technological enhancement but in the resurrection, where believers are transformed into the image of the risen Christ (Rom 8:29, Phil 3:21). In contrast, the transhumanist vision offers a counterfeit form of salvation, where the pursuit of self-perfection and autonomy replaces humanity's dependence on divine grace.[60]

C. S. Lewis, in *The Abolition of Man*, warned against the dangers of using technology to manipulate and control human nature. Lewis argued that by attempting to overcome the natural order, humanity risks losing its very humanity. He describes this as the "abolition of man," wherein the qualities that make us truly human—moral agency, relationality, and our capacity for love—are sacrificed in the pursuit of technological mastery. For Lewis, the ultimate danger of such manipulation is that humans, in their desire to control nature, become enslaved by the very tools they create. "Man's conquest of Nature," he writes, "turns out, in the moment of its consummation, to be Nature's conquest of Man."[61]

This loss of humanity, according to Lewis, is not a path to liberation but to enslavement, as technology becomes the new master rather than the servant of human flourishing. His critique anticipates the theological concerns surrounding AI, genetic modification, and consciousness uploading. When human nature is subjected to technological manipulation,

---

60. Sutherland, "God's Narrative of Redemption," 52–55.
61. C. S. Lewis, *The Abolition of Man* (New York: HarperOne, 2001), 77.

it leads not to freedom but to the loss of essential human qualities—moral responsibility, dependence on God's grace, and the capacity for genuine relationship. Lewis's vision is profoundly theological: by attempting to control human nature, humanity forfeits its relationship with the Creator, thereby undermining its created purpose.

This critique ties closely to the Christian understanding of salvation as a return to the original design of the *imago Dei*. In seeking to manipulate and "improve" human nature through technology, transhumanism echoes the ancient idolatry of placing trust in creation rather than the Creator. The restoration of the *imago Dei*, however, cannot be achieved through technological means but through divine grace, which transforms humanity into the likeness of Christ. As 2 Cor 3:18 declares, "And all of us, with unveiled faces, seeing the glory of the Lord as though reflected in a mirror, are being transformed into the same image from one degree of glory to another; for this comes from the Lord, the Spirit."

Dietrich Bonhoeffer, in his *Ethics*, argued that humanity's true nature can only be understood in relationship with God. Bonhoeffer's theology of freedom emphasizes that true human freedom is not found in self-determination or technological autonomy, but in being bound to God and to others. "Freedom is not something man has for himself but something he has for others," Bonhoeffer writes.[62] In this way, Bonhoeffer saw freedom not as self-assertion but as participation in God's will and a life lived in service to others. Any attempt to achieve salvation or self-perfection apart from God, Bonhoeffer argues, inevitably leads to a distortion of human nature. The transhumanist dream of immortality through technological enhancement directly contradicts this theological vision, as it seeks freedom and perfection in isolation from God's grace.

Bonhoeffer's concept of "the world come of age," where humanity believes itself no longer in need of God, can also be applied to the transhumanist ethos. Transhumanism, with its promise of mastery over human destiny, exemplifies the ultimate expression of humanity "come of age," where dependence on technology replaces dependence on divine grace. Yet, for Bonhoeffer, the true mark of maturity is not self-sufficiency but surrender to the will of God. It is through this surrender that the *imago Dei* is restored, and humanity finds its true purpose.

John Sailhamer, in his work on biblical theology, emphasizes that the *imago Dei* is not merely a static image but is linked to humanity's

---

62. Bonhoeffer, *Ethics*, 215.

purpose and destiny in God's redemptive plan. Sailhamer highlights the biblical theme of restoration, where God's ultimate goal is to renew the creation and restore humanity to its intended role as stewards of creation.[63] Transhumanism's attempt to redefine human destiny through technological enhancement overlooks this biblical trajectory of restoration. Rather than leading to salvation, the technological manipulation of human nature risks further alienating humanity from its true identity as bearers of the *imago Dei*.

In conclusion, the promise of salvation through technological enhancement offered by transhumanism stands in direct conflict with the Christian understanding of salvation by grace. While transhumanism seeks to transcend human limitations through human effort, the Christian narrative emphasizes that true immortality and perfection can only be achieved through divine intervention. By relying on technology to achieve what can only be granted through God's grace, transhumanism risks not only distorting the *imago Dei* but also leading humanity away from the true source of eternal life. As Lewis, Bonhoeffer, Sailhamer, and the biblical narrative remind us, salvation and the restoration of the *imago Dei* come not through human striving but through participation in the redemptive work of God.

TRANSHUMANIST ESCHATOLOGY

The eschatological vision of transhumanism represents a secularized form of salvation, where humanity achieves its ultimate destiny not through divine intervention but through technological mastery. Bostrom, in his foundational essay, "Transhumanist Values," outlines a future where human beings evolve into "posthumans," entities with vastly superior cognitive, physical, and emotional capacities. Bostrom's vision is one of radical enhancement, where suffering, disease, and even death are overcome through technological means. Advances such as CRISPR gene editing, biotechnology, and AI-driven cognitive enhancement are making this vision seem increasingly attainable. Gene editing offers the potential to eradicate hereditary diseases, while AI promises to enhance cognitive functioning and problem-solving abilities far beyond human

---

63. John H. Sailhamer, *The Pentateuch as Narrative: A Biblical-Theological Commentary*, Library of Biblical Interpretation (Grand Rapids: Zondervan, 1992), 22–25.

limitations.⁶⁴ In these endeavors, there is certainly a noble pursuit at work—the alleviation of human suffering. In fact, the biblical mandate to help others and bring healing to the world (Isa 58:6–7, Luke 10:9) aligns with the desire to address the ailments and limitations of the human condition. However, such advancements must be tempered with ethical and moral guardrails that align with the *imago Dei*. The danger lies in distorting humanity's divine identity by overstepping the boundaries of ethical enhancement, thereby moving from the pursuit of healing to the idolatrous goal of achieving control over life and death itself.

In a similar way, ancient civilizations sought divine intervention to meet their needs through ritual sacrifices. The Canaanites, for instance, sacrificed children to the god Moloch, believing this would ensure prosperity and fertility. Similarly, the Aztecs offered human sacrifices to Huitzilopochtli, their sun god, to sustain the cosmic order. These sacrifices were part of a larger pattern where human beings attempted to trade something valuable—whether crops, lives, or resources—for divine favor, protection, or abundance. This anthropomorphic conception of gods, who required appeasement through sacrifice, reflected an exchange-based relationship between humans and the divine. While these ancient practices may seem distant, the underlying behaviors mirror modern attempts to secure transcendence or immortality through technological mastery. In the same way that people once sought divine favor through sacrifices, transhumanism represents a contemporary quest to trade elements of our humanity—such as embodiment and autonomy—in exchange for the promise of personal enhancement and control over life and death. Ecclesiastes 1:9 reminds us, "What has been is what will be, and what has been done is what will be done; there is nothing new under the sun." This cyclical human behavior, though modernized, reflects the ancient tendency to strive for control over the ultimate questions of existence.⁶⁵

In Christian theology, the future is not one of individual enhancement but of communal resurrection, where all of creation is restored

---

64. Bostrom, "Transhumanist Values." Bostrom outlines a future in which transhumanist advancements such as CRISPR gene editing, biotechnology, and AI-driven cognitive enhancement will enable humanity to evolve into "posthumans"—entities with vastly superior cognitive, physical, and emotional capacities. His vision of radical enhancement aims to overcome suffering, disease, and even death through technological means, yet raises significant ethical concerns regarding the nature of human identity, social inequality, and the limits of human autonomy.

65. Sutherland, "God's Narrative of Redemption," 72–76.

and redeemed through Christ. First Corinthians 15:42–44 emphasizes the transformation of the body in the resurrection: "So it is with the resurrection of the dead. What is sown is perishable, what is raised is imperishable." The Christian eschaton is not a singular event where a few individuals transcend the human condition; it is a cosmic event involving the renewal of all things. The resurrection of the body is central to this hope, affirming the goodness of creation and the integrity of embodied existence. Transhumanism's vision of posthumanity, by contrast, seeks to escape the limitations of the body, viewing embodiment as an obstacle to be overcome rather than a gift to be redeemed.

Theologians like N. T. Wright emphasize that the resurrection is not about escaping the physical world but about the renewal of creation. In *Surprised by Hope*, Wright argues that the Christian hope is focused on the transformation of the physical body in the new creation, where heaven and earth are united in a cosmic restoration. Wright critiques any vision of the future that separates the spiritual from the physical, noting that the resurrection of Christ affirms the goodness of the created order, which is to be renewed, not discarded.[66] This sharply contrasts with transhumanism's rejection of embodiment as a limitation to be transcended.

Similarly, O'Donovan, in *Resurrection and Moral Order*, argues that the resurrection confirms the moral goodness of the body, which plays an essential role in human identity and ethical action. O'Donovan emphasizes that the body is not something to be discarded in favor of cognitive or spiritual enhancement but is integral to how humans relate to one another and to God. The resurrection, according to O'Donovan, reveals that human flourishing is achieved not through personal enhancement but through the transformation of the body in communion with God.[67]

The theological critique of transhumanism is further deepened by David Bentley Hart, who argues that the Christian hope is fundamentally communal and relational, where the redemption of the body is tied to the restoration of relationships with God, others, and the created order. In *The Beauty of the Infinite*, Hart critiques the individualistic nature of transhumanist salvation, noting that true fulfillment is found not in self-perfection but in participation in the divine life.[68] Transhumanism's

---

66. N. T. Wright, *Surprised by Hope: Rethinking Heaven, the Resurrection, and the Mission of the Church* (New York: HarperOne, 2008), 92–96.

67. O'Donovan, *Resurrection and Moral Order*, 22–25.

68. David Bentley Hart, *The Beauty of the Infinite: The Aesthetics of Christian Truth* (Grand Rapids: Eerdmans, 2003), 293–98.

WHY THEOLOGY? 27

vision of posthumanity risks alienating individuals from the communal and relational aspects of human nature, offering instead a salvation grounded in personal achievement and immortality.

In this way, transhumanism echoes an ancient error: the desire to be like God through human effort rather than divine grace (Gen 3:5). The theological critique, as N. T. Wright, O'Donovan, and Hart have shown, is that true hope is found not in personal transcendence but in the communal resurrection of all creation. The sacrificial pursuit of individual enhancement in transhumanism—whether through the body, mind, or both—becomes a modern manifestation of idolatry, where humanity sacrifices its embodied, relational existence in pursuit of secular salvation. As I outlined in "God's Narrative of Redemption," this form of idolatry is particularly insidious because it promises salvation while severing humanity from its dependence on God.[69]

In conclusion, transhumanism's eschatology, while presenting a compelling vision of secular salvation, ultimately contradicts the Christian hope of resurrection and new creation. It replaces communal redemption with individual enhancement and seeks to overcome the body rather than affirming its role in human destiny. As Wright, O'Donovan, and Hart remind us, the resurrection offers a vision of cosmic renewal, where the body is not something to be transcended but transformed in union with God's redemptive plan.

CONCLUSION: THEOLOGY AS A FRAMEWORK

As we conclude this foundational chapter, we have explored why theology is not merely an ancillary tool but the central framework for navigating the ethical, spiritual, and metaphysical crises posed by AI and transhumanism. At the heart of this book is the argument that modern technologies, such as AI and human enhancement, represent new forms of idolatry that distort human identity and divine purpose, and only a theologically grounded understanding of the *imago Dei* can provide the robust framework necessary for addressing these challenges.

This chapter has laid the groundwork for understanding AI and transhumanism as more than technical or ethical issues; they are deeply theological at their core. By attempting to overcome human limitations through technological means—whether through cognitive enhancement,

---

69. Sutherland, "God's Narrative of Redemption," 293–98.

the pursuit of immortality, or the creation of autonomous entities—these movements echo ancient forms of idolatry. Theologians from Augustine to Bonhoeffer have wrestled with the dangers of humanity striving for control over life and death rather than accepting its role as stewards of creation. Just as the Tower of Babel story reflects humanity's attempt to transcend divine boundaries, so too does transhumanism challenge the limits placed upon humanity by God.

Yet it is not enough to critique these movements solely through a theological lens; we must also engage with their potential benefits. There is undeniable value in seeking to alleviate suffering, improve human capabilities, and heal disease. Such pursuits align with biblical mandates to care for the sick and marginalized, as demonstrated in Isa 58:6–7 and Luke 10:9. However, as this chapter has shown, these advancements must be carefully guided by a theological anthropology that affirms the *imago Dei*, ensuring that technological innovation does not distort humanity's identity or sever its relational bond with the Creator.

In addition to cautioning against the dangers of AI and transhumanism, theology also offers a constructive path forward. Rather than rejecting technology outright, Christian theology encourages its use in ways that enhance human dignity, relationality, and moral responsibility. By grounding technological advancements in the framework of the *imago Dei*, Christians can promote innovations that serve the common good—using AI to support healthcare, education, and social justice, while safeguarding the inherent worth of each person. This means that technology should complement human relationships, not replace them, and should be harnessed to foster community, compassion, and justice rather than exacerbate inequalities or diminish human agency.

The transition from theory to application is critical to demonstrate how these theological principles can directly shape our engagement with AI. As we consider the potential of AI, the following case studies will explore how these technologies are currently impacting key sectors of society, starting with healthcare. By examining practical examples, we can better understand how AI may either support or undermine the ethical standards theology provides.

In the chapters that follow, we will delve deeper into the specific ways AI and transhumanism challenge theological doctrines such as the resurrection, salvation, and the integrity of the human body. Chapter 2, "The *Imago Dei* and the Crisis of Human Identity," will expand on the doctrine of the *imago Dei*, examining how AI and transhumanist pursuits risk undermining the divine image in humanity by redefining what it means to be human. Through a combination of biblical exegesis, theological reflection, and contemporary case studies, we will explore how this crisis can be addressed by reclaiming a theologically sound understanding of human identity in a rapidly advancing technological world.

By grounding this conversation in the rich traditions of Christian thought and biblical truth, this book seeks to provide not just a critique but a pathway forward—one that embraces the possibilities of technology while firmly rooted in the dignity, purpose, and relationality of humanity as created in the image of God.

CASE STUDY #1: OPACITY IN HEALTHCARE DECISION-MAKING

In 2023, AI has increasingly taken on a critical role in healthcare, particularly in areas like diagnostics and decision-making in surgery. For example, AI systems are being integrated into oncology departments, where they analyze large datasets to determine optimal treatment protocols for cancer patients. One such AI platform, designed by a leading tech company, processes data from thousands of clinical studies, along with individual patient histories, to recommend highly personalized treatment plans. The accuracy and efficiency of these systems often surpass that of human doctors, offering the potential to revolutionize healthcare by providing quicker, data-driven recommendations.[70]

However, this rapid integration of AI into healthcare raises profound ethical and theological questions. Who bears the responsibility when AI systems make mistakes? While surgeons traditionally hold responsibility for treatment outcomes, AI introduces a layer of complexity. If an AI-driven treatment plan results in a negative outcome, such as the death of a patient, who is accountable? Is it the doctor who relied on AI's recommendation, or the institution that implemented the technology? Can AI systems truly be held accountable if their decision-making process is not fully understood?

One major concern is AI's "black-box" decision-making, where the internal logic of the AI's algorithms is opaque, even to its developers and

---

70. McKinsey & Company, *Transforming Healthcare with AI*, McKinsey & Company, Mar. 2020, https://www.mckinsey.com/~/media/McKinsey/Industries/Healthcare%20Systems%20and%20Services/Our%20Insights/Transforming%20healthcare%20with%20AI/Transforming-healthcare-with-AI.ashx.

users. This lack of transparency makes it difficult to understand how AI arrives at certain conclusions or recommendations, which can lead to ethical dilemmas regarding patient consent and trust. If patients don't understand how decisions about their care are made, can they meaningfully consent to those decisions? How should healthcare providers navigate the trust gap created by AI's opaque processes? The American Medical Association has raised concerns that this "black-box" nature can diminish patient trust and create complications around ethical decision-making in critical healthcare scenarios.[71]

Additionally, while AI can process medical data with remarkable speed and precision, it lacks the relational and moral dimensions inherent to human decision-making, raising concerns from a theological perspective. How can AI reflect the moral agency that humans possess as bearers of the *imago Dei*? If AI lacks the capacity for relational understanding, can it fully consider the holistic well-being of a patient, beyond data points and outcomes? Does reliance on AI risk dehumanizing patients and medical professionals alike by reducing healthcare decisions to calculations? This tension between human dignity, moral responsibility, and machine efficiency becomes central to the ethical debates surrounding AI in healthcare.[72]

---

71. Danton S. Char et al., "Implementing Machine Learning in Health Care—Addressing Ethical Challenges," *New England Journal of Medicine* 378:11 (2018) 981–83, https://doi.org/10.1056/NEJMp1714229. The authors highlight the ethical dilemmas posed by AI's "black-box" nature in medical decision-making, emphasizing that opacity in AI-driven healthcare systems can erode patient trust and complicate informed consent. They argue that without clear explanations of AI-generated recommendations, patients and providers may struggle to assess the reliability and fairness of treatment options, raising significant concerns about transparency, accountability, and autonomy in clinical settings.

72. Emilio Gómez-González et al., "Artificial Intelligence in Medicine and Healthcare: A Review and Classification of Current and Near-Future Applications and Their Ethical and Social Impact" (preprint, last revised Feb. 6, 2020), https://arxiv.org/abs/2001.09778. In this comprehensive review, the authors discuss how AI's lack of relational and moral dimensions raises ethical concerns in healthcare. They emphasize that while AI can process vast amounts of medical data with remarkable speed and precision, it lacks the capacity for human-like moral agency and relational understanding. This deficiency poses challenges in ensuring that AI systems fully consider the holistic well-being of patients, beyond mere data points and outcomes. The authors also highlight the risk of dehumanization in healthcare, where reliance on AI could reduce patients and medical professionals to mere components in a data-driven process, potentially undermining human dignity and moral responsibility.

Case Study #1: Takeaway

The use of AI in healthcare presents both opportunities and challenges for ethical decision-making, particularly when it comes to human autonomy and moral agency. While AI-driven technologies (like NeoGenesis, discussed in Case Study #3) offer promising advances in enhancing human abilities and addressing disabilities, they also raise concerns about the potential dehumanization of medical care. By prioritizing technological solutions over relational and moral considerations, such systems risk undermining the intrinsic dignity of human beings as bearers of the *imago Dei*. In this context, Christian ethics calls for a balanced approach, where technology is used to serve humanity without replacing the relational and moral dimensions that define human identity.

Case Study #1: Discussion Questions

1. *Ethics of AI in Decision-Making*: How does AI's growing role in healthcare decision-making challenge the traditional understanding of medical responsibility and accountability? In what ways does this shift toward shared responsibility affect the physician-patient relationship, and how should Christian ethics engage with these changes?

2. *Theological Reflection on AI and Autonomy*: If AI systems increasingly dictate healthcare decisions, how do we ensure that patient autonomy and the moral agency of physicians are preserved? What role should the doctrine of the *imago Dei* play in developing ethical guidelines for AI in healthcare?

3. *Transparency and Trust*: Can patients provide informed consent to medical decisions when AI's decision-making processes are opaque? How can healthcare providers bridge the trust gap that arises from AI's "black-box" nature?

4. *Theological Framework and the* Imago Dei: Given that AI lacks relationality and moral agency, how does its integration into healthcare challenge the theological doctrine of the *imago Dei*? Can AI systems be considered agents of care in the same way that humans, as image-bearers of God, are?

5. *Philosophical Reflection on Human Nature and Agency*: Drawing from classical philosophy, such as Aristotle's concept of *phronesis* (practical

wisdom), how should healthcare decisions be approached differently from an AI-driven model? Can AI systems, lacking the moral virtues emphasized by Aristotle or Kantian notions of autonomy, truly make decisions in the best interest of human flourishing?

6. *Soteriology and Technological Salvation:* Transhumanism and AI often promise to overcome suffering and disease, which aligns with some of the biblical mandate for healing. However, does this promise of technological salvation conflict with the Christian understanding of salvation through divine grace? How should we approach technological advancements that seem to promise a form of "secular salvation"?

7. *Idolatry and Technological Mastery:* Reflecting on biblical critiques of idolatry, how does the use of AI in healthcare risk becoming a modern form of idolatry, where we place our trust in created technologies rather than the Creator? In what ways might our reliance on AI for life-and-death decisions mirror ancient sacrifices to appease anthropomorphic gods?

8. *Eschatology and AI's Promises:* How do the promises of AI—overcoming human limitations and even extending life—interact with Christian eschatological hope? Does reliance on AI to solve problems of mortality represent a misplaced hope, replacing divine intervention with technological mastery?

CASE STUDY #2: PREDICTIVE POLICING

In 2035, the city of Metroville implemented a new AI-powered predictive policing system known as Sentinel.[73] Sentinel was designed to analyze vast amounts of data—social media posts, surveillance footage, criminal records, and geographical crime patterns—to predict areas of potential criminal activity. The AI system could suggest where law enforcement officers should be deployed and identify individuals who may be more likely to commit crimes based on historical data and behavioral analysis.

Initially, Metroville's city council praised the system for its efficiency in lowering crime rates. Officers were sent to high-risk areas before crimes

[73]. Metroville is a fictional city and Sentinel is fictional technology created for illustrative purposes within this case study. Any resemblance to real companies, technologies, places, or individuals is purely coincidental. The case study is intended to explore ethical and theological questions related to AI-powered predictive policing and does not reference any actual existing entity.

occurred, and several crimes were prevented through preemptive action. However, over time, concerns began to arise. Civil rights activists noted that Sentinel disproportionately targeted certain neighborhoods, often those with higher minority populations, raising concerns of bias. These communities were heavily policed based on the AI's analysis, which mirrored historical injustices and reinforced existing stereotypes.

Ethicists and theologians began to question the moral implications of using AI in this way. What does it mean for moral agency when an AI system is responsible for determining who is more likely to commit a crime? If a person's actions are predicted and preempted by technology, does this not undermine their autonomy and the Christian understanding of moral responsibility and repentance? Additionally, the system's deployment raised broader theological questions about justice and fairness. By targeting individuals based on patterns and predictions, the AI appeared to strip away the possibility of transformation and redemption, which are central to Christian theological anthropology.

Religious leaders pointed to the importance of human dignity and relational justice, emphasizing that decisions about law enforcement should not be left to technology alone. True justice requires context, relational understanding, and compassion—qualities that an AI, driven by data and efficiency, cannot possess. Sentinel, though lauded for its efficiency, had inadvertently dehumanized entire communities by reducing them to data points and probabilities.

Case Study #2: Takeaway

The application of AI in governance, particularly in predictive policing, highlights significant ethical concerns about justice, fairness, and human dignity. While AI systems like Sentinel can improve efficiency in law enforcement, they risk reinforcing societal biases and dehumanizing individuals by reducing them to data points. Christian theology emphasizes the importance of relational justice and moral responsibility, reminding us that true justice requires context, compassion, and the possibility of transformation. The use of AI in governance must be carefully guided to ensure that technology serves humanity and upholds the dignity of each person as a reflection of the *imago Dei*.

Case Study #2: Discussion Questions

1. *Moral Agency and Transformation:* How does AI in predictive policing challenge the Christian understanding of moral agency, repentance, and transformation? Does this system conflict with the theological belief in the possibility of personal change and redemption?

2. *Justice and Inequality:* What ethical implications arise when AI systems reinforce historical patterns of injustice? How can a Christian response ensure that technology promotes fairness and human dignity rather than perpetuating inequality?

3. *Human Responsibility vs. AI Decision-Making:* To what extent should AI be involved in decision-making processes that affect human lives, especially in matters of justice and law enforcement? How can Christians advocate for systems that prioritize human moral responsibility?

CHAPTER 2

The *Imago Dei* and the Crisis of Human Identity

CLEARLY, AI AND TRANSHUMANISM have ushered humanity into a new era of ethical and spiritual complexity. These technological advancements are not merely tools; they are catalysts that reshape human cognition, identity, and even mortality. In light of this, the doctrine of the *imago Dei*—the foundational belief that humanity is created in the image of God—demands renewed theological scrutiny. What does it mean to bear the divine image in an age where the lines between humanity and machine become increasingly blurred? Furthermore, how can a traditional Christian understanding of human dignity and relationality hold firm against the increasing pressure to redefine humanity through artificial enhancement? These questions form the crux of this chapter.

As we engage with both the ancient and contemporary dimensions of this debate, it becomes clear that the *imago Dei* is not merely a relic of theological history but a vital concept for addressing the deepest questions of human identity. The concept is far from static; it is dynamic, rooted not only in creation but in relationship with God. The divine image reveals itself as dynamic and relational—one that grounds human purpose not in technological mastery but in communion with God and creation. However, the desire for human enhancement through AI and transhumanism, while innovative, ultimately threatens to erode the moral and relational dimensions that are intrinsic to the *imago Dei*. In this way, the rise of these technologies calls into question not just what humans can do but what humans are, making this theological reflection all the more urgent.

The Christian narrative, rooted in the *imago Dei* and embodied in Christ, offers an alternative to these technological aspirations. It calls for a holistic vision of human flourishing that embraces the totality of the person—mind, body, and soul—and resists reductionist views of human identity. Such a vision stands in stark contrast to transhumanist ideals, which often prioritize individual autonomy and cognitive enhancement over relational and moral wholeness. This chapter seeks to demonstrate how a theological understanding of the *imago Dei* is essential for framing the crises presented by AI and transhumanism. Through biblical exegesis, theological reflection, and the critique of modern scholarship, we will explore how the redemptive work of Christ not only restores the fractured *imago Dei* but also calls humanity to live out its true purpose, rejecting the false promises of technological transcendence.

EXEGESIS OF GENESIS 1:26–27

Genesis 1:26–27 stands as a foundational text in Christian theology, establishing the concept of humanity's creation in the *imago Dei*. The passage reads,

> Then God said, "Let us make humans in our image [*b'tsalmenu*], according to our likeness [*kid'mutenu*], and let them have dominion over the fish of the sea and over the birds of the air and over the cattle and over all the wild animals of the earth and over every creeping thing that creeps upon the earth. So God created humans [*b'tselem Elohim*] in his image, in the image of God he created them; male and female he created them. (Gen 1:26–27)

The Hebrew terms *tselem* (image) and *demut* (likeness) provide insight into what it means for humanity to bear the image of God. In Gen 1:26, both terms appear—*tselem* (*b'tsalmenu*) and *demut* (*kid'mutenu*)—yet in verse 27, only *tselem* is retained (*b'tselem Elohim*). This distinction suggests that while *tselem* conveys the idea of representation or reflection, *demut* emphasizes qualitative similarity in nature or attributes. The presence of both terms in verse 26 highlights the fullness of humanity's intended identity, while the exclusive use of *tselem* in verse 27 affirms that the divine image is the defining characteristic of human creation. Together, these terms indicate that the *imago Dei* encompasses not only physical representation but also relational, rational, and moral dimensions.

Humanity as Created in the Image of God

The doctrine of the *imago Dei* emphasizes that humanity reflects God's image, both physically and spiritually. The Hebrew word *tselem* refers to an image, idol, or representation, suggesting that human beings, in some way, function as divine representatives on earth.[1] This concept of image-bearing is unique to humanity within the biblical creation narrative, and scholars have debated its meaning for centuries, but the consensus highlights three key aspects: relationality, rationality, and moral agency, each reflecting different facets of God's character.

Relationality: The relational aspect of the *imago Dei* finds its roots in the triune nature of God. The plural language used in Gen 1:26, "Let us make humankind in our image," has long been interpreted as a reflection of the relational nature of God—Father, Son, and Holy Spirit. Early church fathers, such as Augustine, suggested that this plurality represents the divine counsel within the Godhead, where God exists in eternal relationship.[2] As a result, humanity, created in the image of this triune God, is inherently relational.

This relationality is mirrored in humanity's composition as mind, body, and soul, and in the creation of male and female, which underscores the communal and complementary aspects of human life.[3] Augustine further posits that human relationality reflects the divine intellect and will, calling human beings to live in communion with God and others. In short, Augustine views humanity's divine image as primarily relational and intellectual, calling us into communion with God and one another. This understanding of relationality contrasts sharply with modern technological advancements, which often prioritize individual autonomy over communal identity.

Rationality: In addition to relationality, the term *tselem* also emphasizes humanity's rational capacity. This concept is further expanded by the Hebrew word *demut*, which connotes likeness in form or function. Humanity's likeness to God, therefore, includes intellectual and reasoning abilities, reflecting divine wisdom.[4]

---

1. Victor P. Hamilton, *Handbook on the Pentateuch*, 2nd ed. (Grand Rapids: Baker Academic, 2005), 26.

2. Augustine, *The City of God*, trans. Marcus Dods (New York: Random House, 1950), XI.26.

3. Augustine, *City of God*, trans. Marcus Dods, XI.26.

4. Robert Jamieson et al., *A Commentary, Critical, Experimental, and Practical, on the Old and New Testaments*, vol. 1, *Genesis–Deuteronomy* (London: Collins, n.d.), 8.

Thomas Aquinas expands on this, arguing that rationality is central to the *imago Dei*—a reflection of divine wisdom that allows humans to engage in moral discernment.[5] Aquinas notes that rationality is not merely an intellectual gift but also a moral capacity that mirrors God's reasoning. This rational capacity enables humans to engage in moral reasoning and ethical decision-making, which distinguishes them from animals. In this light, rationality is seen not only as the ability to think but as the ability to act in ways that align with God's will, showing how human reasoning mirrors divine wisdom.

Moral Agency: The moral dimension of the *imago Dei* is closely tied to humanity's capacity for moral agency. The phrase "let them have dominion" in Gen 1:26 reflects the Hebrew verb *radah*, meaning to rule or reign.[6] This dominion is not arbitrary but is rooted in humanity's role as God's representative on earth, exercising authority in a manner that mirrors God's justice and mercy. As Kilner notes, moral agency is foundational to the *imago Dei*, because it reflects humanity's ability to align with divine righteousness.[7]

Humanity, created in God's image, was initially sinless and capable of living in perfect harmony. This moral dimension calls humanity to reflect divine justice through righteous rule and stewardship of the earth. In essence, moral agency within the *imago Dei* emphasizes that humans are accountable to God for their actions, particularly in how they exercise authority over creation.

The Triune Nature of God and Its Reflection in Humanity

The plural language in Gen 1:26—*na'aseh adam b'tsalmenu* ("Let us make humankind in our image")—has sparked considerable theological reflection This plural form has been interpreted in various ways, but its most significant meaning is as an allusion to the relational and communal nature of the Godhead—the divine Trinity. Early church fathers, including Augustine, interpreted this plurality as a reflection of the Trinitarian nature of God, where Father, Son, and Holy Spirit collaborate in the creation of humanity. Augustine believed that this communal nature of God

---

5. Thomas Aquinas, *Summa Theologiae*, I.93.5.
6. Hamilton, *Handbook on the Pentateuch*, 28.
7. Kilner, *Dignity and Destiny*, 28.

is mirrored in human relationships, where memory, intellect, and love reflect the inner workings of the Godhead.[8]

Although the Trinity is fully revealed in the New Testament, Augustine saw in this Genesis passage a hint of the inner life of the triune God, suggesting that the communal and relational aspects of God's nature are intrinsic to the *imago Dei*. However, Augustine's contribution extends beyond simply affirming human relationality. His reflections in *De Trinitate* suggest that the human mind, in its ability to know and love, actively participates in this divine relationship, not only as an image-bearer but as one capable of reflecting God's memory, intellect, and will.

Moreover, humanity's relational nature is not confined to human-to-human relationships but extends to our communion with the divine. Theologians such as Gregory of Nyssa emphasized that humanity was created for the purpose of participating in the life of God.[9] This participation is not merely a reflection of God's nature but an invitation into divine communion. As Gregory writes, "Man was created to participate in the divine. . . . This participation is the *telos*, or ultimate purpose, of human existence."[10] Gregory's insight highlights that humanity's ultimate purpose is found in this divine relationship, not merely in individual achievement or autonomy.

This theological vision of relationality provides a stark contrast to modern technological aspirations of autonomy and self-enhancement. While Augustine and Gregory offer foundational perspectives, modern theologians like Dietrich Bonhoeffer expand on this relational framework.[11] In contrast to the biblical vision of humanity's relational identity, transhumanist ideals promote autonomy and individual enhancement. Theologians like Bonhoeffer have critiqued this emphasis on autonomy as fundamentally opposed to the Christian understanding of human identity. Bonhoeffer argued that human beings are not defined by their autonomy, but by their relationships with others and with God. In his *Ethics*, Bonhoeffer wrote, "Man is not alone; he is not an isolated being, but exists only in community with others. He is created for the 'other,' and it is in this community that the *imago Dei* is most fully realized."[12]

---

8. Augustine, *De Trinitate*, trans. Edmund Hill (New York: New City, 1991), XI.6.

9. Gregory of Nyssa, *On the Making of Man*, trans. Philip Schaff (Edinburgh: T&T Clark, 1888), 5.

10. Gregory of Nyssa, *On the Making of Man*, 12.

11. Bonhoeffer, *Ethics*, 269.

12. Bonhoeffer, *Ethics*, 251.

This relational framework becomes particularly significant when viewed in contrast to AI and transhumanist ideals, which often prioritize self-determined enhancement over communal identity. Bonhoeffer emphasizes the fulfillment of the *imago Dei* in relationality, directly countering transhumanist ideals that isolate identity from community.

The image of God in humanity, according to Bonhoeffer, calls for interdependence, cooperation, and communal flourishing—values that are often neglected in the technological aspirations of individual enhancement and autonomy. Bonhoeffer's work in *Ethics* critiques the isolationist tendencies of modern autonomy by emphasizing that human beings are fundamentally relational, created for community. In a world increasingly shaped by AI and transhumanist ideals, which prioritize self-sufficient and autonomous enhancement, Bonhoeffer's theology offers a vital counterpoint.[13] He contends that human identity is not shaped in isolation but through relationships with others and God. AI and transhumanist ambitions that focus on enhancing individual cognitive or physical abilities risk dehumanizing individuals by severing the bonds that define personhood.

In his critique, Bonhoeffer presents a theology where fulfillment is found not in the enhancement of individual capacities but in mutual interdependence and ethical responsibility toward others. He writes, "Let him who cannot be alone beware of community. Let him who is not in community beware of being alone."[14] According to Bonhoeffer, man is not meant to be an isolated being but rather to exist in healthy community while also nurturing the self. This theological framework challenges the autonomous ideals of transhumanism, suggesting that the fulfillment of the *imago Dei* cannot be achieved through technological augmentation of the self but rather through participation in a communal life marked by love and service. Bonhoeffer's emphasis on relationality serves as a critique of the self-centered pursuit of transcendence through technology, arguing that true transcendence is found in a life lived for the other, in alignment with God's purposes. Thus, Bonhoeffer's ethics pose a direct challenge to the notion of AI autonomy, where systems operate independently of human moral agency, further isolating humans from meaningful relationality.

---

13. Bonhoeffer, *Ethics*.

14. Dietrich Bonhoeffer, *Life Together*, trans. John W. Doberstein (New York: Harper and Row, 1954), 77.

Moltmann echoes this critique, warning that the reduction of human identity to autonomy and control distorts the relational nature of humanity.[15] Moltmann's theology of relationality and participation critiques technological determinism by affirming that humans are inherently relational beings, called to live in communion not only with one another but with God and creation. His emphasis on "participation in the divine life" contrasts sharply with the transhumanist vision of individual enhancement and control over one's destiny. In *Theology of Hope* and *The Spirit of Life*, Moltmann advocates for an understanding of human identity that is fundamentally participatory, where individuals find their true meaning not in self-determined mastery over life but in their relationship with God and the larger created order.[16]

Moltmann also warns against the dangers of technological determinism, where human freedom is subsumed by the inexorable logic of technological progress. In a world increasingly driven by AI and technological systems, Moltmann's critique is essential, as it challenges the idea that technology can define or control human destiny. Moltmann's theology reminds us that true freedom and flourishing come from participating in the divine life, not in attempting to transcend human limitations through technology. His call for a participatory theology challenges the assumption that human flourishing can be achieved through the autonomous manipulation of life and death—a core aspiration of transhumanism.

By advocating for relationality and participation, both Bonhoeffer and Moltmann critique the core assumptions of AI autonomy and transhumanist control. Their theologies present a compelling vision of human identity that is rooted in relational dependence on God and others, resisting the allure of technological self-sufficiency. In this sense, both theologians offer a framework that resists the reductionist tendencies of modern technology and AI, where human beings are often seen as isolated, autonomous entities rather than deeply interconnected participants in God's creation.

Aquinas adds to this by highlighting that the *imago Dei* is expressed not only through rationality and relationality but also through the will. For Aquinas, the image of God in humanity reflects the eternal processions

---

15. Jürgen Moltmann, *The Spirit of Life: A Universal Affirmation*, trans. Margaret Kohl (Minneapolis: Fortress, 1992), 32–33.

16. Moltmann, *Spirit of Life*, 32–33; Jürgen Moltmann, *Theology of Hope: On the Ground and the Implications of a Christian Eschatology*, trans. James W. Leitch (Minneapolis: Fortress, 1993).

within the Trinity, where the intellect generates the Word, and love proceeds from both.[17] Thus, Aquinas's understanding emphasizes that the *imago Dei* involves not just autonomy but a participation in divine love and knowledge, reinforcing the relational and moral dimensions of human existence. Aquinas, like Augustine, underscores that relationality is integral to human identity, but he expands the discussion by connecting it to divine love and will. This emphasis on participation—where intellect and love reflect the divine processions—offers a deeper view of human relationality as not just communal but also intellectual and volitional.

In sum, the relational aspect of the *imago Dei*—as articulated by Augustine, Aquinas, and modern theologians like Bonhoeffer—offers a powerful critique of transhumanist ideals. It calls for a return to understanding human identity not as isolated autonomy but as participation in the divine life, which is central to human flourishing.

Humanity's Role in Creation: Dominion and Responsibility

The phrase *radah* (have dominion) in Gen 1:26 underscores humanity's responsibility as stewards of creation. In the ancient Near Eastern (ANE) context, the term *radah* often referred to the authority exercised by kings and rulers, especially over their subjects and lands. The use of this term in the biblical creation narrative suggests that humanity's role is to govern creation as a reflection of God's righteous and benevolent rule.[18] In this sense, dominion is not about domination or exploitation but about stewardship and care, where human authority mirrors the justice and mercy of God's own governance.

Scholars such as John Walton have noted that *radah* places humanity in the position of vice-regents under God, exercising authority derived from divine kingship. This authority is not an invitation to exploit the natural world but a call to responsible stewardship, reflecting God's justice and mercy. Humanity's dominion over creation is, therefore, a call to preserve and cultivate the goodness of creation rather than dominate it.[19]

The concept of dominion in Genesis is closely tied to the *imago Dei*, which implies that humanity's rule over creation is meant to reflect

---

17. Thomas Aquinas, *Summa Theologiae*, I.93.

18. John H. Walton, *The Lost World of Genesis One: Ancient Cosmology and the Origins Debate* (Downers Grove, IL: InterVarsity, 2009), 63–66.

19. Walton, *Lost World of Genesis One*, 72.

God's creative and sustaining power.[20] According to scholars like Brown, Fausset, and Jamieson, this dominion is not a mandate to subdue or exploit the natural world but rather a responsibility to care for it, reflecting the divine mandate to "cultivate and keep" the earth (Gen 2:15). This relational dynamic between humanity, God, and creation emphasizes that human beings are not autonomous rulers but stewards entrusted with the task of maintaining the harmony and flourishing of the world.[21]

However, this model of stewardship stands in stark contrast to the transhumanist vision of dominion as technological mastery. Transhumanism, in seeking to transcend human limitations through AI and human enhancement technologies, often reframes dominion as a form of control over nature and even life itself. AI systems, designed to optimize, control, and dominate various aspects of human life—from labor to social interactions—risk distorting humanity's original vocation as stewards of creation. Instead of caring for the world and one another in accordance with God's justice and mercy, technological advancements tend to redefine dominion as domination, reducing the complexity of creation to data-driven manipulation.

In Genesis, dominion exercised in a state of original righteousness signifies that humanity's authority over the earth was intended to mirror God's just and merciful rule. The moral agency given to humanity in the *imago Dei* was initially untainted by sin, allowing human beings to govern creation in accordance with divine wisdom and justice. However, this moral agency was contingent on humanity's relationship with God.[22] When Adam and Eve disobeyed God's command by eating from the tree of the knowledge of good and evil, their exercise of dominion became distorted by sin. The Hebrew word *radah* thus transforms from a benevolent rule into one marked by exploitation and disharmony. As Augustine notes, sin disrupted the harmonious relationship between humanity, God, and creation, leading to alienation and decay.[23]

The *imago Dei* was marred through disobedience, resulting in a broken relationship not only between humanity and God but also between humanity and the natural world. As theologian Ellen Davis points out, this rupture is reflected in the subsequent curse upon the ground in Gen 3, where the earth, once a place of fruitful labor, becomes resistant to

---

20. Brown et al., *Genesis-Deuteronomy*, 8–9.
21. Brown et al., *Genesis-Deuteronomy*, 8–9.
22. Thomas Aquinas, *Summa Theologiae*, I-II.91.2.
23. Augustine, *City of God*, trans. Bettenson, XIII.14.

human cultivation. This not only represents the fracturing of humanity's dominion over creation but also signals the deeper cosmic consequences of sin.[24] The creation, once a space of divine-human cooperation, is now subject to futility, groaning under the weight of corruption, as Paul describes in Rom 8:20–22. Similarly, AI and transhumanist technologies risk deepening this alienation by promoting domination over creation rather than cooperation with it. The focus shifts from responsible stewardship to self-centered control, as seen in the pursuit of digital immortality or AI-driven decision-making that marginalizes human relationality and moral agency.

Nevertheless, the restoration of the *imago Dei* is central to the redemptive work of Christ, who is described in Col 1:15 as "the image of the invisible God" (*eikon tou Theou tou aoratou*). Through Christ's life, death, and resurrection, the broken relationship between humanity, God, and creation is restored, offering the possibility of renewed dominion grounded in righteousness and justice. This restored dominion is not a return to prelapsarian innocence but an elevation of human vocation in Christ, where believers are called to exercise authority over creation in a way that reflects the self-giving love of God.[25]

Thus, humanity's role in creation is a reflection of divine stewardship, calling for an ethic of care and responsibility that resists the exploitation of natural resources and prioritizes the flourishing of all creation. As this chapter will continue to explore, the restoration of the *imago Dei* through Christ enables humanity to fulfill its original vocation of stewardship, offering a counternarrative to the transhumanist vision of dominion as self-determined mastery over the created order. In a world where technological advancements threaten to redefine dominion as domination—where AI systems are increasingly tasked with autonomous control—the biblical concept of *radah* calls us back to our original vocation. This vocation is one of stewardship, humility, and care for the earth, grounded in the *imago Dei* and restored through Christ's redemptive work. AI and transhumanist ambitions, which prioritize mastery over creation, represent a distorted view of dominion, one that ultimately erodes the relational and moral dimensions intrinsic to humanity's identity as bearers of the divine image.

---

24. Ellen F. Davis, *Scripture, Culture, and Agriculture: An Agrarian Reading of the Bible* (Cambridge: Cambridge University Press, 2009), 41–43.

25. N. T. Wright, *Paul and the Faithfulness of God* (Minneapolis: Fortress, 2013), 123.

The Moral Aspect of the Imago Dei and Original Righteousness

In the pre-fall state, humanity was endowed with original righteousness, a condition that reflected the very holiness and moral purity of God. This sinless state allowed human beings to act in ways fully aligned with God's will. As Kilner argues, original righteousness underscores the intrinsic value of humanity's moral nature, which was imbued with the ability to freely live in accordance with God's perfect order.[26]

Augustine of Hippo emphasized that this righteousness was part of humanity's original nature, allowing human beings to reflect the divine character before the fall distorted their desires and moral inclinations. In this light, original righteousness can be seen not merely as a passive state but as an active moral agency in service to God's will.[27]

Thomas Aquinas elaborated on this idea, asserting that original righteousness was a precondition for humanity's natural inclination toward good. In this state, humans were naturally disposed to act in accordance with reason, allowing them to exercise dominion over creation as part of God's moral order.[28] This moral harmony was lost with the fall, but, as Paul notes in Col 3:10, humanity is "renewed in knowledge after the image of its creator." This renewal, which involves the whole human person—mind, body, and soul—restores the *imago Dei* through Christ.[29]

As noted by David Brown and his colleagues, the blessing given to humanity in Gen 1:28 was not merely a mandate to populate the earth but also a calling to live in harmony with God's moral order.[30] This stewardship of creation was a direct outworking of humanity's moral agency, demonstrating that the *imago Dei* is not a static quality but one that requires active engagement with God's purposes for the world. In the New Testament, Paul's theology emphasizes the restoration of this moral agency through Christ. In Col 3:10, Paul speaks of humanity being "renewed in knowledge after the image of its creator." This renewal, according to scholars like N. T. Wright, is not limited to the intellect or

---

26. Kilner, *Dignity and Destiny*, 55–57.
27. Augustine, *City of God*, trans. Bettenson, XIII.14.
28. Thomas Aquinas, *Summa Theologiae*, I-II.91.2.
29. John F. Wippel, *The Metaphysical Thought of Thomas Aquinas* (Washington, DC: Catholic University of America Press, 2000), 112.
30. Brown et al., *Genesis-Deuteronomy*, 8–9.

spirit but involves the entirety of the human person—mind, body, and soul—reflecting the holistic nature of the *imago Dei*.[31]

Paul's assertion that the *imago Dei* is restored through Christ underscores the importance of moral transformation as part of Christian salvation. This renewal process is not just a return to original righteousness but an elevation of human identity in Christ, who perfectly embodies the *imago Dei*.[32] For theologians like Karl Barth, this restoration is the fulfillment of humanity's true purpose: to live in perfect communion with God, reflecting his image not just in being but in doing.[33] The restoration of the *imago Dei* through Christ serves as a counternarrative to transhumanist aspirations of achieving human perfection through technological means. While AI and transhumanism seek to enhance human capacities artificially, the Christian narrative affirms that true human flourishing is found in the restoration of moral agency through divine grace.[34]

The moral dimension of the *imago Dei*, therefore, is not simply a relic of humanity's pre-fall state; it is an ongoing call to live in accordance with God's will, restored through the redemptive work of Christ. As modern technologies like AI and transhumanism threaten to redefine human identity and agency, the doctrine of the *imago Dei* provides a theological framework for resisting these reductionist tendencies. In Christ, the *imago Dei* is not only restored but perfected, offering humanity a vision of moral agency that transcends the limits of human autonomy and technological enhancement. Ultimately, the moral aspect of the *imago Dei*, rooted in humanity's original righteousness and restored through Christ, calls us to resist the allure of self-made transcendence and instead embrace the transformative power of divine grace, which alone can restore us to our true identity as bearers of God's image.

---

31. Wright, *Paul and the Faithfulness of God*, 123.

32. Karl Barth, *Church Dogmatics*, vol. 3/2, *The Doctrine of Creation*, ed. G. W. Bromiley and T. F. Torrance, trans. Harold Knight et al (Edinburgh: T&T Clark, 1960), 202. Barth argues that humanity's restoration in Christ is the fulfillment of its true purpose: to exist in perfect communion with God. This restoration is not merely a return to an original state but a dynamic participation in God's ongoing work, reflecting the divine image not only in being but in action. Barth's emphasis on the *imago Dei* as an active, relational identity contrasts sharply with transhumanist aspirations that seek to achieve perfection through technological means rather than through divine grace.

33. Kilner, *Dignity and Destiny*, 133–36.

34. David Kelsey, *Eccentric Existence: A Theological Anthropology* (Louisville: Westminster John Knox, 2009), 219–21.

PATRISTIC AND MEDIEVAL UNDERSTANDINGS

The patristic and medieval periods played a crucial role in the development of the doctrine of the *imago Dei*, particularly in its theological and philosophical dimensions. Building upon the biblical foundations laid in Genesis, early church fathers and medieval theologians sought to unpack the rich meaning of being made in the image of God. Their reflections, rooted in both Scripture and classical philosophy, provide a multifaceted understanding of the divine image that emphasizes rationality, relationality, moral agency, and humanity's unique role within creation.

Early Church Fathers: Augustine and the Imago Dei

Among the early church fathers, Augustine stands as one of the most significant contributors to the doctrine of the *imago Dei*. For Augustine, the image of God in humanity was primarily intellectual and rational. In his seminal work, *De Trinitate*, he developed a profound connection between the *imago Dei* and the human mind's capacity to grasp divine wisdom. According to Augustine, human rationality reflects God's nature, particularly in the intellect's ability to contemplate eternal truths and seek after God.[35] In this sense, the *imago Dei* was not merely a static attribute of human nature but a dynamic capacity to participate in the divine wisdom.

However, Augustine's understanding of the *imago Dei* was not limited to rationality alone. In his later writings, Augustine expanded upon the relational aspect of the divine image, highlighting humanity's capacity for love and self-knowledge. He argued that just as the Trinity exists in a relationship of love between Father, Son, and Holy Spirit, so too does humanity reflect this relational dynamic.[36] This relationality is a key component of the *imago Dei*, as human beings are created not for isolated existence but for communion with God and one another. In emphasizing relationality, Augustine's theology critiques the isolationist tendencies found in modern transhumanism, which prioritize individual enhancement over communal responsibility.

Augustine also connected the *imago Dei* to humanity's capacity for moral discernment. He contended that the human ability to know and

---

35. Augustine, *De Trinitate*, IX.3.
36. Augustine, *De Trinitate*, XI.6.

choose between good and evil was a reflection of the moral dimension of the divine image. This moral capacity was deeply intertwined with human free will, which Augustine viewed as essential to human flourishing.[37] His framework stands in opposition to AI systems that remove moral agency from humans, reducing them to passive recipients of technological control.

Medieval Theology: Thomas Aquinas and the Expansion of the Imago Dei

Building upon Augustine, Thomas Aquinas developed a more nuanced and comprehensive understanding of the *imago Dei*, particularly in his synthesis of Aristotelian philosophy with Christian theology. For Aquinas, the *imago Dei* included not only rationality and intellect but also the human will and moral decision-making. Aquinas emphasized that reason and volition were essential aspects of the divine image, as they reflected humanity's unique capacity for moral agency and participation in the divine order.[38]

Aquinas understood the *imago Dei* as primarily located in the rational soul, which was endowed with the faculties of intellect and will.[39] In Aquinas's view, these faculties enable humans to engage in divine wisdom and love, and to make moral decisions that reflect God's justice. Aquinas expanded upon Augustine's emphasis on moral agency by articulating a vision of humanity's participation in the divine order. He argued that human beings, as rational creatures, were capable of understanding and participating in the natural law, which was a reflection of God's eternal law. This participation in the divine order is an essential aspect of the *imago Dei*, as it allows humans to exercise moral agency in a way that mirrors God's governance of the universe.[40] This focus on moral agency is particularly relevant in modern critiques of AI, which often removes human decision-making from the moral sphere by prioritizing algorithmic control over ethical discernment.

---

37. Augustine, *On Free Choice of the Will*, trans. Anna Benjamin and L. H. Hackstaff (New York: Bobbs-Merrill, 1964), II.19.
   38. Thomas Aquinas, *Summa Theologiae*, I.93.
   39. Thomas Aquinas, *Summa Theologiae*, I.93.
   40. Thomas Aquinas, *Summa Theologiae*, I-II.91.

Stewardship and Dominion in Patristic and Medieval Thought

The theme of stewardship and dominion, rooted in the Genesis mandate to "have dominion" (*radah*) over the earth (Gen 1:26), was further developed by both the patristic and medieval theologians. In the patristic period, theologians such as Gregory of Nyssa viewed humanity's dominion over creation as a reflection of the *imago Dei*, emphasizing that this dominion was not one of exploitation but of responsible stewardship.[41] Gregory argued that humans, as image-bearers of God, were called to care for creation in a way that mirrored God's own providential care, ensuring the flourishing of all creatures.

Aquinas also took up the theme of dominion, but he framed it within the context of humanity's moral responsibility. He argued that humanity's dominion over creation was contingent upon their relationship with God. When aligned with God's will, humanity's exercise of dominion would reflect God's justice and mercy.[42] However, when this relationship was broken by sin, humanity's dominion became distorted, leading to the exploitation and degradation of creation. Aquinas thus connected the moral agency of the *imago Dei* with the ethical responsibility of stewardship, underscoring that human dominion over creation must always be exercised in a way that reflects God's righteousness.

In conclusion, the patristic and medieval understandings of the *imago Dei* provided a rich and multifaceted theological framework that emphasized rationality, relationality, and moral agency. Augustine and Aquinas, in particular, laid the groundwork for understanding how humanity, as bearers of the divine image, are called to live in relationship with God, others, and creation. This theological foundation challenges the modern aspirations of AI and transhumanism, which often prioritize individual autonomy over relational and communal existence. By returning to the insights of the early church and medieval theologians, we are reminded that humanity's true identity and purpose are found not in self-enhancement but in participation in the divine life. Patristic and medieval theological reflections on the *imago Dei* correlate to the exegesis of Gen 1:26–27 and present a profound understanding of human identity, grounded not in self-sufficiency or technological enhancement but in relational participation with God, creation, and community—offering

---

41. Gregory of Nyssa, *On the Making of Man*, 5.
42. Thomas Aquinas, *Summa Theologiae*, I.96.

a powerful counternarrative to the reductionist inclinations of AI and transhumanism.

REFORMATION AND MODERN INTERPRETATIONS

The Reformation marked a significant shift in theological reflection on the *imago Dei*, challenging medieval scholasticism and renewing an emphasis on the relational and covenantal aspects of humanity's divine image. While earlier thinkers like Augustine and Aquinas had focused on the intellectual and rational dimensions of the *imago Dei*, Reformation theologians like John Calvin brought the relational nature of humanity's image-bearing identity to the forefront.[43] This shift not only deepened the understanding of human dignity but also illuminated the way in which the divine image is restored through Christ's redemptive work. By emphasizing the covenantal and communal aspects of the *imago Dei*, Reformation theologians provided a theological foundation that critiques the individualistic tendencies of AI and transhumanism.[44]

43. With regard to Reformation theology and the *imago Dei*, John Calvin's contributions have been highly influential in shaping Christian understandings of humanity's relationship with God. Calvin's *Institutes of the Christian Religion* emphasized that the *imago Dei* is not merely an intellectual or rational quality but rather a relational and covenantal reality. As Calvin wrote, "Nearly all the wisdom we possess, that is to say, true and sound wisdom, consists of two parts: the knowledge of God and of ourselves." Calvin, *Institutes*, trans. Battles, 1.1.1. This focus on the relational nature of the *imago Dei* reflects Calvin's broader theological system, where the human being is designed to live in relationship with God, in faithful obedience to the divine covenant. Calvin's covenantal theology shapes his view that the divine image in humanity encompasses both relationality and moral agency. However, Calvin has been critiqued for his emphasis on human depravity post-fall, which some argue overshadows the *imago Dei* in human beings. Despite these critiques, Calvin's theology remains a cornerstone for understanding the covenantal dimensions of the *imago Dei*. As Richard Muller notes, "Calvin's doctrine of the image of God is pivotal for understanding his entire system of theology and his views on human nature." Muller, *The Unaccommodated Calvin: Studies in the Foundation of a Theological Tradition* (Grand Rapids: Baker Academic, 2000), 58. Nonetheless, this research focuses primarily on Calvin's contributions to relationality and covenant, leaving aside debates over his interpretation of human depravity.

44. With regard to modern *imago Dei* research advances, Karl Barth has been considered one of the most important figures advancing the research in the twentieth century. Barth was suggested as the premier scholar on *imago Dei* studies between 1919–1960 by Gunnlaugur A. Jónsson, *The Image of God: Genesis 1:26-28 in a Century of Old Testament Research*, trans. Lorraine Svedsen (Stockholm: Almqvist and Wiksell, 1988), 146. In *Church Dogmatics*, Barth writes that, "'In our image' means to be created as a being which has its ground and possibility in the fact that . . . in God's own sphere and being, there exists a divine and therefore self-grounded prototype to which this being can

In the face of contemporary technological advancements, including AI and transhumanism, the Reformation and modern interpretations of the *imago Dei* offer a timely and necessary corrective. They remind us that human identity cannot be reduced to intellectual or physical capacities but must be understood within the broader framework of relationality, community, and moral agency. This section will explore how theologians like Calvin and Barth developed these ideas, providing a foundation for engaging with the ethical and spiritual challenges of our technological age.

John Calvin

John Calvin's theology of the *imago Dei* significantly shaped Reformation thought. He emphasized the *imago Dei* not merely as an intellectual reflection of God, as Augustine had done, but as rooted in a covenantal relationship between God and humanity. For Calvin, the divine image reflected humanity's role as partners in the divine covenant, emphasizing faith and obedience as central to this identity. This covenantal framework placed relationality at the heart of the divine image, suggesting that humans were created not only to reflect God intellectually but to live in faithful relationship with the Creator.[45] This relational framework challenges transhumanist ideals of self-determined mastery by reasserting the importance of human dependence on God and community.

---

correspond." Karl Barth, *Church Dogmatics*, vol. 3/1, *The Doctrine of Creation*, ed. G. W. Bromiley and T. F. Torrance, trans. J. W. Edwards et al. (London: T&T Clark, 2010), 183. Barth has been criticized because of the duality of gender imposed on the perfected image, but this aspect of Barth's findings is not the focus of this research. In Barth's own words, "We cannot say man without having to say male or female and also male and female. Man exists in this differentiation, in this duality." Barth, *Church Dogmatics*, vol. 3/2, 286. As Niskanen outlines, "Even though the theological and philosophical underpinnings of Barth's exegesis were called into question, his dialectical model would prove to be the most influential interpretation of the *imago Dei* for almost half a century, and its influence can still be seen today." Paul Niskanen, "The Poetics of Adam," *Journal of Biblical Literature* 128:3 (2009) 417–36, 418. A development in Barth's dialectical understanding of the image of God is found in the work of Claus Westermann; Claus Westermann, *Genesis* (Darmstadt: Wissenschaftliche Buchgesellschaft, 2016). Though Westermann's work gets into the exegetical weeds of Genesis the importance here is that the author follows Barth in stressing the relational and participatory nature of human beings in God's image, which is pursuant with the patristic leads discussed herein.

45. John Calvin, *Institutes of the Christian Religion*, trans. Henry Beveridge (Grand Rapids: Eerdmans, 2001), 1.15.3.

Calvin argued that the image of God in humanity was deeply marred by sin, but not completely eradicated. Therefore, the capacity for communion with God—both individually and corporately—remained intact, though fractured.[46] For Calvin, the *imago Dei* was therefore central to understanding humanity's redemption and restoration.[47] In contrast to AI's emphasis on enhancing individual capacities, Calvin's theology insists that true human flourishing occurs through restored relationships with God and others rather than technological self-enhancement.

Karl Barth

Karl Barth, a towering figure in twentieth-century theology, offered a modern interpretation of the *imago Dei* that emphasized relationality, but in a way distinct from Calvin's covenantal framework. Barth focused on the *imago Dei* as realized through human relationships and community. Barth argued that humans reflect the image of God when they live in relationships of love, trust, and mutual respect.[48] This shift from the individual to the communal emphasizes the interconnectedness of human beings, countering the autonomy-centric worldview promoted by AI and transhumanist ideologies.

According to Barth, the image of God in humanity cannot be understood in isolation but must be seen in the context of human community.[49] This relational vision critiques transhumanism's focus on individual enhancement by reaffirming that humans are fulfilled through interdependent relationships. Barth's theology thus offers a powerful counternarrative, reminding us that the *imago Dei* calls humans to live not in self-sufficient isolation but in interdependent relationships.[50]

Contemporary Reflections

In contemporary theology, scholars continue to engage with the *imago Dei* in light of modern challenges, particularly AI and transhumanism. These technological movements often emphasize cognitive or physical

---

46. Calvin, *Institutes*, 1.15.4 (trans. Beveridge).
47. Calvin, *Institutes*, 3.7.5 (trans. Beveridge).
48. Karl Barth, *Church Dogmatics*, vol. 3/2, 195.
49. Barth, *Church Dogmatics*, vol. 3/2, 196.
50. Barth, *Church Dogmatics*, vol. 3/2, 198.

enhancement as the pinnacle of human achievement, yet in doing so, they risk distorting the relational and moral dimensions of the *imago Dei*. Modern theologians express concern that focusing on individual cognitive enhancements, rather than fostering communal and relational identities, reflects a reductionist view of humanity.[51]

Brent Waters, in his exploration of technological ethics, argues that transhumanist ideologies often reduce the human person to a mere collection of biological functions, stripping away the deeper, relational aspects that make humans bearers of God's image.[52] Waters critiques the idea that technology can deliver human transcendence, stating that such pursuits often disregard the social and moral responsibilities intrinsic to human nature. His concern is that in striving for immortality or cognitive enhancement, society risks devaluing the essential qualities that constitute human dignity—our relationality, moral agency, and dependence on God.[53]

Sherry Turkle offers a complementary critique from a psychological perspective, highlighting the ways in which technology shapes our interactions and self-understanding.[54] She argues that our increasing reliance on AI and digital communication can erode authentic relationships, leading to a diminished sense of self. Turkle warns that the more we rely on technology to mediate our relationships, the more we risk losing our capacity for empathy and deep connection with others. Her work underscores the theological concerns regarding AI and the *imago Dei*, particularly the idea that technological progress, while useful, can alienate us from our God-given relational identity.[55]

---

51. Brent Waters, *Christian Moral Theology in the Emerging Technoculture*, 2nd ed. (Farnham, Surrey, UK: Ashgate, 2014), 34.

52. Brent Waters is recognized for his critique of transhumanism and technological advancements that threaten to undermine the relational and embodied aspects of human identity. He emphasizes that the *imago Dei* must inform our approach to technology, particularly when it comes to human enhancement. See Waters, *From Human to Posthuman*, 62–64.

53. Waters, *From Human to Posthuman*, 34–35.

54. Sherry Turkle has been a prominent critic of how digital technologies, including AI, affect human relationships and identity. Her work highlights the dangers of technological isolation and the erosion of genuine human connections, providing an important psychological lens for discussions about the *imago Dei* in an age of AI. See Sherry Turkle, *Alone Together: Why We Expect More from Technology and Less from Each Other* (New York: Basic Books, 2011), 150–53.

55. Turkle, *Alone Together*, 79.

Jordan Peterson's reflections on responsibility and meaning further deepen these concerns. Peterson suggests that modern technological advancements, particularly those driven by the transhumanist agenda, often prioritize individual autonomy over collective responsibility, neglecting the moral and relational dimensions of human existence.[56] He asserts that true meaning and fulfillment are not found in technological enhancement but in the acceptance of moral responsibility and the pursuit of a life grounded in service to others. Peterson's critique aligns with theological concerns, as he emphasizes the importance of human interdependence and the dangers of individualism.[57] His work highlights the tension between technological autonomy and the moral responsibility that is central to the *imago Dei*.

Additionally, contemporary philosophical critiques challenge the idea of human autonomy, which undergirds much of the transhumanist agenda. These critiques, supported by Peterson's observations, point out that the *imago Dei* cannot be understood solely through the lens of individual accomplishment or technological transcendence. Instead, theologians argue that the *imago Dei* involves a holistic view of human identity, encompassing body, mind, and soul, as well as the relational and communal aspects that are often overlooked in technological discourse. The relational nature of the *imago Dei*—emphasizing human interdependence, moral agency, and divine purpose—offers a necessary counterbalance to the individualistic ethos of transhumanism.

In response to these pressing concerns, the *imago Dei* remains an essential theological lens, offering a robust defense against the simplistic and reductionist tendencies of modern technological ambitions. As Christian Lous Lange wisely noted, "Technology is a useful servant but a dangerous master," reminding us that without careful ethical and theological guidance, the tools of human advancement can easily become mechanisms of dehumanization.[58]

---

56. Jordan Peterson often critiques reductionist approaches to human identity, particularly in the context of technological advancements like AI. He emphasizes the need for a deeper understanding of human dignity, grounded in the *imago Dei*. See Jordan B. Peterson, *12 Rules for Life: An Antidote to Chaos* (Toronto: Random House Canada, 2018), 243–46. Additionally, Peterson's lectures frequently explore the Genesis creation narrative as a foundational text for understanding the moral and relational dimensions of human life. See Jordan B. Peterson, "Biblical Series 2: Genesis 1—Chaos and Order," May 27, 2017, YouTube video, https://www.youtube.com/watch?v=hdrLQ7DpiWs.

57. Peterson, *12 Rules for Life*, 101–3.

58. Christian Lous Lange, *Technology and Human Progress* (New York: Harper and Row, 1936), 45.

THE RESTORATIVE ASPECT OF THE *IMAGO DEI*

In Christian theology, the doctrine of the *imago Dei* not only addresses humanity's unique status as bearers of God's image but also emphasizes the dynamic process of restoration through Christ. While the fall marred the image of God in humanity, the redemptive work of Christ offers a way for that image to be restored, renewing the relational, rational, and moral dimensions that were originally intended in creation. Key New Testament passages, such as Col 1:15 and Rom 8:29, point to Christ as the "image of the invisible God" and the model for human transformation.

This section will explore how Christ's redemptive act restores the broken *imago Dei*, framing redemption as a holistic and dynamic process that contrasts sharply with modern technological attempts at human enhancement. Rather than seeking transcendence through human achievement, the Christian vision of redemption through Christ centers on relationality, moral responsibility, and the sanctification of the entire human person—mind, body, and soul. In contrast to the transhumanist pursuit of immortality and cognitive enhancement through technology, the Christian narrative offers the restoration of human identity through Christ's resurrection, emphasizing eternal life as a gift of grace rather than a product of human control. Through this lens, the *imago Dei* becomes the guiding framework for understanding human identity in an age of AI and transhumanism, offering a redemptive narrative that restores humanity's dignity and purpose.

Redemption Through Christ

In Christian theology, the *imago Dei* is not simply a static condition; it is a dynamic reality, both affirmed at creation and marred by the fall. However, this image is not irreparably lost but is restored through Christ, as highlighted in key New Testament passages.

Exegesis of Colossians 1:15

Paul's declaration in Col 1:15 that Christ is the "image of the invisible God" (*eikōn tou theou tou aoratou*) serves as a cornerstone for understanding Christ's role in redeeming humanity's fractured identity. Unlike fallen humanity, whose ability to fully reflect God's image is compromised by sin, Christ stands as the perfect embodiment of what it means to bear the *imago Dei*. Paul does not merely assert that Christ is an image of God; rather, he presents Christ as the visible manifestation of the invisible God. Christ reveals the character, will, and purpose of God in a way that the Old Testament's (OT) images and shadows could not. This language resonates deeply with the Jewish wisdom tradition, where divine wisdom is seen as God's agent in creation (Prov 8). Yet Paul applies this to Christ, presenting him not just as a reflection of wisdom but as its ultimate source.

Michael Gorman emphasizes the participatory nature of this image.[59] For Paul, Christ is not only the exemplar of the divine image but also the means through which humanity is restored to that image. Gorman argues that believers are called to embody this restored *imago Dei* by participating in Christ's redemptive mission.[60] In this sense, Col 1:15 is not only a theological statement about Christ's identity but also a call to action for the church, which must live out the restored image through humility, justice, and self-giving love.

Paul's use of the term *eikōn* here parallels the language in Rom 8:29, where believers are described as being "conformed to the image of his Son." This suggests that the restoration of the *imago Dei* is an ongoing process of transformation, where Christians are progressively being shaped into the image of Christ.[61] This transformative process is central to Pauline theology and affirms that the *imago Dei* is not merely a static condition but a dynamic calling. The role of Christ as the perfect image of God serves both as the model and the means of this transformation.[62]

Stanley E. Porter further expands on this by highlighting the cosmic scope of Christ's redemptive work. In Col 1:16–20, Paul elaborates that Christ is not only the image of God but the agent through whom all things were created and are sustained. This affirms Christ's preeminence, not merely as a historical figure but as the eternal Son through whom creation and new creation are brought into being.[63] Thus, human-

---

59. Michael J. Gorman, *Becoming the Gospel: Paul, Participation, and Mission* (Grand Rapids: Eerdmans, 2015), 197.

60. Gorman, *Becoming the Gospel*, 199.

61. Gorman, *Becoming the Gospel*, 201.

62. N. T. Wright, *Colossians and Philemon: An Introduction and Commentary*, Tyndale New Testament Commentaries 12 (Downers Grove, IL: InterVarsity, 1986), 72.

63. Stanley E. Porter, *The Apostle Paul: His Life, Thought, and Letters* (Grand Rapids: Eerdmans, 2016), 335–36. Porter highlights the cosmic scope of Christ's redemptive work in Col 1:16–20, emphasizing that Christ is not only the image of God but also

ity's redemption through Christ is not limited to individual salvation; it has cosmic implications, encompassing the reconciliation of all things in heaven and on earth.

Theologically, Christ's role as the *eikōn tou theou* highlights the tension between fallen humanity and its potential for restoration. Paul's choice of the word *eikōn* suggests both a reflection and a manifestation of divine glory. As Porter explains, Christ, as the firstborn (*prototokos*) of all creation, does not hold this position chronologically but as a declaration of his preeminence and sovereignty.[64] In him the fullness of God dwells, and through him humanity finds its ultimate redemption and restoration to the divine image.[65]

This restoration, rooted in Christ's resurrection, contrasts sharply with the transhumanist quest for immortality through technology. While transhumanism seeks to avoid death through cognitive enhancement or artificial means, the Christian promise of eternal life is based on the transformative power of Christ's resurrection. The restored *imago Dei* points to a future where human identity is fully realized in communion with God, not in technological transcendence but in the eschatological hope of resurrection.

Exegesis of Romans 8:29

Romans 8:29 further develops this theme, emphasizing that those who are "conformed to the image of [God's] Son" (*symmorphous tēs eikonos tou huiou autou*) are being restored in the *imago Dei*, articulating a profound theological insight into Christian identity. Unlike technological or transhumanist aspirations, which often aim to enhance the human condition through external means, Paul envisions a transformation grounded in divine grace and centered on Christ's redemptive work.

Paul uses the word *symmorphous* to describe how believers are progressively molded into the image of Christ. This term emphasizes the process of spiritual transformation, wherein believers reflect Christ's

---

the divine agent through whom all things were created and sustained. Porter argues that Paul's language affirms Christ's preeminence, not merely as a historical figure but as the eternal Son through whom both creation and new creation come into being. This interpretation reinforces Christ's role in restoring the *imago Dei* and countering reductionist, human-centered approaches to identity and transformation.

64. Porter, *Apostle Paul*, 371.
65. Porter, *Apostle Paul*, 372.

nature through their lives. As Fitzmyer notes, Paul's vision of conformation to Christ is not a superficial change but a deep, inward transformation that encompasses every aspect of human existence—mind, body, and soul.[66] This progressive transformation reaches its fulfillment in the eschatological hope of glorification, where believers fully embody the image of Christ.

Rather than achieving transformation through self-effort or technological means, Paul asserts that the process of sanctification—wherein believers are progressively conformed to Christ's image—flows from divine predestination and the work of the Spirit.[67] The use of *eikōn* (image) here is consistent with Paul's theology in Col 1:15, where Christ is described as the *image of the invisible God*. Therefore, the restoration of humanity's image-bearing status is closely tied to Christ's role as the perfect *imago Dei*.

This trajectory of salvation mirrors the restoration of the *imago Dei*, reinforcing the idea that human transformation is part of God's broader plan to renew creation. In stark contrast to the transhumanist pursuit of immortality through technological enhancement, Paul's vision presents transformation as a divine process that is holistic, encompassing not just physical or cognitive aspects but the whole human person. Gorman emphasizes that being "conformed to the image of [God's] Son" is not about individual human achievement but about participating in the divine life through union with Christ.[68] Through this union, believers not only reflect Christ's image but also participate in the divine process of sanctification, moving toward the fullness of their identity as image-bearers of God, realized the fullest in eschaton.

---

66. Joseph A. Fitzmyer, *Romans: A New Translation with Introduction and Commentary*, Anchor Yale Bible 33 (New Haven: Yale University Press, 2008), 524.

67. While Rom 8:29 discusses themes of predestination, it is important to note that this passage can be interpreted without necessarily adhering to a strict doctrine of predestination. Many Christian traditions emphasize human free will and the cooperative relationship between divine grace and human response, as seen in Arminian, Wesleyan, and other non-Calvinist theological frameworks. For example, Arminian theology holds that God's foreknowledge does not negate human freedom but rather anticipates human decisions. For a fuller treatment, see Roger E. Olson, *Arminian Theology: Myths and Realities* (Downers Grove, IL: InterVarsity, 2006), 18–19. Additionally, N. T. Wright highlights that Rom 8 can be understood as a broader description of God's ultimate purpose for humanity, focusing on the process of sanctification and transformation rather than rigid predestination: N. T. Wright, *Paul for Everyone: Romans, Part 1; Chapters 1–8* (Louisville: Westminster John Knox, 2004), 151.

68. Gorman, *Becoming the Gospel*, 197.

The restoration of the *imago Dei* occurs through the process of sanctification. Paul's language of being conformed to Christ reflects this transformation as a return to the original divine intent for humanity. As previously discussed in the exegesis of Col 1:15, Christ embodies the perfect *imago Dei*, and through union with him believers reflect this image once again. This restoration is not merely an intellectual or moral renewal but involves the entirety of the human person—mind, body, and soul. Christ's resurrection, as the first fruits of this new creation, reveals that the restoration of humanity's image-bearing status is not a return to a pre-fallen state but the realization of humanity's full potential in communion with God.

Paul's theology offers a direct critique of transhumanist aspirations for technological immortality and enhancement. For Paul, the restoration of the *imago Dei* is both holistic and transformative, addressing the entirety of the human person, and offering an alternative vision of redemption grounded in Christ. Through this process, believers are gradually transformed into the image of Christ, reflecting his glory and fulfilling their divine purpose.

Transhumanism's focus on escaping death through technology fails to account for the holistic restoration of humanity that Paul envisions—a restoration that finds its fulfillment not in human effort or technological progress but in divine grace. For Paul, the image-bearing status of humanity is progressively restored through Christ, whose own role as the *eikōn* serves as both the model and the means of this transformation. This vision invites believers to reflect God's glory not through external enhancement but through union with Christ and participation in his redemptive work. Unlike transhumanist aspirations, which seek immortality through technological enhancement, the Christian narrative offers an alternative vision of redemption that is both holistic and transformative.[69] Christ's resurrection reveals that the restoration of humanity's image-bearing status is not a return to a pre-fallen state but the realization of humanity's full potential in communion with God.[70] This

---

69. Gorman, *Becoming the Gospel*, 197. Gorman argues that Paul's theology of participation is central to Christian transformation, emphasizing that believers are not merely recipients of salvation but are called to embody the gospel. He highlights that this transformation into Christ's image is not achieved through human effort or external enhancement but through participation in Christ's redemptive mission, reflecting God's glory through self-giving love.

70. N. T. Wright, *The Resurrection of the Son of God* (Minneapolis: Fortress, 2003), 415. Wright's interpretation emphasizes the holistic transformation of the human

transformation, as James D. G. Dunn argues, is not simply a reversal of the fall but a fulfillment of humanity's divine vocation.[71]

The Restoration of Human Identity

The restoration of the *imago Dei* in Christ is the theological response to transhumanism's quest for immortality. The *imago Dei*, understood through the lens of redemption, is dynamic, reflecting a process that involves not just ethical or intellectual improvement but a total reorientation of the human person toward God. This redemptive process, known as sanctification, continually shapes and reforms human identity in light of Christ's example.[72]

The *imago Dei* is, therefore, not a static state that is perfected in creation and then broken beyond repair in the fall. Rather, it is a continual process of renewal and restoration, one that can only be completed through Christ. In contrast to the transhumanist vision of self-deification—where human beings seek to overcome their physical and cognitive limitations through technological means—the Christian vision affirms that immortality is a divine gift, not a human accomplishment.[73] The restoration of the *imago Dei* reclaims human dignity in its fullest sense, affirming relationality and moral agency in a way that transhumanism cannot.

The Role of the Imago Dei in Shaping Christian Identity

This restorative process is critical for shaping a Christian vision of human identity, particularly in an age where technological advancements promise to transcend mortality and bodily limitations. The *imago Dei* offers a counternarrative to transhumanist ideals of autonomy and

---

person in Christ, in contrast to transhumanist aspirations for immortality. He argues that resurrection is not merely about extending life but about fully realizing humanity's vocation in God's renewed creation.

71. James D. G. Dunn, *The Theology of Paul the Apostle* (Grand Rapids: Eerdmans, 1998), 296. Dunn discusses the transformative aspect of the resurrection in relation to the *imago Dei*, asserting that resurrection does not simply restore humanity to its original state but moves it toward the fulfillment of its divine purpose in communion with God.

72. Sutherland, "God's Narrative of Redemption," 82.

73. Sutherland, "God's Narrative of Redemption," 84.

self-enhancement, insisting that true human flourishing comes not through the rejection of embodied existence but through its redemption. The Christian vision of human identity, grounded in the *imago Dei*, affirms that our ultimate transformation comes not from within, through technological mastery, but from beyond, through the transformative grace of Christ.

As Christians, the *imago Dei* is not merely an abstract theological concept but a lived reality that informs every aspect of human existence. This relational and dynamic view of the *imago Dei* stands in stark contrast to the reductionist tendencies of transhumanism, offering a holistic and theologically grounded framework for understanding human identity in a technological age. In the end, the restoration of the *imago Dei* through Christ reaffirms the dignity and purpose of humanity, inviting us to participate in the divine nature while resisting the temptations of technological transcendence.

CONCLUSION: THE *IMAGO DEI* AND HUMAN IDENTITY

In this chapter, we have explored the profound theological, biblical, and philosophical reflections on the *imago Dei* as a lens through which to engage with the challenges posed by AI and transhumanism. From the creation narrative in Genesis to the redemptive work of Christ, the *imago Dei* emerges not as a static attribute but as a dynamic and relational concept that touches every dimension of human identity. By examining historical interpretations from Augustine to Aquinas, and drawing on modern voices like Karl Barth and contemporary scholars, we have seen that the *imago Dei* offers a robust theological framework that affirms human dignity, relationality, and moral agency in the face of technologies that threaten to reduce humanity to mere cognitive or physical enhancement.

The crisis of human identity brought on by AI and transhumanism is not just a technological issue but a spiritual one. As this chapter has demonstrated, the *imago Dei* critiques the reductionist tendencies of these movements by offering a vision of human flourishing that is rooted in divine purpose rather than technological mastery. It is through Christ, the perfect *eikōn tou theou* (image of God), that the fractured image of humanity is restored. In this, we see a powerful theological counternarrative to the promises of AI and transhumanism—one that reaffirms the dignity, relationality, and purpose of embodied human existence.

As we look ahead, the next chapter will delve into the ethical implications of these technological advancements, with a focus on the challenges posed to human freedom, moral agency, and responsibility. Chapter 3, "Idolatry and Technology: Gods of Our Own Making," will explore the ancient practice of idolatry, drawing critical parallels between the anthropomorphism of ancient gods and the modern creation of AI and enhanced human beings. By analyzing biblical warnings against idolatry and their modern equivalents, we will examine how AI and transhumanism might be leading us into new forms of self-deification, where we attempt to remake ourselves in the image of our own desires. The exploration of these ethical and theological issues will offer further insights into the deep spiritual questions surrounding AI and its potential to distort the *imago Dei*.

CASE STUDY #3: HUMAN ENHANCEMENT

In 2040, a cutting-edge biotech company, Genomic Horizons, unveils its latest AI-driven technology, NeoGenesis,[74] designed to enhance human intelligence and physical capabilities. The technology works by integrating neural and genetic modifications powered by AI algorithms. The enhancements allow users to boost their cognitive abilities, eliminate genetic predispositions to disease, and even extend their lifespans.

Initially, the technology is marketed to individuals with severe disabilities or genetic disorders, promoting a more equitable future. However, as the technology proves successful, demand increases among the general population. Wealthy individuals begin to use NeoGenesis for enhancements beyond medical necessity, seeking heightened intelligence, physical prowess, and even aesthetic modifications. This development sparks debates about the ethical implications of AI-enhanced human beings, particularly regarding questions of moral agency, identity, and freedom.

---

74. Genomic Horizons is a fictional company and NeoGenesis is fictional technology created for illustrative purposes within this case study. Any resemblance to real companies, technologies, places, or individuals is purely coincidental. The case study is intended to explore ethical and theological questions related to AI-driven human enhancement and does not reference any actual existing entity.

Religious leaders, including a group of Christian theologians, raise concerns about the theological implications of such enhancements. They argue that NeoGenesis reflects a transhumanist aspiration for self-deification, attempting to transcend human limitations without addressing the deeper, relational aspects of human brokenness and redemption. From a theological perspective grounded in the *imago Dei*, these enhancements prioritize autonomy and cognitive perfection over the relational and moral dimensions that define humanity's identity as bearers of God's image.

This distortion of the *imago Dei* becomes evident when examining the purpose of these enhancements. Rather than seeking redemption and restoration through Christ, the users of NeoGenesis aim to transcend their natural limitations through human achievement. This quest for autonomy, theologians argue, leads to a diminished understanding of moral agency. If technology is used to artificially enhance cognitive and moral capacities, it raises the question of whether individuals still retain true moral autonomy or whether their moral decision-making is influenced by AI algorithms.

In response, Genomic Horizons defends their innovation, claiming that enhancing human capacities aligns with humanity's mandate to "subdue the earth" (Gen 1:28) and that technology can serve as a means of exercising dominion over creation. However, this defense fails to address the deeper theological critique that moral agency—grounded in human relationality and freedom—cannot be reduced to mere enhancements. The debate intensifies as theologians, ethicists, and tech advocates argue about whether AI-driven enhancements promote human flourishing or diminish what it means to be truly human.

Case Study #3 Takeaway

AI-driven technologies like NeoGenesis present both opportunities and ethical challenges, particularly regarding human autonomy and the *imago Dei*. While such enhancements promise improved cognitive and physical capacities, they risk distorting the relational and moral dimensions of human identity. By prioritizing autonomy and perfection, these technologies may undermine the intrinsic dignity of humanity as bearers of God's image. Christian ethics calls for caution, ensuring that technology serves human flourishing without replacing the relational and moral responsibilities central to the *imago Dei*.

Case Study #3: Discussion Questions

1. *Theological Perspective:* How does the concept of the *imago Dei* challenge or support the use of AI and genetic technology to enhance human capacities? Does this technology risk distorting humanity's identity as bearers of God's image?
2. *Moral Agency and Responsibility:* What impact might AI-driven human enhancement have on moral agency and responsibility? If humans enhance their cognitive and moral capacities artificially, do they still retain true moral autonomy?
3. *Relationality vs. Autonomy:* How does the emphasis on autonomy in transhumanism conflict with the theological understanding of humanity as fundamentally relational beings? Can NeoGenesis be used in ways that foster human relationships and communal flourishing, or does it inevitably lead to greater isolation and individualism?
4. *Technological Ethics:* Considering NeoGenesis was originally developed for medical purposes, should there be ethical limits to its application? Should enhancements be restricted to therapeutic uses, or should individuals be free to enhance themselves as they wish?
5. *Human Flourishing:* From a Christian theological standpoint, how does human flourishing relate to technological enhancement? Is the pursuit of extended life, heightened intelligence, and physical perfection compatible with the Christian vision of flourishing, or does it risk becoming a form of idolatry?
6. *Transhumanism and Redemption:* How does the Christian doctrine of redemption, which seeks the restoration of the *imago Dei*, offer an alternative vision to the transhumanist quest for immortality and perfection through technology?

CASE STUDY #4: END-OF-LIFE HEALTHCARE DECISION-MAKING

In 2050, a major healthcare organization, LifeTech Solutions, launches an AI system designed to assist in end-of-life decision-making. The system, known as VitalChoice,[75] collects massive amounts of patient data, including medical history, genetic predispositions, and even social and psychological factors, to recommend the best course of action for patients facing terminal illnesses. The AI analyzes data to suggest whether to pursue aggressive treatments, palliative care, or, in some cases, assisted death.

Initially, VitalChoice is celebrated for its ability to process complex information and provide patients and families with clear options. However, as the AI begins to be adopted more widely, concerns emerge about its impact on moral agency and the ethical implications of allowing AI systems to play such a significant role in life-and-death decisions. Theologians and ethicists argue that relying on AI in these decisions risks diminishing the inherent dignity of human life, as well as the relational and moral responsibilities of patients, families, and medical professionals.

From a theological perspective grounded in the *imago Dei*, the use of AI to make life-and-death decisions raises significant concerns. Human beings, as image-bearers of God, are endowed with the capacity for moral discernment, and this capacity is not merely intellectual but deeply relational and communal. VitalChoice, by offering algorithm-driven solutions, risks reducing these moral decisions to data points and probabilities, undermining the relational dynamics between patients, families, and caregivers. Additionally, the Christian doctrine of the sanctity of life challenges the very premise that AI systems can accurately measure the worth of a life or make recommendations about its end.

In defending its system, LifeTech Solutions argues that AI enhances human decision-making by providing objective data to inform difficult choices. However, theologians counter that reducing life-and-death decisions to algorithmic outputs ignores the spiritual and relational dimensions of human life, which cannot be quantified by AI. In this context, the *imago Dei* calls for human dignity to be preserved in these moments

---

75. LifeTech Solutions is a fictional company and VitalChoice is fictional technology created for illustrative purposes within this case study. Any resemblance to real companies, technologies, places, or individuals is purely coincidental. The case study is intended to explore ethical and theological questions related to the use of AI in end-of-life decision-making and does not reference any actual existing entity.

of vulnerability, affirming that moral agency is not something that can be transferred to machines.

Case Study #4 Takeaway

The VitalChoice AI system raises critical ethical and theological concerns about the role of AI in life-and-death decision-making. While offering practical solutions to complex medical dilemmas, its use risks dehumanizing the sacredness of life by reducing moral agency to algorithmic outputs. From a Christian perspective, the *imago Dei* affirms the inherent dignity of human life and the relational nature of moral decisions, especially in moments of vulnerability. AI should support, not replace, the moral and relational responsibilities entrusted to humans in these profound decisions.

Case Study #4: Discussion Questions

1. *Theological Perspective:* How does the concept of the *imago Dei* challenge or support the use of AI systems like VitalChoice in making life-and-death decisions? Does relying on AI undermine the sanctity of human life?

2. *Moral Agency and Responsibility:* How might the use of AI in end-of-life decisions affect moral agency? Can AI systems fully account for the relational and ethical dimensions involved in these choices?

3. *Relationality vs. Autonomy:* In what ways does AI-driven decision-making risk prioritizing efficiency and autonomy over human relationships and communal care? How might VitalChoice impact the relational responsibilities of patients, families, and medical professionals?

4. *Technological Ethics:* Should AI systems like VitalChoice be limited to providing recommendations, or is there a role for them in making final decisions in healthcare? What ethical boundaries should be in place to preserve human dignity and autonomy?

5. *Human Flourishing:* From a Christian standpoint, how does human flourishing relate to decision-making in healthcare, particularly in end-of-life situations? Can AI enhance human flourishing, or does it risk reducing complex moral decisions to impersonal data points?

CHAPTER 3

Idolatry and Technology: Gods of Our Own Making

IN THIS CHAPTER, WE explore the theological implications of AI and human enhancement technologies, revealing how these advancements serve as contemporary forms of idolatry. Where ancient idols were crafted from stone or wood, today's idols emerge in the form of technological innovation. These new idols are often revered for their ability to fulfill deep-seated human desires for control, autonomy, and immortality, much like their ancient counterparts. While the physical materials have changed, the underlying theological crisis remains the same: humanity's ambition to exert dominance over life and death, and to transcend the natural limitations placed upon us.

The pursuit of immortality through AI-driven technologies—particularly in the realms of mind uploading and brain-computer interfaces—reflects this ancient drive to manipulate divine power for personal gain. Just as ancient religious practices sought to harness the divine, today's technologies offer the illusion of control over mortality. Likewise, the anthropomorphization of AI—designing machines to mirror our own image—reveals a theological crisis rooted in idolatry. Instead of acknowledging technology as a reflection of divine creativity, humanity projects its fractured and sinful image onto these machines, molding them to fulfill human desires and frailties. These technologies are no longer merely tools; they begin to assume an idolatrous role, replacing God's sovereignty with human autonomy.

This chapter argues that AI and human enhancement technologies function as modern idols, distorting the *imago Dei* by recreating humanity in its own image rather than reflecting the divine image. In this distortion, AI alters not only human identity but also the theological relationship between creation and Creator, severing the relational aspect central to the *imago Dei*. By placing ultimate trust in human creations rather than in God, these technologies lead humanity away from its intended purpose and deeper into a crisis of identity and autonomy.

THE BIBLICAL CRITIQUE OF IDOLATRY

Idolatry is a central theme of critique in both the Old and New Testaments (NT). At its core, idolatry involves ascribing divine power and worth to created things, distorting the proper relationship between Creator and creation. It is not merely about crafting graven images; idolatry represents an inversion of the *imago Dei*—the image of God in humanity is corrupted when humans seek to create gods in their own image.[1] In this way, idolatry reflects human autonomy and control elevated above God's sovereignty, serving as a theological antithesis to divine order.

Exodus 20:3–5 serves as a cornerstone in this critique. The first two of the Ten Commandments forbid both the worship of other gods and the crafting of idols. The Hebrew text of Exod 20:3 commands, "You shall have no other gods before me" (לא יהיה־לך אלהים אחרים על־פני, Lōʾ yihyeh-ləkā ʾĕlōhîm ʾăḥērîm ʿal-pānāy). This phrasing, rendered literally, suggests monotheistic exclusivity, emphasizing Yahweh's unique authority and Israel's exclusive devotion to him. This commandment was not merely an injunction to prioritize Yahweh but a direct challenge to the idolatrous worship prevalent in the ANE, forbidding his followers from ascribing divine status to the created world.[2]

This critique of idolatry speaks to the heart of modern concerns with AI and human enhancement technologies. Just as ancient idols reflected humanity's attempt to control divine power, modern AI technologies are imbued with anthropomorphized characteristics, mirroring human desires for autonomy, perfection, and control. By crafting AI systems in our image, we run the risk of creating a new form of idolatry—one that reflects our own fractured humanity rather than the divine image we were intended to reflect. Like the ancient idols, AI systems become "gods" that

---

1. Lints, *Identity and Idolatry*, 35.

2. Johann David Michaelis, *Commentaries on the Laws of Moses*, vol. 1, trans. Alexander Smith (London: Rivington, 1814), art. 33.

humans turn to for transcendence, distorting our relationship with God and elevating technological autonomy over divine sovereignty.

Definitions and Characteristics of Idolatry

Idolatry distorts worship by ascribing divine power and worth to created things, whether statues, natural elements, or human figures. Theologically, this represents a disordered relationship between humanity and God. The attempt to control the divine is central to idolatry, where humans craft false gods to reflect their own desires for power and autonomy.

In Exod 32:1–6, we witness the Israelites creating a golden calf, declaring, "These are your gods, O Israel, who brought you up out of the land of Egypt" (Exod 32:4). The act of worshiping the calf reflects a deep-seated desire to control the divine, as the people substitute a visible, manageable image for the God who transcends their comprehension. Similarly, Isa 44:9–20 offers a searing critique of idol-making, exposing the futility of crafting a god from wood or metal. In this passage, Isaiah points out the absurdity of using the same piece of wood to cook food and then fashioning a god from the leftover material.

The NT continues this critique with Paul's words in Rom 1:21–23, where he describes humanity's idolatry as a rejection of God's glory in favor of images that mirror created things. This exchange of divine glory for idols, Paul argues, is a perversion of the *tselem* (צֶלֶם) found in Gen 1:26–27, where humanity is created in God's image. The *tselem* signifies rationality, moral agency, and relationality with God, but through idolatry, humans invert this divine image, projecting their desires onto lifeless objects. Idolatry, as Lints emphasizes, becomes an inversion of the *imago Dei*, where humans, created to reflect God's image, instead create gods in their own image.[3] The result is a loss of dignity and identity, as people become enslaved to the very idols they create.

In modern terms, AI and transhumanism present new forms of idolatry, where technology is imbued with anthropomorphized characteristics, designed to reflect and fulfill human desires for autonomy and control. Like ancient idols, these technologies foster a false sense of mastery over life and death, as humanity seeks to transcend its limitations without acknowledging divine sovereignty. The theological danger here is that AI and human enhancement technologies, in their pursuit

---

3. Lints, *Identity and Idolatry*, 42.

of cognitive and physical perfection, distort the relationship between humanity and God, leading to the elevation of human autonomy over relational dependence on God.

Idolatry and Anthropomorphism

A significant aspect of idolatry is anthropomorphism—the projection of human attributes onto divine beings. In the ANE, gods were often depicted with human traits such as anger, jealousy, and lust. This anthropomorphism was not merely symbolic but shaped the way people understood and interacted with the divine. Rather than revealing the true nature of God, these idols reflected human desires, particularly the desire for power, control, and security. As noted by G. K. Beale, "What people revere, they resemble, either for ruin or restoration." When humans worship anthropomorphic idols, they begin to reflect the flawed, limited nature of those idols, leading to moral and societal degradation.[4]

As discussed in chapter 2, the term *tselem* (צֶלֶם), used in Gen 1:26–27 to describe humanity's creation in the image of God, stands in direct contrast to the false images created in the ANE. Humanity, as the *tselem Elohim*, is called to reflect God's moral and relational nature, living in righteous dominion over creation. However, when humans project their desires onto idols, as in the case of Nebuchadnezzar's golden image in Dan 3, the result is a distortion of this divine calling. Nebuchadnezzar's *tselem* represents human pride and control, a direct inversion of the humble relationality inherent in the biblical *imago Dei*.[5] The anthropomorphized gods of the ANE, such as Baal or Molech, exemplify this inversion by embodying human lust for power and control rather than divine holiness and justice.

In modern terms, AI systems represent a new kind of anthropomorphism, where machines are designed to mirror human cognition, autonomy, and decision-making. Like the false gods of the ANE, AI is imbued with human attributes, but these technologies reflect humanity's fractured image, distorting our desires for control, immortality, and perfection. The result is a form of self-idolatry, where humans seek to create in machines an idealized version of themselves, mirroring their

---

4. G. K. Beale, *We Become What We Worship: A Biblical Theology of Idolatry* (Downers Grove, IL: InterVarsity, 2008), 16.

5. Sutherland, "God's Narrative of Redemption," 31.

own ambitions rather than reflecting divine order. Just as the ancient gods were crafted to embody human traits, AI systems become vessels for humanity's pursuit of autonomy and self-sufficiency, leading to a theological crisis.

This anthropomorphism extends beyond mere technological advancement—it reshapes human identity. Just as Nebuchadnezzar's golden image led to a perversion of divine authority, modern AI systems distort human moral agency by granting machines increasing autonomy over decisions previously made by humans. The creation of AI mirrors the biblical warnings against crafting false images, as these systems become idols that absorb and reflect humanity's deepest fears and desires. Rather than pointing to God, they turn humanity inward, fostering a self-referential cycle of dependence on technology that alienates us from our intended relationship with God.

Idolatry, then, distorts not only the divine image but also human identity. By worshiping created things, humans degrade their own status as image-bearers of God. Similarly, by projecting our desires onto AI systems, we risk degrading human dignity, making moral responsibility subservient to technological autonomy. As Lints further observes, the act of constructing idols from wood, stone, or metal represents an attempt to domesticate the divine, to reduce the infinite into the finite, and to make the transcendent God manageable and manipulable. This parallels modern efforts to create AI systems that promise control and mastery over life itself, transforming machines into false gods. The consequences of this are disastrous, both spiritually and ethically, leading to moral decay that alienates individuals and communities from the true God.

Theological Exegesis of Exodus 20:3–5

> You shall have no other gods before me. You shall not make for yourself an idol, whether in the form of anything that is in heaven above, or that is on the earth beneath, or that is in the water under the earth. You shall not bow down to them or worship them; for I the Lord your God am a jealous God, punishing children for the iniquity of parents, to the third and the fourth generation of those who reject me.

Understanding the theological depth of Exod 20:3–5 is critical for framing the argument that AI and human enhancement technologies serve as modern-day idols, mirroring ancient distortions of worship. This passage contains the first two commandments of the Decalogue, establishing the prohibition against idolatry and highlighting the dangers of human attempts to redefine divinity and power. The command to have "no other gods before me" and the prohibition against graven images resonate not just historically but in the contemporary context of AI and transhumanism. The creation of false images—whether through physical idols or technological systems—represents a corruption of the *imago Dei*, where humanity seeks to define itself on its own terms. The theological implications of these verses reveal God's deep concern for his people's spiritual and moral well-being, reflecting his role as a protective father.[6]

Verse 3

The Hebrew commandment לֹא יִהְיֶה־לְךָ אֱלֹהִים אֲחֵרִים עַל־פָּנָי (*Lōʾ yihyeh-ləkā ʾĕlōhîm ʾăḥērîm ʿal-pānāy*), often translated as "You shall have no other gods before me," carries relational implications. The phrase עַל־פָּנָי (*ʿal-pānāy*), commonly translated as "before me," suggests proximity and intimacy, evoking the image of a protective father who desires exclusive relational closeness with his children.[7] The command is not merely about exclusivity in worship but also about warning against false deities that offer no real power.

In the ANE context, where polytheism dominated, the Israelites were constantly tempted to adopt the worship of surrounding deities like Baal and Asherah.[8] This prohibition serves not just as a declaration of monotheism but as a protective measure, warning Israel of the dangers of idolatry, which distorts their relational integrity with God. As Michaelis notes, this command highlights Yahweh's deliverance of Israel from Egyptian bondage, making him alone worthy of their devotion. Yahweh's concern is for the well-being of his people, ensuring they remain aligned with the true source of life and blessing, avoiding the destructive paths of idolatry.[9]

The idea of having "other gods before me" is thus a relational and covenantal demand, grounded in God's desire to protect Israel from the

---

6. Michaelis, *Laws of Moses*, art. 33.

7. John H. Walton, ed., *Zondervan Illustrated Bible Backgrounds Commentary: Old Testament*, vol. 1, *Genesis, Exodus, Leviticus, Numbers, Deuteronomy* (Grand Rapids: Zondervan, 2009), 230.

8. Lints, *Identity and Idolatry*, 63.

9. Michaelis, *Laws of Moses*, art. 33.

destructive paths of idolatry. Yahweh's concern is not for his own honor, but for the spiritual, ethical, and relational integrity of his people. By commanding Israel to have no other gods, Yahweh ensures that they remain aligned with the true source of life and blessing, avoiding the destructive paths of idolatry.

Verse 4

The prohibition against idols in verse 4 (לֹא תַעֲשֶׂה־לְךָ פֶסֶל, *Lōʾ taʿăseh-ləkā pésel*) emphasizes God's concern for the relational purity of his covenant people. The term *pesel* (פֶסֶל, *pésel*) refers to a "carved image," while *temunah* (תְמוּנָה, *təmūnāh*) expands this to include any physical representation of creatures. This prohibition highlights the aniconic nature of Israelite worship, contrasting sharply with the iconic worship of surrounding cultures.[10]

In prohibiting the creation of idols, Yahweh protects his people from the relational and spiritual consequences of idol worship. In the ANE, idols were believed to house the presence of a deity, serving as intermediaries between the divine and the human. However, Yahweh's prohibition reflects his desire for a direct, unmediated relationship with his people.[11] As Walton notes, this commandment underscores the unique nature of Yahweh's relationship with Israel, in which his presence is not mediated through objects but through the covenantal relationship itself.[12]

Likewise, the creation of idols introduces a transactional and manipulative form of worship, where humans attempt to control the divine through images and offerings. Such practices undermine the covenantal relationship between Yahweh and Israel, which is based on trust, obedience, and love rather than manipulation. As Lints observes, the act of crafting an idol is an inversion of the *imago Dei*, whereby humanity, instead of reflecting God's image, seeks to recreate God in its own image.[13] This fundamentally distorts the relationship between the Creator and the creation, as it reduces the transcendent God to an object that humans can manage, thereby undermining divine sovereignty and leading to moral and spiritual degradation.

10. Walton, *Zondervan Illustrated Bible Backgrounds*, 232.
11. Beale, *We Become What We Worship*, 60.
12. Walton, *Zondervan Illustrated Bible Backgrounds*, 230.
13. Lints, *Identity and Idolatry*.

The prohibition against idolatry in Exod 20:4 is, therefore, more than just a command to avoid physical images; it is a command to protect the relational purity of the covenant between God and his people. By avoiding the temptation to manipulate or control the divine, Israel is called to live in trust and obedience, preserving their identity as bearers of the divine image. In the context of AI and transhumanism, this warning against creating idols mirrors modern technological aspirations. By creating systems that reflect human desires for control and mastery, humanity risks domesticating the divine, elevating technological creations to the status of false gods. The prohibition serves as a timeless reminder of the dangers of reducing the transcendent God to something manageable and finite.

Verse 5

Exodus 20:5 presents a theological tension, particularly surrounding the concept of divine jealousy. The Hebrew word *qannā'* (קַנָּא), often translated as "jealous," is better understood as "zeal" or "passionate concern." God's zeal is not rooted in possessiveness but in his deep care for his people, guarding them against the harm caused by idolatry. This reflects the heart of a protective father, invested in the well-being of his children.[14]

The phrase "visiting the iniquity of the fathers on the children" (פֹּקֵד עֲוֹן אָבוֹת עַל־בָּנִים, *pōqēd ʿăwōn ʾābōt ʿal-bānīm*) requires a nuanced reading. The word *paqad* (פָּקַד), translated as "visiting," carries the sense of oversight or accountability, not unjust punishment. This passage reflects the generational consequences of sin, where idolatry leads to communal and spiritual degradation.[15] As Brown and others argue, the effects of idolatry ripple through generations, causing moral and spiritual decay.[16]

God's zeal is not rooted in possessiveness or insecurity but in his profound care for his people. He is passionately protective of them, guarding them against idolatry, which he knows leads to harm, degradation, and the fracturing of the relationship between humanity and the divine. His zeal, therefore, reflects the heart of a father deeply invested

---

14. Christopher J. H. Wright, *Old Testament Ethics for the People of God* (Downers Grove, IL: InterVarsity, 2004), 53–54.

15. Lints, *Identity and Idolatry*, 34–36.

16. David Brown et al., *A Commentary, Critical, Experimental, and Practical, on the Old and New Testaments*, vol. 6, *Acts–Revelation* (London: Collins, n.d.).

in the well-being of his children.[17] This protective concern is further understood in the covenantal relationship God shares with Israel, where his commands are not arbitrary rules but guiding principles for flourishing within that covenant.[18]

The phrase that follows, "visiting the iniquity of the fathers on the children" (פֹּקֵד עֲוֹן אָבוֹת עַל־בָּנִים, pōqēd ʾăwōn ʾābōt ʿal-bānīm), requires a careful theological lens. Paqad (פָּקַד), translated here as "visiting," carries the sense of oversight, observation, or holding accountable. This does not imply unjust punishment of innocent children but highlights the generational consequences of sin, particularly in a communal and covenantal context.[19] In ANE society, familial and communal identities were intertwined, and the actions of one generation could have lasting effects on subsequent generations, both in terms of material conditions and spiritual disposition. The idolatrous practices of one generation often led to the moral and spiritual degradation of future ones. As David Brown and others argue, the effects of false worship—particularly in its ethical dimensions—can ripple through generations, causing spiritual and moral decay.[20]

Rather than portraying God as vindictive, verse 5 communicates a profound truth about the long-reaching effects of sin, particularly idolatry, within a community. Idolatry, as seen throughout the Hebrew Scriptures, is not just a spiritual misstep but a socially and morally destructive practice that leads to oppression, injustice, and the breakdown of communal solidarity.[21] By engaging in idol worship, the Israelites were not only breaking their covenant with God but also exposing themselves and their descendants to systems of thought and worship that dehumanize

---

17. John Goldingay, *Old Testament Theology: Israel's Faith* (Downers Grove, IL: InterVarsity, 2006), 74.

18. Nahum M. Sarna, *Exploring Exodus: The Heritage of Biblical Israel* (New York: Schocken, 1986), 185.

19. Umberto Cassuto, *A Commentary on the Book of Exodus* (Jerusalem: Magnes, 1967), 244; Walter Brueggemann, *Theology of the Old Testament: Testimony, Dispute, Advocacy* (Minneapolis: Fortress, 1997), 355.

20. Jamieson et al., *Genesis–Deuteronomy*, 230. Jamieson, Fausset, and Brown argue that false worship leads to moral and spiritual degradation, not only for individuals but across generations. Their commentary highlights how idolatry erodes ethical structures within societies, creating a ripple effect of spiritual decline. Rather than portraying God as vindictive, they interpret the biblical warnings as emphasizing the long-term consequences of abandoning true worship.

21. Lints, *Identity and Idolatry*, 89.

and exploit, a reality still seen in the social and moral consequences of idolatry today.[22]

Rather than portraying God as vindictive, verse 5 communicates the profound truth that idolatry brings long-lasting harm, both spiritually and communally. Idolatry is not merely a spiritual misstep; it is socially destructive, leading to injustice and oppression. Yahweh's zeal, therefore, is protective, calling his people away from the moral decay inherent in idol worship. This protective warning applies just as powerfully today, where the idolatry of technology and AI threatens to disrupt human identity, moral agency, and relational dependence on God.[23] This call to a higher form of worship, grounded in the covenantal relationship between God and his people, stands in stark contrast to the destructive practices of idolatry that permeated the ancient world. Far from being merely spiritual deviations, these acts of idol worship brought tangible harm to individuals and communities, distorting the very fabric of moral and societal order.

The Moral Dimension of Idolatry: Harm to People and Communities

Idolatry's consequences extend far beyond spiritual transgressions; they create tangible moral and societal harm. In the ANE, the worship of idols was often tied to ritualistic practices that devalued human dignity and promoted exploitation. Cults like those of Molech and Asherah did not merely involve the reverence of false gods but engaged practices that caused profound ethical harm to individuals and communities. These religious systems corrupted the *imago Dei* in humanity, as they endorsed violence, inequality, and the oppression of vulnerable populations.

MOLECH: HISTORICAL CONTEXT AND ARCHEOLOGICAL EVIDENCE

Molech worship, one of the most heinous forms of idolatry practiced in the ANE, is historically linked with child sacrifice, a practice that is referenced multiple times in the Hebrew Bible and corroborated by archaeological evidence and ancient texts. The worship of Molech, associated with the god of the Ammonites, involved the ritualistic killing of

---

22. Beale, *We Become What We Worship*, 36.
23. Terence E. Fretheim, *Exodus* (Louisville: Westminster John Knox, 1991), 230.

children, as explicitly condemned in Lev 18:21, where God forbids the Israelites from passing their children "through the fire" to Molech.[24] The horror of this practice is underscored by the moral weight of the command, signifying that child sacrifice was a transgression not only against divine law but also against the very fabric of human dignity and familial life.

Evidence of child sacrifice in Canaanite and Phoenician cultures is not limited to biblical texts. Excavations at Carthage, a Phoenician colony, have uncovered *tophets*—burial grounds for children who were sacrificed to appease deities, including Molech and Baal. These burial sites, replete with urns containing the charred remains of infants, are grim archaeological confirmations of a widespread and culturally embedded ritual.[25] Inscribed stelae found in these *tophets* provide further evidence, detailing the offerings of children as part of votive sacrifices intended to secure divine favor or protection. The ancient Greek historian Diodorus Siculus also recorded these sacrifices, noting how the people of Carthage, in times of crisis, would increase their sacrifices, sometimes including the children of noble families, in a desperate bid to stave off disaster.[26]

The normalization of such practices within these societies reveals a disturbing erosion of the sanctity of life, particularly the lives of the most vulnerable. The sacrificial system was often tied to sociopolitical structures that manipulated religious devotion to consolidate power. By portraying these gruesome rituals as necessary acts to secure divine protection, the elites maintained control over the populace, fostering a culture of fear and desperation. Families, driven by the belief that such sacrifices would avert disaster, were indoctrinated into this system, which ultimately disrupted familial bonds. The act of offering a child—one's own flesh and blood—into the fires of Molech represents a profound

---

24. Leviticus 18:21.

25. Lawrence E. Stager and Samuel R. Wolff, "Child Sacrifice at Carthage—Religious Rite or Population Control?" *Biblical Archaeology Review* 10:1 (1984) 31–51.

26. Diodorus Siculus, *Library of History*, vol. 12, *Fragments of Books 33–40*, trans. Francis R. Walton, Loeb Classical Library 423 (Cambridge, MA: Harvard University Press, 1967), 2014. Diodorus records the Carthaginian practice of child sacrifice, particularly in moments of crisis, when the nobility sought divine favor through increasingly extreme offerings. His account, though written from a Greek perspective, corroborates archaeological findings from Carthaginian tophets, where urns containing the charred remains of sacrificed children have been discovered. This historical testimony, alongside inscribed stelae detailing votive sacrifices, provides an external, nonbiblical confirmation of child sacrifice as a culturally embedded ritual among the Phoenicians and their Carthaginian descendants.

moral and theological distortion, where the gift of life is subverted into an instrument of death.

This culture of fear and manipulation not only devalued individual lives but also had broader societal implications. By turning to idolatry for protection, communities created an environment where life was commodified, and the well-being of the community became secondary to appeasing deities. The familial structure, which in many ANE societies was the bedrock of social and moral order, was perverted, with parents indoctrinated into sacrificing their offspring, a direct violation of the divine commandment to "be fruitful and multiply" (Gen 1:28). The erosion of these familial bonds had lasting effects, fostering a communal ethos that was grounded in fear and despair rather than mutual care and justice.

The societal structures that supported and normalized child sacrifice are emblematic of the moral failures inherent in idolatry. These practices reflect a worldview in which divine favor could be bought through human suffering, and where the powerless—children, the most vulnerable members of society—were viewed as expendable. This was antithetical to the biblical understanding of justice, which emphasized the protection of the weak and the marginalized (Deut 10:18). The ritual of child sacrifice to Molech thus stands as one of the clearest examples of how idolatry leads to moral degradation, creating a society that devalues life and undermines the very relationships that are meant to foster human flourishing.

In the context of AI and human enhancement technologies, the comparison with Molech worship is instructive. While modern society does not physically sacrifice children to appease gods, concerns are rising over how technological advancement, particularly in areas like genetic engineering and AI, commodifies human life. Just as Molech worship commodified children as sacrificial offerings, contemporary practices risk reducing human beings to data points or products of technological manipulation, thereby eroding the sanctity of life and the inherent dignity of the individual. The historical and theological critique of Molech worship offers a sobering reminder of the dangers inherent in any system—ancient or modern—that dehumanizes and commodifies life for the sake of perceived progress or security.

IDOLATRY AND TECHNOLOGY   79

Asherah and Fertility Cults

The worship of Asherah, often associated with fertility cults in the ANE, exemplifies the commodification of human bodies and the exploitation of women, reducing the sacredness of human relationships to transactional and ritualistic exchanges. Asherah, regarded as a mother goddess and consort to Baal, was venerated through fertility rites, which included ritualistic sex acts intended to promote agricultural and human fertility. These fertility cults commodified human bodies, particularly female bodies, to appease deities and ensure prosperity.

One of the most egregious forms of exploitation linked to Asherah worship was temple prostitution, a ritual practice in which women and, at times, men would engage in sexual acts as part of religious ceremonies. This practice was deeply embedded in the socioreligious fabric of certain Canaanite and Phoenician cultures, where it was believed that mimicking the sexual union of the gods would ensure fertility for the land and its people.[27] Once inducted into this system, women had little to no agency over their own bodies, and their sexual exploitation was sanctified under the guise of religious devotion. This exploitation not only dehumanized individual women but also eroded the familial unit, undermining the covenantal understanding of marriage and sexual union that was meant to reflect mutual respect and love. The commodification of women's bodies for religious ends systematically degraded genuine human relationships.

The coercion inherent in temple prostitution points to the systemic inequality that these fertility cults perpetuated. Women, particularly those from lower socioeconomic backgrounds, were frequently forced into these roles, either by familial obligation, economic desperation, or outright coercion by religious authorities.[28] Once drawn into this system, women had minimal control over their own bodies, as their exploitation was legitimized under the guise of religious piety. This systemic abuse not only stripped women of their dignity but also fractured the familial structure, distorting the covenantal vision of marriage as a relationship grounded in mutual respect and love. As sacred spaces became markets for the commodification of women's bodies, authentic human

---

27. Othmar Keel and Christoph Uehlinger, *Gods, Goddesses, and Images of God in Ancient Israel* (Minneapolis: Fortress, 1998), 265–70.

28. Susan Ackerman, *Under Every Green Tree: Popular Religion in Sixth-Century Judah* (Atlanta: Scholars, 1992), 44–50.

relationships suffered, replaced by transactions that prioritized religious ritual over individual autonomy and well-being.

As bodies were commodified for religious ends, genuine human relationships were systematically degraded. Within Asherah cults, this commodification reinforced a cycle of exploitation, reducing women's worth to their role in fertility rites and their perceived sexual utility. The institutionalization of inequality between men and women was deeply embedded in the religious system, where men, as the primary beneficiaries of fertility rites, exercised control over women's bodies, reinforcing patriarchal norms that devalued female agency. This system sustained a hierarchy in which women were not only objectified but also stripped of autonomy, perpetuating the normalization of gender-based exploitation in sacred spaces.

The breakdown of familial relationships, coupled with the normalization of sexual exploitation, weakened the moral foundation of society. Children, born into communities where their mothers were often ritually exploited, grew up in environments that lacked the stability of strong, supportive family structures. In this way, fertility cults not only dehumanized the women involved but also perpetuated cycles of poverty, inequality, and social instability. Wealthy and powerful men, who often had the means to engage in and support these cult practices, further entrenched their dominance by controlling access to temple prostitutes and using religious ritual as a means to assert their sociopolitical power. The commodification of human life in Asherah worship parallels modern concerns about the objectification of the human body in society today.

The worship of Asherah and its associated practices represent a profound distortion of the *imago Dei*. Instead of seeing human beings as reflections of God's image, deserving of dignity and respect, fertility cults reduced people to mere objects, tools for religious transactions. The ritualistic practices associated with Asherah worship were centered on indulgence, control, and the manipulation of human sexuality for divine favor, all of which stood in stark contrast to the virtues of justice, charity, and chastity that are foundational to human flourishing.[29]

The institutionalization of temple prostitution, therefore, not only destroyed the dignity of women but also undermined the societal structures necessary for moral and communal health. In a culture where the body was commodified, family relationships and communal bonds

---

29. Thomas Aquinas, *Summa Theologiae*, II-II.153.2.

weakened, leading to social fragmentation. The exploitation fostered by these fertility cults parallels modern concerns about the objectification and commodification of the body in contemporary society, raising important questions about how humanity continues to grapple with the moral implications of treating human beings as objects of manipulation rather than as bearers of the divine image.

Thus, the commodification of the human body and exploitation of gender roles in Asherah worship parallels how modern society grapples with the objectification of human bodies in consumerist cultures. The moral failures of these practices highlight the profound danger that idolatry poses—not only as a spiritual misstep but as a systemic force of dehumanization and exploitation.

Baal Worship and Agricultural Rituals

Baal, one of the primary deities worshiped throughout the ANE, was regarded as the storm god responsible for fertility, rainfall, and agricultural prosperity. The veneration of Baal was closely tied to the cycles of nature, especially the fertility of the land. As the storm god, Baal was believed to control the rains, essential for the sustenance of crops and livestock. This deep connection to agriculture led to the development of elaborate religious rituals intended to appease Baal and ensure the prosperity of crops, often at the expense of human dignity and societal equity.

The worship of Baal involved ritual sacrifices, which frequently included bloodshed. Animal sacrifices were a common practice in ancient Canaan, with bulls and sheep often slaughtered as offerings to Baal in the hope of securing his favor. However, in more extreme cases, human sacrifice, particularly the offering of children, also became part of Baal worship. In times of extreme drought or crisis, when agricultural prosperity was threatened, such sacrifices were believed to placate Baal and encourage the return of fertility to the land.[30] These offerings, often made by desperate individuals or communities facing starvation, were acts of both religious devotion and fear, illustrating the extent to which Baal worship perverted the understanding of divine-human relationships.

The socioeconomic implications of these practices were profound, particularly for the poor. During times of drought, when crops failed and

---

30. Othmar Keel, *The Symbolism of the Biblical World: Ancient Near Eastern Iconography and the Book of Psalms* (Winona Lake, IN: Eisenbrauns, 1997), 290–95.

resources were scarce, the demands of Baal worship placed an additional burden on the most vulnerable members of society. Rituals that required sacrifices—whether of animals or, in some cases, humans—were costly, consuming essential resources that could otherwise have been used to sustain life. In such desperate times, the poorest members of society were often left with few options but to comply with the demands of these religious practices, even when it meant the loss of vital livestock or, tragically, their children.[31] In this way, the worship of Baal exacerbated existing inequalities, as the wealthy could afford to make offerings without the same existential risks that the poor faced.

Baal worship reinforced societal inequalities by fostering a system in which the elite, particularly the priestly and ruling classes, could manipulate religious devotion for personal gain. The kings and priests of Canaanite cities often controlled the temples and determined the required sacrifices, using religious rituals as a means of consolidating power and maintaining control over the populace. In many cases, they exploited the fear of drought and famine to exact costly tributes from the lower classes, who were desperate to secure Baal's favor and ensure the survival of their families and crops. This religious manipulation entrenched socioeconomic disparities, as the poor bore the brunt of the ritual demands while the wealthy and powerful benefited from the system.[32]

Moreover, the agricultural dependence on Baal worship had a cyclical effect on societal structures. As droughts persisted, communities increasingly turned to Baal with more fervent and costly offerings, leading to a deeper reliance on a religious system that perpetuated inequality. Instead of addressing the real socioeconomic issues—such as the equitable distribution of resources or the creation of sustainable agricultural practices—the system of Baal worship intensified the exploitation of the vulnerable. The poor, already suffering from a lack of resources, were required to make ever more significant sacrifices, deepening their economic desperation and reinforcing their dependence on a religious structure that offered no tangible relief.

Theologically, the worship of Baal represented a fundamental distortion of the relationship between humanity and the divine. Rather than seeing the gods as benevolent providers, Baal worship framed the divine

---

31. John Day, *Yahweh and the Gods and Goddesses of Canaan* (Sheffield: Sheffield Academic, 2000), 102–8.

32. Michael D. Coogan, *The Old Testament: A Historical and Literary Introduction to the Hebrew Scriptures* (New York: Oxford University Press, 2017), 142–44.

as capricious and demanding, requiring constant appeasement through sacrifices that often resulted in human suffering. This transactional relationship with the divine degraded human dignity and placed undue stress on communities already struggling to survive. In contrast to the covenantal relationship presented in the Hebrew Bible, where Yahweh seeks the flourishing of his people through justice and mercy, Baal worship promoted a system of fear and exploitation.[33]

Ultimately, the worship of Baal, especially through agricultural rituals, illustrates how idolatry can have far-reaching socioeconomic and moral consequences. By fostering a culture of sacrifice that disproportionately affected the poor, Baal worship contributed to the breakdown of community bonds, exacerbated economic inequality, and distorted the proper understanding of divine providence. The bloodshed and exploitation inherent in these rituals reveal the deep moral failures of a religious system that prioritized appeasing the gods over the well-being of human communities.

The societal harm caused by Baal worship, with its bloodshed and exploitation, serves as a powerful example of how idolatry corrupts not only spiritual devotion but also the moral and social fabric of a community. These practices reveal the fundamental misdirection of human purpose that lies at the heart of idolatry—a misdirection that can be further illuminated through the theological framework of *exitus-reditus*, which Augustine and Aquinas both employed to explain humanity's intended relationship with God.

Idolatry and the Disruption of Divine Order: The Framework of Exitus-Reditus

The moral failings of idolatry can also be understood through the theological framework of *exitus-reditus*, which Augustine and later Aquinas adapted from Neoplatonism. This framework posits that all creation flows out from God (*exitus*) and is intended to return to him (*reditus*) through virtuous living and communion with the divine. This flow and return express humanity's ultimate purpose, to move toward communion with God, the *summum bonum*. As Aquinas explains, "Man's last end is that to which he looks for the fulfillment of his nature," emphasizing the

---

33. William F. Albright, *From the Stone Age to Christianity: Monotheism and the Historical Process* (Baltimore: Johns Hopkins Press, 1940), 202–6.

natural orientation of human life toward God as the source of all goodness and truth.³⁴ Idolatry disrupts this harmonious process by diverting human devotion away from God and toward finite, created things that can never bring about the ultimate return to God. Instead of directing their will toward the eternal, humans become ensnared in the temporal and material.

As Augustine reflects in *City of God*, idolatry is an exile from God's presence, as it substitutes for the living Creator things that are dead.³⁵ He likens it to a form of slavery, where the human soul becomes entangled in temporal and corruptible things.³⁶ The *exitus* is thus misdirected, and the possibility of *reditus*—the return to God—becomes impossible, leading to both spiritual and moral estrangement. Augustine's critique here is not merely theological but deeply moral: idolatrous worship results in a disordered love, whereby humans exchange the eternal for the fleeting, the incorruptible for the corruptible, ultimately disrupting the *ordo amoris*—the proper ordering of love.³⁷

Child sacrifice to Molech represents a perversion of this process, where life, meant to return to God, is destroyed. Similarly, the fertility rites of Asherah transform intimate relationships into acts of manipulation and control, further illustrating the degradation caused by idolatry. This distortion is mirrored in modern technological idolatry, where humanity seeks to manipulate life and death, breaking the natural flow of *exitus* and preventing a return to God.

Idolatry's harm is not limited to individual degradation; it also affects communities and societies as a whole. When idol worship becomes entrenched in a culture, it fosters systems of injustice and oppression. Political and religious leaders often used idol worship to consolidate power, manipulating the populace into performing degrading rituals to maintain control. The prophetic literature of the OT reveals this moral failure clearly. The prophets Amos and Isaiah, for example, both denounce Israel's infidelity to Yahweh through idolatry, showing how it directly leads to social inequality, oppression, and the exploitation of the poor (Amos 5:11–12; Isa 10:1–2). Idolatry thus becomes a vehicle for systemic injustice, legitimizing social hierarchies based on fear and domination rather than the equality and justice commanded by God. Amos warns

---

34. Thomas Aquinas, *Summa Theologiae*, I-II.1.8.
35. Augustine, *City of God*, trans. Bettenson, XV.23.
36. Augustine, *City of God*, trans. Bettenson, IV.4.
37. Augustine, *City of God*, trans. Bettenson, X.1.

that, "Because you trample on the poor and take from them levies of grain, you have built houses of hewn stone, but you shall not live in them" (Amos 5:11). Here, the correlation between idolatry and social injustice is explicit—infidelity to God is directly linked to the exploitation of the vulnerable.[38]

Aquinas further argues that the moral order, rooted in divine law, is intended to guide societies toward the common good. When societies deviate from worshiping the true God and instead turn to idols, this natural order is disrupted. Aquinas asserts that "laws directed toward an unjust good fail to uphold the common good" and therefore contribute to societal harm.[39] Such laws result in practices that harm human dignity rather than uphold it. Justice, for Aquinas, is not simply a legal construct but a reflection of God's will for human flourishing, and idolatry fundamentally undermines this divine justice by promoting the worship of false and destructive gods.

Thus, the moral dimension of idolatry is not merely about personal sin or spiritual deviation; it encompasses the broader social and communal implications of turning away from the worship of the true God. As Augustine and Aquinas both emphasize, idolatry distorts the moral fabric of societies, leading to practices that harm both individuals and communities by promoting exploitation, injustice, and the perversion of human nature. The theological framework of *exitus-reditus* provides a lens through which to understand this disruption, as idolatry prevents humanity from fulfilling its true purpose of returning to God. Understanding these moral failures is crucial for applying the critique of idolatry to contemporary issues such as AI and human enhancement technologies, where the human desire to control and manipulate mirrors the ancient practices of idol worship.

God's Sovereignty vs. Human Control

The theological tension between divine sovereignty and human control has long been a critical issue in Christian thought, especially as humanity navigates its capacity for self-determination. In the contemporary context of AI and human enhancement technologies, this tension takes on new dimensions. These technologies offer humanity unprecedented

---

38. R. E. Clements, *Amos: A Commentary* (Philadelphia: Westminster, 1989), 138.
39. Thomas Aquinas, *Summa Theologiae*, I-II.93.3.

power to shape, extend, and manipulate life, but they also raise significant theological and ethical challenges. At the heart of this challenge is a foundational question: What happens when humanity assumes a role that belongs to God alone?

In Scripture, the sovereignty of God is consistently emphasized as the basis for the relationship between Creator and creation. Genesis 1–2 portrays God as the sole Creator, who, in his infinite wisdom, gives order and purpose to the cosmos. Humanity, created in the *imago Dei*, is called to reflect God's image by exercising dominion over creation, but this dominion is not meant to rival divine sovereignty. It is, instead, a derivative authority, limited by human finitude and moral accountability.[40] This limitation is foundational to understanding God's sovereignty. In the words of Aquinas, "The Creator alone, by His infinite power, governs the world, while humans, in their finitude, must remain subordinate to divine will."[41]

The prohibition against idolatry in Exod 20:3–5 further clarifies the boundary between divine sovereignty and human control. Idolatry is not merely the crafting of physical images; it represents the deeper sin of seeking to control the divine by attributing divine power to created things.[42] This distortion of the *imago Dei* occurs when humanity inverts its intended reflection of God and instead projects its desires onto the created world. The creation of idols is a symbolic grasp for autonomy, where humans seek to manage or control what is ultimately under God's jurisdiction.[43]

In the modern context, the aspirations surrounding AI and transhumanism echo these ancient temptations of idolatry. AI-driven technologies promise to revolutionize healthcare, extend life, and even transcend death. These ambitions mirror the idolatrous desire to control life and death, a power reserved for God alone.[44] As my dissertation underscores, such pursuits place humanity in direct opposition to divine sovereignty, reflecting the hubris of ancient idolatries. Just as the Israelites sought to

---

40. Augustine, *City of God*, trans. Henry Bettenson, XIX.15.

41. Thomas Aquinas, *Summa Theologiae*, I.2.3.

42. Wilfried Michaelis, "Idolatry in the Old Testament," in *Theological Dictionary of the Old Testament*, vol. 3, ed. G. Johannes Botterweck and Helmer Ringgren, 145–65 (Grand Rapids: Eerdmans, 1978).

43. Lints, *Identity and Idolatry*, 43.

44. Catherine Walsh, "AI and the Temptation of Transhumanism," *Journal of Theological Ethics* 23:1 (2020) 33–45.

manipulate their fate through idols of wood and stone, so does modern humanity seek to redefine existence through technological manipulation, challenging the limitations placed upon it by God.[45]

The pursuit of technological control over life, particularly through AI, also disrupts the theological understanding of human mortality. The Bible consistently portrays death as a consequence of the fall, a marker of human limitation. Genesis 3:19 reminds us, "For you are dust, and to dust you shall return." The transhumanist quest to overcome mortality is a form of idolatry that denies this essential limitation, presenting a distorted view of humanity as capable of overcoming divine judgment.[46] In essence, the technological manipulation of life and death in the modern era mirrors the very errors condemned in the worship of Baal and Molech, where humanity sought to secure control over existence through ritualistic practices.[47]

Moreover, the drive for control through technology can be understood through the *exitus-reditus* framework articulated by Augustine and Aquinas. Creation flows from God (*exitus*) and is intended to return to him (*reditus*) through virtuous living and submission to divine will.[48] By seeking autonomy through AI and technological enhancement, humanity disrupts this process. Augustine warns that idolatry, ancient or modern, is ultimately a form of spiritual exile, where humanity exchanges eternal communion with God for temporal control over creation.[49]

Aquinas further emphasizes the limits of human power, noting that "the finite cannot contain the infinite, and humanity must recognize its own limitations in the face of divine omnipotence."[50] Attempts to tran-

---

45. Sutherland, "God's Narrative of Redemption," 152.

46. Jamieson et al., *Genesis–Deuteronomy*, 89. Jamieson et al. emphasize that Gen 3:19 underscores the inescapable reality of human mortality as part of divine judgment. They argue that this passage serves as a theological boundary marker, reminding humanity of its dependence on God and the futility of attempting to transcend created limitations. In contrast to transhumanist aspirations, which seek to defy death through technological advancement, the commentary reinforces that human finitude is divinely ordained and integral to the biblical narrative of redemption.

47. Harold Lindsell, *The Battle for the Bible* (Grand Rapids: Zondervan, 1976), 120.

48. Thomas Aquinas, *Summa Theologiae*, I.105.5.

49. Augustine, *City of God*, trans. Bettenson, IV.1, II.10. Augustine argues that idolatry alienates humanity from God, leading to a form of spiritual exile where temporal concerns replace eternal communion with the Creator. As Augustine warns, idolatry ultimately results in humanity "forsaking Him who is the fountain of life." *City of God*, II.10.

50. Thomas Aquinas, *Summa Theologiae*, I.45.3.

scend these limits, whether through ancient idol worship or modern technological manipulation, are not only theological errors but also moral failings. They elevate human control over God's sovereignty, distorting the *imago Dei* and subverting the natural order established at creation.[51]

God's sovereignty, as revealed in Scripture, is not merely a matter of power but also of relationship. The covenant between God and his people, as seen in Exod 20, underscores his concern for humanity's well-being. The prohibition against idols is not a selfish demand for worship but a protective measure intended to guard against spiritual and moral harm. As discussed in my dissertation, God's "jealousy" (קַנָּא, *qannā*) reflects his protective love for his people, safeguarding them from the destructive consequences of idolatry.[52] This concern remains relevant in modern debates about AI, where the desire for control over life and death mirrors ancient idolatrous impulses, risking a severance of the covenantal relationship established by God.[53]

As we move beyond the ancient expressions of anthropomorphism and idolatry, the technological advancements of the modern era, particularly in AI and transhumanism, echo similar themes of human desire for control and self-deification. Today, this anthropomorphic impulse is evident in the development of AI systems designed to mirror human traits and the transhumanist vision of transcending human limitations.

ANTHROPOMORPHIZING THE DIVINE

The projection of human qualities onto nonhuman entities—known as anthropomorphism—has a long history that stretches from ancient idol-making to contemporary technological design. In the realm of AI and transhumanism, this anthropomorphic tendency is reflected in the creation of AI systems and humanoid robots designed to replicate human physical and cognitive traits. Today's humanoid robots, from Sophia by Hanson Robotics to Atlas by Boston Dynamics, are constructed to replicate human cognitive and physical traits.[54] These machines extend

---

51. Sutherland, "God's Narrative of Redemption," 152.
52. Sutherland, "God's Narrative of Redemption," 212.
53. Sutherland, "God's Narrative of Redemption," 215.
54. Hanson Robotics, "Sophia," Hanson Robotics, https://www.hansonrobotics.com/sophia; BostonDynamics, "Atlas and Beyond: The World's Most Dynamic Robots," BostonDynamics, https://bostondynamics.com/atlas.

human capabilities, often fulfilling human desires for companionship, mastery, and control.

However, the theological implications of this pursuit extend beyond technological convenience. The anthropomorphization of AI systems—where machines are designed in our image—invokes the same theological concerns seen in ancient idol worship. Just as ancient peoples created deities to reflect their desires for control and immortality, today's AI developments serve a similar function. In settings like elder care or social isolation, robots like Sophia are constructed to fulfill human desires for companionship by simulating emotional engagement.[55] Robots such as Atlas enhance human control over labor-intensive tasks, providing a sense of mastery over physical environments.[56] These technological advancements serve as modern-day analogues to ancient idolatry, where human creations were designed to manipulate divine forces for personal gain.

The parallels deepen when examining transhumanist aspirations to upload human consciousness into machines. Companies like Neuralink, which develop brain-computer interfaces (BCIs), are engaged in meaningful work aimed at restoring motor functions and alleviating suffering, aligning with biblical calls to care for the sick and oppressed.[57] Yet alongside these noble goals, the transhumanist agenda harbors a deeper, more troubling desire: the quest to achieve immortality by merging human consciousness with machines.[58] This pursuit, still speculative but technologically plausible, introduces the possibility of digital immortality. By transferring consciousness into a digital realm, humans seek to bypass death, echoing ancient religious and magical attempts to transcend mortality.

This quest for digital immortality raises profound theological concerns. In the Christian tradition, mortality is seen as intrinsic to the human experience following the fall (Gen 3:19). Efforts to overcome death through technological means reflect a misunderstanding of human finitude and disrupt the divine order established by God. The pursuit

55. Hanson Robotics, "Humanizing AI," Hanson Robotics, https://www.hansonrobotics.com/humanizing-ai.

56. BostonDynamics, "Atlas and Beyond."

57. Neuralink, "PRIME Study Progress Update," *Neuralink* (blog), Apr. 12, 2024, https://neuralink.com/blog/prime-study-progress-update.

58. Nick Bostrom and Anders Sandberg, *Whole Brain Emulation: A Roadmap* (Oxford: Future of Humanity Institute, 2008), https://www.fhi.ox.ac.uk/Reports/2008-3.pdf.

of digital immortality mirrors ancient idolatrous practices, such as the sacrifices made to Baal and Molech, where humans sought to exert control over life and death through ritual offerings. While AI and BCIs offer real potential for alleviating suffering and restoring health, their use in the pursuit of immortality reflects a modern inversion of the *imago Dei*, where humans seek to replace divine authority with technological power.

At its core, the anthropomorphization of AI and the transhumanist pursuit of digital immortality reflect humanity's ongoing struggle with mortality, autonomy, and relationality. Theologically, these pursuits raise significant concerns about the distortion of the *imago Dei*. While the ethical use of AI and BCIs can align with Christian values of compassion and healing, the broader push for control over life, death, and human relationships through technology mirrors the ancient idol-making practices that distorted humanity's relationship with the divine.

As AI systems continue to shape identity, decision-making, and conceptions of immortality, the theological parallels to ancient idolatry become increasingly evident. Just as ancient idols were created to embody and manipulate divine power, modern AI technologies are designed to fulfill human desires for control and self-sufficiency, often at the expense of relationality and moral agency. Moving forward, Christian theology must engage critically with these technologies, offering a framework that upholds the relational, moral, and finite aspects of human existence as central to the *imago Dei*.

AI's Impact on Identity and Decision-Making

AI systems now significantly influence human identity and guide critical decision-making processes, often without users fully realizing the depth of their impact. From healthcare to finance, AI can predict diagnoses, manage treatments, and recommend life-altering decisions. In more personal domains, algorithms in dating apps and social media influence human relationships, shaping preferences and interactions. These technologies do more than assist human choices; they often replace the moral deliberation central to theological understandings of humanity.

Grounded in the *imago Dei* anthropology, Christian theology upholds human beings as moral agents with relational and self-governing capacities that reflect God's image. Karl Barth emphasized that humans are designed to live in relational community, both with God and with others.⁵⁹ However, as AI increasingly mediates human judgment, especially in critical areas such as healthcare or finance, it risks undermining the relational and moral dimensions of human agency. AI systems reduce individuals to mere data points rather than moral agents created in the divine image. This mechanization of decision-making reflects a modern form of idolatry, where control is handed over to human-made creations.

In ancient idol worship, humans crafted deities that embodied their desires, hoping to manipulate divine forces for personal or communal gain. Similarly, today's AI systems are designed to optimize decision-making in ways that mirror human preferences and biases, often with little regard for the relational and moral complexities involved. Andrew Torrance critiques this dynamic, noting that by surrendering decision-making to AI, humans relinquish their God-given capacity for moral discernment.⁶⁰ Just as ancient idol worship reduced human-divine relationships to transactional exchanges, AI risks reducing complex moral decisions to mere calculations, devoid of the relational and ethical depth required by the *imago Dei*.

Digital Avatars and the Promise of Immortality

The pursuit of digital immortality, particularly through concepts like mind uploading, presents one of the most profound challenges to the Christian understanding of human finitude. Companies like Neuralink and proponents of mind-uploading technologies suggest that human consciousness could one day be transferred into machines, offering a form of eternal existence in cyberspace. This concept reflects a transhumanist aspiration to overcome mortality, an aspiration that parallels ancient religious practices where humans sought divine favor to transcend death.

Theologically, this pursuit mirrors ancient idolatrous practices. The desire for digital immortality taps into the same longing for control over life and death that underpinned worship in cultures that sacrificed to Baal or Molech. In these contexts, offerings were made to secure power over fertility, life, and death. Transhumanist ideals are modern iterations of these ancient desires, repackaged through technological promises

---

59. Barth, *Church Dogmatics*, vol. 3/2, 200–201.
60. Andrew Torrance, "Artificial Intelligence and the Crisis of Human Agency," *Journal of Theological Ethics* 45:2 (2021) 150–65, 156.

rather than divine manipulation. Nicholas Agar, in his critique of mind uploading, argues that this desire for immortality reflects a fundamental misunderstanding of human nature and identity.[61]

Human beings, as understood in the Christian tradition, are relational and embodied creatures. Mortality is a central part of human experience and efforts to bypass this limitation, whether through ancient sacrifice or modern technology, disrupt the divine order. In Christian theology, eternal life is a gift from God through resurrection, not a goal to be achieved through technological enhancement. The pursuit of digital immortality, therefore, reflects a rejection of the theological significance of death as part of God's design for humanity's redemption.

Algorithmic Decision-Making and the Breakdown of Relationality

A key theological concern with AI is its potential to sever the relational aspect of the *imago Dei*. Human beings are designed to live in community, reflecting the relational nature of the triune God. The anthropologist Sherry Turkle warns that as AI technologies mediate human interactions, they can foster isolation rather than authentic community.[62] Social media algorithms, dating apps, and even surveillance technologies shape human relationships in ways that prioritize efficiency over genuine relational engagement.

From a theological standpoint, these AI-mediated interactions undermine the relational fabric that is central to human identity. Bonhoeffer's work on community and ethics emphasized that humans are made to encounter others in genuine relationship, where moral discernment and mutual care are exercised.[63] When human relationships are filtered through AI algorithms that prioritize data optimization and behavioral manipulation, the depth of relationality diminishes. In a sense, AI

---

61. Nicholas Agar, "Enhancement, Mind-Uploading, and Personal Identity," in *The Ethics of Human Enhancement: Understanding the Debate*, ed. Steve Clarke et al., 184–97 (Oxford: Oxford University Press, 2016), 184. Agar critiques the philosophical assumptions underlying transhumanist aspirations for mind-uploading, arguing that such technological pursuits misunderstand human nature and identity by attempting to separate consciousness from the embodied experience. This critique aligns with concerns about the theological implications of reducing human existence to purely computational processes.

62. Turkle, *Alone Together*, 22.

63. Bonhoeffer, *Life Together*, 47–48.

functions as a modern idol, replacing authentic human connection with curated, transactional exchanges.

As these technologies become more pervasive, theologians must grapple with their impact on relationality and moral agency. Theologian Paul Tillich warned against reducing the divine to the "finite," suggesting that such reduction distorts the true nature of God and, by extension, humanity. AI, by filtering human relationships and decision-making through mechanistic processes, contributes to a similar reduction, undermining the depth and complexity of human interactions that reflect the divine image.[64]

CONCLUSION: AI AND THEOLOGICAL BOUNDARIES

AI's influence on identity, decision-making, and concepts of immortality demands focused theological reflection. These technologies echo ancient desires to transcend human limitations—desires historically associated with idolatry. The push for algorithmic decision-making, the pursuit of digital immortality, and the mechanization of human relationships all reflect humanity's drive for autonomy and control, ultimately risking a disruption of the divinely ordained order.

Theologians like Bonhoeffer and Barth emphasize that true human flourishing is not found in asserting autonomy but in submitting relationally to divine sovereignty. As AI technologies increasingly resemble idols, they invert this divine order, replacing relationality and moral agency with mechanistic control. This disruption reflects a fundamental distortion of the *imago Dei*, where humans seek to mirror their own fractured image through technology rather than reflecting God's.

The key theological critique of AI centers on its capacity to become a modern form of idolatry, distorting both human identity and relationality. Moving forward, Christian theology must provide a robust framework to navigate the ethical and spiritual challenges these technologies pose. While AI and transhumanism hold potential for healing and alleviating suffering, the broader push for autonomy and immortality through technology risks severing the relational and moral dimensions that are central to the *imago Dei*. Grounded in a theological framework that prioritizes divine sovereignty and human finitude, Christian reflection

---

64. Paul Tillich, *The Courage to Be* (New Haven: Yale University Press, 1952), 40.

on AI must affirm the primacy of relationality, moral discernment, and dependence on God.

CASE STUDY #5: DIGITAL IMMORTALITY

In 2035, the tech company SynapTech introduces its groundbreaking brain-computer interface (BCI), NeuroSync,[65] initially designed for medical applications—restoring mobility to patients with spinal cord injuries and alleviating neurological disorders. These applications gain widespread acclaim for their ability to improve quality of life, aligning with Christian ethics that emphasize care for the sick and vulnerable. However, as NeuroSync develops further, the company suggests that the technology might one day facilitate the "uploading" of human consciousness into a digital realm, offering what some are calling "digital immortality."

The transition from medical healing to the pursuit of immortality sparks ethical and theological debate. Proponents of mind-uploading technology see this as a way to overcome biological limitations, transcending death and achieving a form of eternal life. However, many theologians and ethicists express deep concern over the implications of attempting to escape human mortality.

Critics argue that SynapTech's research reflects a desire to assume divine power over life and death, echoing ancient idolatrous practices where humans sought control over divine forces for personal benefit. They worry that this pursuit distorts the *imago Dei*—humanity's reflection of God—by prioritizing autonomy, control, and self-preservation over relationality, mortality, and dependence on God.

The central theological issue is how "digital immortality" attempts to bypass the God-given limitations of mortality, which the Christian tradition views as integral to human finitude after the fall. In the Bible, mortality is both a reminder of human dependence on God and a marker of the hope for resurrection, where life is restored not by human effort but by divine grace. The idea of uploading consciousness challenges this,

---

65. SynapTech is a fictional company and NeuroSync is fictional technology created for illustrative purposes within this case study. Any resemblance to real companies, technologies, places, or individuals is purely coincidental. The case study is intended to explore ethical and theological questions related to brain-computer interface (BCI) research and does not reference any actual existing entity.

presenting immortality as a technological achievement rather than a gift of divine grace.

In response, SynapTech emphasizes the benefits of the technology for improving human life and assures the public that ethical standards are being upheld. Still, many Christians wrestle with the theological implications, asking whether there are limits to the merging of human consciousness and machines. As technology progresses, questions about embodiment, relationality, and what it means to be human become central to the ethical debate.

Case Study #5: Takeaway

The pursuit of digital immortality through technologies like NeuroSync raises profound ethical and theological concerns, particularly regarding human mortality, identity, and autonomy. While AI-driven advancements offer potential healing and restoration in line with Christian ethics, the quest to transcend death through technology mirrors ancient idolatrous practices that sought control over life and death. Christian theology emphasizes the relational, embodied nature of humanity and the divine gift of resurrection, warning against the dangers of technological autonomy that distorts the *imago Dei* and the natural limits of human existence.

Case Study #5: Discussion Questions

1. *Theological Reflection on Mortality*: How does the concept of "digital immortality" conflict with the Christian understanding of human mortality as a consequence of the fall? In what ways does the pursuit of escaping death through technology parallel ancient practices of idolatry, where people sought divine control over life and death?

2. Imago Dei *and Identity*: If human consciousness could one day be transferred into a digital environment, how might this impact the theological understanding of *imago Dei*—the belief that humans are created in God's image? Does the idea of "digital immortality" diminish or distort what it means to be a human being, particularly in relation to embodiment and relationality?

3. *Human Autonomy vs. Divine Sovereignty*: How does the development of technologies like NeuroSync challenge the balance between human

autonomy and divine sovereignty? Are there theological limits to how far humans should seek to extend their control over life and death? What might be the consequences of pursuing technologies that offer extended or eternal life without regard for divine limitations?

4. *Moral Agency and AI:* If mind-uploading technology were to become a reality, how might it affect human moral agency? Would individuals uploaded into a digital system retain moral autonomy, or would this autonomy be diminished by reliance on algorithms and data-driven systems?

5. *Transhumanism and Resurrection:* How does the Christian doctrine of resurrection offer a counternarrative to the transhumanist aspiration for immortality through technology? In what ways does transhumanism represent a form of idolatry by attempting to "redeem" humanity through technological means rather than through divine grace?

6. *Relationality and Isolation:* In what ways does the pursuit of digital immortality risk undermining the relational aspect of human identity? Can technology foster genuine human relationships, or does it inherently lead to greater isolation and a distortion of community? How does this align with the *imago Dei*, which emphasizes relationality?

CASE STUDY #6: EMPLOYMENT DISCRIMINATION

In 2032, a multinational corporation implements an AI-powered system called EmployMatch[66] to manage its hiring process. The AI system uses extensive data to match candidates with job openings, assessing not only qualifications but also personality traits, communication styles, and work preferences. The company promotes EmployMatch as a way to eliminate human bias, create a more diverse workforce, and increase efficiency in hiring. The system rapidly becomes the industry standard, with many organizations adopting it to streamline hiring decisions.

However, within a year of implementation, ethical concerns emerge. Several candidates file lawsuits, claiming that EmployMatch discriminated against them based on gender, race, and socioeconomic background.

---

66. EmployMatch is fictional technology created for illustrative purposes within this case study. Any resemblance to real companies, technologies, places, or individuals is purely coincidental. The case study is intended to explore ethical and theological questions related to AI and employment discrimination and does not reference any actual existing entity.

Investigations reveal that the AI was unintentionally reproducing historical biases present in the training data it was fed. This leads to a major debate about the fairness and ethics of relying on AI in employment decisions.

Religious leaders and ethicists express concern that using AI in such critical decisions reduces human beings to data points, stripping away the relational and moral dimensions of hiring. Theologians critique this practice, arguing that it undermines the *imago Dei* by reducing human value to productivity metrics and personality traits that can be measured and manipulated by algorithms.

In response, the company asserts that the use of AI reduces overt human biases, but they acknowledge the need for adjustments to the algorithm. The debate highlights the tension between efficiency and justice, raising questions about the ethical use of AI in contexts where human dignity and moral discernment are essential.

Case Study #6: Takeaway

The use of AI in employment decisions presents significant ethical challenges, particularly regarding fairness and human dignity. While AI may reduce overt human biases, it risks dehumanizing individuals by reducing them to algorithmic data points. Christian ethics calls for a careful balance between efficiency and relational justice, ensuring that technology serves humanity without undermining the inherent dignity and moral responsibility that define human identity as bearers of the *imago Dei*.

Case Study #6: Discussion Questions

1. Imago Dei *and Human Dignity:* How does the use of AI in employment decisions impact the theological understanding of the *imago Dei*? Does reducing individuals to data points for algorithmic decision-making diminish their inherent dignity as bearers of God's image?

2. *Bias and Fairness:* How can AI systems that unintentionally reproduce historical biases challenge Christian concepts of justice and equality? What theological principles can guide the development of fair and unbiased AI systems?

3. *Relationality vs. Efficiency:* In what ways does the use of AI in employment decisions erode the relational aspect of work, where personal discernment and moral consideration play a key role? Can AI ever fully capture the relational and moral nuances involved in human decision-making?

4. *Autonomy and Control:* What are the risks of ceding control over important human decisions—such as employment—to machines? How might this challenge the balance between human moral agency and divine sovereignty?

5. *Justice in the Workplace:* From a Christian perspective, what responsibilities do organizations have in ensuring that their hiring practices are just and fair? How does the involvement of AI in these decisions affect the pursuit of justice in the workplace?

CHAPTER 4

Human Hubris and Divine Boundaries

THE NARRATIVE OF THE Tower of Babel in Gen 11:1–9 offers a profound commentary on humanity's relentless ambition to reach beyond the boundaries set by divine authority. Human effort on the tower stands as a mirror to the fall in Gen 3, where Adam and Eve, seduced by the allure of forbidden knowledge, sought to become "like God" by eating from the tree of the knowledge of good and evil (Gen 3:5). Both narratives depict a shared theme of humanity's attempt to achieve self-sufficiency and autonomy—direct challenges to divine sovereignty. Just as the serpent in Eden offered the false promise of wisdom and god-like power, the builders of Babel sought elevation to divine equality through technological advancement. The unified language of the builders became a tool for collective ambition and pride, further exacerbating humanity's estrangement from God. Rather than embracing the relational nature of the *imago Dei*, humanity continually strives for autonomy apart from God, leading to fragmentation and division.

In the modern context, AI represents a contemporary form of humanity's attempt to transcend its limitations and achieve god-like control, much like the builders of Babel. The unification of knowledge through technology, particularly in AI's aggregation of data, forms a "new language" that mirrors the collective ambition of the Babel builders. This "language" extends beyond mere communication, embodying power and control as AI synthesizes the collective inputs of humanity into predictive patterns and decision-making frameworks that promise unprecedented accuracy and insight.[1] By harnessing data from millions of human inputs,

---

1. Michael Wooldridge, *A Brief History of Artificial Intelligence* (New York: Flatiron, 2021), 87–91.

AI systems aggregate diverse knowledge into cohesive frameworks, positioning themselves as gatekeepers of human decision-making—a process analogous to the collective action enabled by the unified language of Babel.

The rise of AI, transhumanism, and biotechnology—often positioned as tools to enhance human abilities and overcome mortality—offers remarkable benefits but also presents theological and ethical risks. In particular, these technologies suggest humanity's desire to transcend the very limitations that define its relationship to the divine, echoing the same hubris that led to Babel's downfall.

This chapter explores how transhumanist ambitions parallel the Babel builders' quest for self-sufficiency and god-like autonomy. By critically examining these modern pursuits through theological and ethical lenses, we uncover the deeper implications they hold for humanity's self-understanding, its limitations, and its relationship with the divine. The unification of knowledge and technological capabilities through AI and transhumanism echoes the ancient attempt to transcend divine boundaries. Just as the builders' unified language and ambition led to divine intervention and dispersal, humanity's current quest for technological transcendence invites reflection on divine sovereignty, human limitation, and the collective dangers of hubris.

In the following section, we will explore how the Babel narrative provides a critical framework for understanding the ethical and theological implications of modern technological advancements, particularly in light of the doctrine of the *imago Dei* and the eschatological vision of humanity's redemption.

EXEGESIS OF GENESIS 11:1-9

The pursuit of self-sufficiency and technological transcendence, seen in the Tower of Babel narrative, reflects humanity's ongoing attempts to surpass the limitations imposed by divine sovereignty. As the narrative unfolds, a critical theological examination reveals the deep-seated human desire for autonomy that parallels modern advancements in AI, transhumanism, and biotechnology. This exegesis will uncover how both ancient and contemporary ambitions to surpass human limitations lead to divine intervention, underscoring the importance of recognizing the boundaries inherent in the created order. Through this analysis, the enduring theological critique of humanity's pursuit of god-like autonomy will be made clear, offering a lens through which to view modern technological advancements.

A Unified Humanity: Linguistic and Ideological Homogeneity

The passage begins with a description of humanity's unified linguistic and ideological state: "Now the whole earth had one language and the same words" (Gen 11:1). The phrase שָׂפָה אֶחָת וּדְבָרִים אֲחָדִים (*safah echat u'devarim achadim*) suggests not only a common language but also a deeper ideological homogeneity—a collective unity in purpose and intent.[2] This unity, which at first appears harmonious and constructive, actually sets the stage for a collective rebellion against divine authority.

Similarly, the unity of language at Babel is not merely a neutral or benign development but a precursor to an imperial-like ambition to assert control over creation, bypassing the limitations set by God. The drive for linguistic and ideological unity often becomes a mechanism for consolidating human autonomy and challenging divine sovereignty. This narrative foreshadows the modern ambitions of AI and transhumanism, which seek to unify knowledge and enhance human capabilities, often in ways that sideline ethical considerations and challenge theological boundaries.

This linguistic and ideological unity mirrors modern technological globalization, where AI systems and transhumanist ideals promote a homogenized vision of human progress and enhancement. Just as the builders of Babel sought to construct a unified society that could transcend divine boundaries, contemporary technologists seek to transcend human limitations through AI, presenting a vision of a unified, enhanced humanity that operates beyond the constraints of biological and cognitive limits.[3]

---

2. Victor P. Hamilton, *The Book of Genesis: Chapters 1–17*, New International Commentary on the New Testament (Grand Rapids: Eerdmans, 1990), 347.

3. Gordon J. Wenham, *Genesis 1–15*, Word Biblical Commentary 1 (Waco, TX: Word, 1987), 238.

The Significance of Shinar: Geopolitical and Theological Context

The narrative continues with the migration of humanity to the plain of Shinar: "As people migrated from the east, they found a plain in the land of Shinar and settled there" (Gen 11:2). The geographical reference to Shinar is significant. Shinar, corresponding to ancient Sumer, was the cradle of early Mesopotamian civilization, known for its technological advancements in urbanization, agriculture, and architecture.[4] The region's association with ziggurats—massive temple-towers designed to bridge the gap between heaven and earth—foreshadows the ambition of the Babel builders to construct a structure that reaches the heavens.[5]

In the context of Gen 11:2, the movement to Shinar and the subsequent decision to build a tower reflects the broader cultural belief in the ability of human innovation and labor to transcend natural and divine boundaries. The ziggurats served as a theological assertion of humanity's control over the sacred, a tangible manifestation of the desire to transcend earthly limitations and to bring heaven under human management. Just as modern transhumanism seeks to overcome human limitations through technological means, the Babel builders sought to do so through architectural innovation, placing themselves as gatekeepers between heaven and earth. This architectural hubris parallels the transhumanist vision of overcoming mortality and human finitude through biotechnology and AI, as both represent humanity's perennial desire to ascend to divine heights and overcome the constraints of nature.

By examining both the Babel project and modern AI and transhumanist ambitions, it becomes clear that the underlying drive is a desire to overcome human vulnerability, mortality, and environmental limitation. This reflects a deeper metaphysical and theological tension between the *imago Dei* and the human tendency to assert god-like autonomy through technological or environmental mastery. These modern endeavors, much like the Babel builders' migration to Shinar, reflect an inherent tension between the desire for security and the spiritual need for dependence on God's providence.[6]

---

4. Kenneth A. Mathews, *Genesis 1–11:26*, New American Commentary 1A (Nashville: Broadman and Holman, 1996), 476.

5. Nahum M. Sarna, *Genesis: The Traditional Hebrew Text with New JPS Translation*, JPS Torah Commentary (Philadelphia: Jewish Publication Society of America, 1989), 81.

6. Jeremy A. Black and Anthony Green, *Gods, Demons, and Symbols of Ancient Mesopotamia: An Illustrated Dictionary* (Austin: University of Texas Press, 1992), 186–87.

Technological Innovation: The Use of Bricks and Bitumen

The technological advancement in the Babel narrative is particularly evident in the shift from using natural stone to kiln-fired bricks and bitumen: "Come, let us make bricks, and burn them thoroughly. And they had brick for stone, and bitumen for mortar" (Gen 11:3).

Theologically, this shift represents more than just a technological leap—it parallels humanity's broader ambition to transcend natural limitations. The use of bricks and bitumen symbolizes the manipulation of natural resources to assert human dominance and autonomy, much like how modern AI and biotechnology manipulate biological processes today. Moving from natural stone to manufactured materials reflects the builders' ability to reshape the natural world to their advantage, signaling a deeper desire for control and immortality. This manipulation echoes modern technology's quest to transcend biological limits through AI and genetic engineering, aiming to achieve dominance over life and death.[7]

This ambition to control natural processes reveals human pride and hubris. Just as the Babel builders sought to create a monument to their greatness, modern pursuits in AI and biotechnology reflect similar desires for god-like autonomy. Both ancient and modern technologies serve as instruments of human power, but they also highlight a spiritual and ethical tension—the conflict between human ambition and divine sovereignty. By manipulating the natural world, humanity risks crossing the boundaries set by God, challenging the created order and inviting the consequences of hubris.

The Tower: A Symbol of Human Ambition and Autonomy

The ambition of the Babel builders is rooted in their desire to construct "a city and a tower with its top in the heavens" (Gen 11:4). The Hebrew term מִגְדָּל (*migdal*), commonly translated as "tower," reveals deeper motivations behind this project. Derived from the Hebrew root גדל (*gadal*), which conveys growth, greatness, and magnification, the word *migdal* in this context symbolizes humanity's aspiration for self-exaltation and immortality. The attempt to "reach the heavens" is not just architectural but laden with theological significance, representing an effort to bridge

---

7. Hamilton, *Book of Genesis*, 348–50.

the human-divine divide.[8] It is an attempt to "bridge" the divide between human and divine realms. The goal of reaching the "heavens" (שָׁמַיִם, *shamayim*) is laden with theological significance.

In ANE cultures, such monumental structures, especially ziggurats, were seen as a way for humanity to connect with the divine, or, at times, to bring the gods down to earth. However, in the Babel narrative, the attempt to construct this tower is not presented as a legitimate religious endeavor to connect with God but rather as an act of human hubris. The act of building a *migdal* with its "top in the heavens" becomes symbolic of a defiant assertion of autonomy, a rebellion against divine sovereignty. This language underscores the builders' intention to construct not merely a physical structure but one that embodies human pride and self-glorification. The use of the verb *gadal* in this context points to humanity's overreach and inflated sense of self-importance, reflecting an aspiration to elevate themselves to the divine level.[9]

In ANE cosmology, towers like ziggurats were considered sacred spaces designed to connect heaven and earth.[10] However, in the Babel narrative, the construction of the *migdal* is a perversion of this symbolic connection, as it is driven by human ambition to assert independence from divine will. This stands in contrast to other ancient cultures that built such structures for worship or communication with their gods, highlighting the narrative's theological critique of human pride. The language of the text, along with the etymological and cultural roots of *gadal* and *migdal*, underscores the theological implications of the Babel project as an act of human defiance and self-exaltation that ultimately leads to divine intervention.

Theological Critique of Technological Transcendence

The theological exegesis of the Tower of Babel narrative in Gen 11:1–9 emphasizes the critical tension between human ambition and divine sovereignty. Through the lens of this story, the desire to transcend limitations

---

8. Bruce K. Waltke, *Genesis: A Commentary* (Grand Rapids: Zondervan, 2001), 181–82. This commentary explores the theological significance of the Tower of Babel narrative, emphasizing that the attempt to "reach the heavens" was not merely an architectural ambition but a symbolic act of human self-exaltation, reflecting a deeper theological challenge to divine authority.

9. Hamilton, *Book of Genesis*, 352.

10. Black and Green, *Gods, Demons, and Symbols*, 58–59.

through technological innovation and self-glorification becomes clear, offering a timeless critique relevant to modern pursuits like AI and transhumanism. In examining the use of bricks, ziggurats, and the ambition to "reach the heavens," the narrative reveals humanity's persistent desire for autonomy—mirrored in the modern drive to overcome mortality and biological constraints through technological means.

The parallels between the Babel builders and contemporary technologists reflect a shared ambition: both seek to manipulate natural and divine boundaries to gain power, control, and immortality. The narrative highlights how such pursuits, whether through ancient architecture or modern AI, transhumanism, and biotechnology, ultimately invite divine intervention and point to the inherent limitations of human efforts.

Ultimately, the Tower of Babel serves as a reminder that human ambition must be tempered by theological reflection. The *imago Dei*, with its inherent limitations, is not something to be overcome through technological means but embraced as part of humanity's relationship with the divine. Drawing on Augustine's critique of human pride, we see that transcendence belongs to God alone, and attempts to bypass human finitude are fraught with moral risks. Aquinas similarly emphasized that human limits were part of the natural order designed by God, with the fulfillment of human nature found in communion with God rather than technological elevation. The pursuit of transcendence is not merely a technical problem; it is a metaphysical and theological one, requiring a return to the humility and dependence on God that the builders of Babel so tragically lacked.

The theological critique of the Tower of Babel reveals how humanity's pursuit of autonomy and technological transcendence leads to divine intervention, underscoring the dangers of collective ambition. In a similar vein, modern advancements in AI and transhumanism reflect a new form of collective intelligence—one that brings both promise and peril. The aggregation of human input through AI parallels the Babel builders' unified effort, demonstrating both the benefits and moral pitfalls of collective ambition. To further explore these parallels, we now turn to the concept of the "wisdom of the crowd," a key framework for understanding how AI aggregates human input to form decisions, and examine its theological and ethical implications in light of the Babel narrative.

WISDOM OF THE CROWD AND AI

The concept of collective intelligence has long intrigued thinkers who have sought to understand the potential of human collaboration to solve complex problems. The emergence of AI amplifies these questions, as AI increasingly draws upon vast human inputs to make decisions and predictions. To grasp how AI mirrors the ancient pursuit of unity in the Tower of Babel and the risks associated with it, one must first turn to the origins of the "wisdom of the crowd" theory and its implications in the digital age.

The Wisdom of the Crowd Theory

The term *wisdom of the crowd* was first coined by Sir Francis Galton, a British polymath, whose 1906 experiment at a country fair became a landmark in understanding collective human judgment. Galton observed a contest in which nearly eight hundred participants were asked to guess the weight of an ox. While individual guesses varied widely—many wildly inaccurate—the median guess of the crowd was remarkably close to the actual weight. The median guess was 1,207 pounds, a mere 0.8 percent off from the actual weight of 1,198 pounds. Galton's finding surprised him, as it demonstrated that the aggregated wisdom of a diverse group could outperform even the most knowledgeable individual experts.

Galton's study laid the foundation for the idea that, under certain conditions, the collective judgment of a group of independent thinkers can produce remarkably accurate results.[11] The principle has since been explored in depth by James Surowiecki in his seminal work *The Wisdom of Crowds*. Surowiecki expands Galton's findings by arguing that groups are remarkably good at solving problems, forecasting, and making decisions, provided that the group is sufficiently diverse, and its members act independently.[12] This diversity ensures that individual errors tend to cancel each other out, resulting in an aggregated decision that approximates the truth.

---

11. Francis Galton, "*Vox Populi*," *Nature* 75 (Mar. 1907), 450–51.
12. James Surowiecki, *The Wisdom of Crowds* (New York: Anchor, 2005), 4–7.

AI's Use of Collective Intelligence

AI, in many ways, is a modern digital manifestation of the "wisdom of the crowd." Much like Galton's ox-weighing experiment, AI systems pull vast amounts of data from diverse human inputs, aggregating these into patterns that can refine and enhance decision-making algorithms. This data, collected from millions of interactions, is synthesized by AI to predict outcomes and make decisions with a precision that would be unattainable through individual human expertise alone. In this sense, AI is an embodiment of collective intelligence, operating at a scale beyond traditional human capabilities.[13]

As Jaron Lanier argues, however, the unification of human knowledge through AI presents a paradox.[14] On one hand, AI has the potential to solve problems and create efficiencies that humans could not achieve individually. On the other hand, this very unification of knowledge risks flattening individuality and creativity. Lanier, a prominent critic of AI and digital centralization, warns that AI systems can lead to a form of "technological monoculture," where the aggregation of human input leads not to enhanced human freedom but to its diminishment. AI's capacity to centralize decision-making power can erode the agency of individuals, mirroring the dangers of collective hubris seen in the Babel narrative.

The theological parallels between AI's use of collective intelligence and the unified language of Babel are striking. Just as the builders of Babel sought to unify their language to achieve a grand technological goal—reaching the heavens—AI unifies human knowledge to achieve unprecedented predictive power. Both endeavors, while promising remarkable advancements, carry inherent risks. At Babel, the unified language became a vehicle for prideful ambition, as the builders sought to transcend human limitations and challenge divine authority. In a similar vein, AI's capacity to aggregate human knowledge and refine decision-making processes has the potential to overreach, leading to ethical challenges about autonomy, privacy, and the limits of technological power.[15]

---

13. Jaron Lanier, *Ten Arguments for Deleting Your Social Media Accounts Right Now* (New York: Henry Holt, 2018), 35–36.

14. Lanier, *Ten Arguments*, 38–39.

15. Surowiecki, *Wisdom of Crowds*, 17–18.

Ethical Dangers of Centralized Intelligence

One of the most significant ethical dangers posed by AI is the centralization of decision-making power. AI systems, by aggregating vast amounts of data, can centralize information in ways that make them immensely powerful—but also potentially dangerous. As AI grows more capable of making decisions in areas such as surveillance, law enforcement, and even healthcare, the risk of social control and surveillance becomes a pressing concern. The power to predict human behavior and outcomes can lead to reduced freedom and autonomy for individuals, as decisions are increasingly shaped by algorithms rather than human deliberation.[16]

Lanier's critique of AI touches on these ethical dangers, emphasizing that the centralization of intelligence through AI risks creating a society in which individuality and creativity are stifled. AI, he argues, has the potential to flatten human diversity, as algorithms prioritize efficiency and optimization over the unpredictability of human decision-making.[17] This critique mirrors the theological concerns raised by the Babel narrative: just as the builders of Babel sought to consolidate power through linguistic unity, AI systems today consolidate power through centralized knowledge, threatening to homogenize human experience and undermine the diversity that characterizes human flourishing.

The Babel narrative offers a theological warning against human ambition when it seeks to rival divine authority. The builders' attempt to reach the heavens, driven by their unified language and technological ambition, was ultimately an act of defiance against divine sovereignty. In the same way, the rise of AI raises profound ethical questions about the boundaries of human autonomy and the dangers of seeking god-like power through technology. By centralizing human knowledge and decision-making, AI risks becoming a new form of idolatry, where technology replaces the divine as the ultimate source of authority.[18]

In both ancient and modern contexts, the unification of human ambition, whether through language or technology, invites ethical and theological scrutiny. As AI systems continue to evolve, it is crucial to reflect on the dangers of overreaching human autonomy and the importance of maintaining ethical boundaries that respect human dignity and freedom. Just as Babel's tower represented an attempt to transcend

---

16. Lanier, *Ten Arguments*, 53–55.
17. Lanier, *Ten Arguments*, 60.
18. Lanier, *Ten Arguments*, 65.

human limitations through collective effort, AI's capacity to unify human knowledge raises questions about autonomy, control, and the theological implications of technological transcendence. It is within this context that the reflection on AI as a new language and a modern tower becomes not only necessary but urgent, as we explore the deeper theological concerns surrounding humanity's pursuit of god-like autonomy in the age of AI.

AI AS A NEW LANGUAGE AND NEW TOWER

As AI and transhumanist technologies increasingly shape the fabric of modern society, they raise profound questions about the nature of human existence, identity, and the boundaries of technological progress. At its core, these innovations serve as a bridge between human potential and a seemingly limitless future, mirroring the theological tension seen in the Tower of Babel narrative. Just as the ancient builders sought to transcend human limitations through a unified effort, modern humanity uses AI as a tool to consolidate knowledge, control, and power in ways that echo the ambitions of Babel. These new technological "towers" are not simply structural marvels or intellectual achievements but carry deep ethical and theological significance, questioning the role of humanity within creation and its relationship with the divine. This section explores how AI functions as a new language and a new tower in the modern age, analyzing the theological implications of humanity's pursuit of self-deification and the risks of technological idolatry.

AI as a Unifying Language

In the modern age, AI serves as a new form of unifying language, much like the single tongue spoken by the builders of Babel. AI bridges diverse cultural and linguistic gaps by creating a universal platform where information and decision-making are consolidated. This "new language" is not merely one of communication but one of patterns, algorithms, and data, representing the synthesis of collective human knowledge. AI operates by aggregating inputs from millions of users, refining algorithms to predict outcomes with remarkable accuracy, a process reminiscent of Babel's unity in purpose and ambition.

Gerhard von Rad's interpretation of the Tower of Babel emphasizes how the linguistic unity in Gen 11 enabled humanity to pursue a collective ambition that glorified human achievement while usurping divine authority.[19] This unified human endeavor, von Rad argues, became a symbol of humanity's prideful overreach, reflecting a deeper theological critique of the dangers inherent in collective power when untethered from divine order.

Similarly, the rise of AI today reflects a new form of centralized power, where the aggregation of human knowledge into a unified technological system echoes Babel's linguistic unity. AI systems gather vast amounts of data, synthesizing human input to predict and control future outcomes, potentially addressing global challenges like climate change and disease. However, this concentration of technological power also carries significant risks. Just as the linguistic unity of Babel facilitated a rebellion against divine authority, the centralization of human knowledge within AI systems poses ethical concerns about autonomy, surveillance, and the erosion of individual freedom. By centralizing decision-making within AI frameworks, humanity risks creating a new form of control that challenges the boundaries established by divine sovereignty, much as the builders of Babel sought to assert their autonomy through their technological accomplishments.

Theologically, AI represents a technological bridge between human intelligence and what could be perceived as a divine realm of omniscience. As AI refines its ability to process vast amounts of information, it increasingly mimics divine attributes such as omnipresence (by being embedded in almost every facet of life) and omniscience (by predicting human behaviors). This shift prompts a theological reflection: Is AI becoming humanity's new attempt to bridge the gap between the finite and the infinite? Augustine's writings on pride and ambition underscore the dangers of humanity's desire to transcend its divinely imposed limits through self-sufficiency. He viewed pride as the root of all sin, a turning away from God toward self-glorification, and warned that such arrogance leads to spiritual downfall. For Augustine, the human attempt to achieve autonomy apart from God's will was a form of rebellion, paralleling the ambition of the builders at Babel, who sought to reach the heavens through their own means. This pursuit of self-exaltation without

19. Gerhard von Rad, *Genesis: A Commentary*, trans. John H. Marks, Old Testament Library (London: SCM, 1972), 146. Von Rad's interpretation emphasizes how the linguistic unity in Gen 11 allowed humanity to pursue a collective ambition that glorified human achievement, usurping divine authority. This unified human endeavor, von Rad argues, became a symbol of humanity's prideful overreach, reflecting the dangers inherent in collective power when untethered from divine order.

divine guidance, he argued, inevitably results in moral and spiritual disintegration.[20]

AI's role as a unifying language also reflects a broader theological concern: the potential loss of relationality that defines the *imago Dei*. As AI becomes the mediator of human interaction and decision-making, there is a risk of reducing human identity to mere data points, stripping away the personal and relational elements of being made in God's image. Like the builders of Babel, who sought to unite themselves through technological innovation, modern humanity's reliance on AI as a universal language can lead to fragmentation—both relationally and spiritually.

AI and Transhumanism: Modern Forms of Self-Deification

The drive behind transhumanism—particularly in its ambition to overcome mortality through AI and biotechnology—bears a striking resemblance to the Babel builders' quest for immortality and divine status. Transhumanists advocate for the use of AI, genetic engineering, and cybernetic enhancements to push beyond the biological limitations of human existence, aspiring to achieve a god-like control over life and death. This mirrors the Babel narrative, where humanity sought to ascend to the heavens, an ultimate act of self-deification that brought about divine judgment.

From a theological perspective, transhumanism fundamentally challenges the *imago Dei*. By seeking to remake humanity through technology, it redefines human nature apart from its God-given dignity and limitations. Ethicist Brent Waters argues that the rise of AI and transhumanism signals a fundamental shift in how humanity perceives itself, marking a significant departure from the biblical understanding of human nature as created in the image of God.[21] This shift not only challenges theological notions of human limitation but also represents an idolatrous move to supplant divine authority with human ingenuity and technological control. By seeking to transcend mortality and finitude through technology, humanity is, as Waters contends, attempting to recreate itself in its own image, thereby positioning human innovation as a new form of divine power.[22]

---

20. Augustine, *City of God*, trans. Bettenson, XII.14.
21. Waters, *From Human to Posthuman*, 89.
22. Waters, *From Human to Posthuman*, 89.

Furthermore, Deepak Chopra has argued that the transhumanist agenda, by prioritizing technological enhancement over spiritual growth, risks reducing human existence to material and biological components, neglecting the metaphysical and divine aspects that define true humanity.[23] Chopra posits that by focusing solely on extending life and enhancing human capacities through technological means, transhumanism overlooks the deeper, spiritual dimensions of human existence that cannot be captured by algorithms or genetic manipulation. In the same way that the builders of Babel sought to transcend their creaturely status through technological means, transhumanism reflects humanity's desire to escape the limitations of mortality and finitude, thus challenging the very essence of what it means to be made in the image of God.

Transhumanism's focus on self-deification through AI and biotechnology brings to light the dangers of seeking autonomy apart from God. The desire to surpass biological and cognitive limits reflects the same prideful ambition that drove the builders of Babel to construct a tower "with its top in the heavens" (Gen 11:4). In both cases, the ambition to achieve divine status through human effort leads not to transcendence but to fragmentation and alienation from the divine. A key theological concern is that transhumanism, much like Babel, neglects the relational aspect of the *imago Dei*. Humanity is not only made in God's image in terms of rationality or moral agency but also for deep, relational communion with God and with one another. By striving for autonomy and rejecting the inherent limitations that come from a relationship with the Creator, both transhumanism and Babel's project distort the communal and relational nature of human identity. This isolation results in alienation, not only from God but also from the community that the *imago Dei* is meant to reflect.

Idolatry and Technological Transcendence

AI and transhumanism can also be viewed as modern forms of idolatry, where human creations assume a god-like status. In the ancient world, idols were crafted to represent divine beings, embodying the attributes of the gods in physical form. Today, AI and biotechnology function as technological idols, where humanity's creations are revered for their

---

23. Deepak Chopra, *The Future of God: A Practical Approach to Spirituality for Our Times* (New York: Harmony, 2014), 152–55.

perceived omniscience, omnipotence, and immortality. Just as ancient idols were believed to grant their creators control over the divine, AI is often viewed as a tool for controlling the future, predicting outcomes, and overcoming human limitations.[24]

AI assumes a pseudo-omniscient status by processing vast human data, not as a reflection of human characteristics but as a transcendent force that analyzes patterns beyond human capacity. Unlike traditional idols, which were crafted to resemble gods or humans, AI transcends those anthropomorphic limits by processing and analyzing massive databases. Through machine learning and algorithmic refinement, AI simulates a form of omniscience, making predictions and guiding decisions with remarkable precision. This precision is achieved through the sheer volume of data and the complexity of the models that learn patterns from it, simulating god-like control over knowledge.[25]

The comparison to ancient idol worship is even more striking when considering the ethical and theological implications. In the Decalogue, idol worship was prohibited not only because it represented a distortion of the divine-human relationship but also because it led to harmful practices like human sacrifice and sexual perversion in worship rituals. These practices dehumanized individuals and corrupted societal morality.[26] Similarly, AI's potential to harm humanity emerges from the ethical risks associated with its power: surveillance, social control, and the erosion of human dignity.

Surowiecki's insights on the collective intelligence of crowds highlight the risks of idolizing AI. While the aggregation of human knowledge through AI can lead to remarkable advancements, it also centralizes power in ways that can be ethically dangerous.[27] Just as the builders of Babel sought to centralize their efforts in a single, towering structure, modern AI systems consolidate human knowledge and decision-making into singular, powerful algorithms. This centralization risks eroding human agency and moral responsibility, as decisions once made by individuals are now deferred to machines. Much like the societal harm caused by ancient idol worship, unchecked AI applied in areas such as

24. Waters, *From Human to Posthuman*, 112–15.

25. Jaron Lanier, *Who Owns the Future?* (New York: Simon and Schuster, 2013), 125–30.

26. Walter Brueggemann, *The Ten Commandments: A Humanist's Reflection* (Louisville: Westminster John Knox, 2012), 45–47.

27. Surowiecki, *Wisdom of Crowds*, 45–49.

law enforcement, healthcare, and governance may cause significant damage if not carefully regulated. The theological prohibition of idols served as a safeguard against such societal harm, and a similar theological and ethical reflection on AI is necessary to prevent it from becoming a destructive force in modern life.[28]

Similarly, the pursuit of technological transcendence through AI mirrors the Babel builders' desire for autonomy and control. As Augustine argued in *The City of God*, idolatry arises when humanity places its trust in created things rather than in the Creator.[29] In the case of AI and transhumanism, the idolatry lies in the belief that technology can solve all of humanity's problems, from disease to death, thereby replacing the need for divine intervention and guidance. This technological idolatry, like the construction of Babel's tower, seeks to establish human autonomy and control over creation, bypassing the divine order.[30]

The theological parallels between Babel's tower and modern AI remind us that the pursuit of autonomy through technology ultimately leads to fragmentation and divine intervention. Just as the Babel builders were scattered across the earth, modern humanity risks alienating itself from its true purpose by placing its trust in technological idols. The theological critique of idolatry, in both the ancient and modern contexts, emphasizes the need for humility and dependence on God rather than on the creations of human hands.[31]

Recognizing the theological boundaries within which humanity must operate is essential for ensuring that technological progress remains ethically sound. As AI and transhumanism push the boundaries of human autonomy, there must be an acknowledgment of the divine limits set to protect human dignity and relationality within the *imago Dei*. The continued development of these technologies will require a sustained ethical vigilance to prevent the distortion of humanity's role as image-bearers of God, ensuring that innovation remains aligned with divine authority.

---

28. Waters, *Christian Moral Theology*, 89–92.
29. Augustine, *City of God*, trans. Bettenson, II.19.
30. Chopra, *Future of God*, 89–91.
31. Augustine, *City of God*, trans. Bettenson, II.19.

BOUNDARIES FOR TECHNOLOGICAL PROGRESS

As technological advancements in AI and transhumanism continue to reshape society, they raise profound theological and ethical questions about the nature of human identity, autonomy, and the limits of human ingenuity. These technologies challenge long-standing theological concepts such as the *imago Dei* and divine sovereignty, particularly in their ability to make decisions, predict outcomes, and enhance human capabilities. As humans seek to transcend their biological and cognitive limitations, the need for a robust theological critique becomes clear. This section will explore the theological and ethical boundaries necessary for technological progress, examining how AI and transhumanism challenge human identity as bearers of God's image and why recognizing divine boundaries and human finitude is essential in guiding these developments.

Theological Critique of Human Autonomy and the Imago Dei

The profound theological challenges posed by AI and transhumanism highlight how these technologies distort the core relational and moral dimensions of the *imago Dei*—the belief that humanity is created in the image of God. As humans seek to transcend their biological and cognitive limitations through technological enhancements, transhumanism promotes autonomy and self-sufficiency. This drive for transcendence mirrors the prideful ambition of the builders at Babel, who sought to elevate themselves to divine status by constructing a tower that would reach the heavens (Gen 11:4).

Augustine's reflections on pride and self-sufficiency are particularly relevant here. He cautioned that true freedom and fulfillment are found in dependence on God, not in the pursuit of autonomy apart from divine authority.[32] In the same way, modern technologies like AI, which centralize decision-making power and reduce human freedom to algorithms, undermine the relational and spiritual dimensions of the *imago Dei*. Ethical reflection on these technologies must be grounded in a biblical understanding of human identity, one that prioritizes community, empathy, and humility before God.

The relational nature of the *imago Dei* affirms that human identity is not rooted in individual autonomy but in relationship—both with God

---

32. Augustine, *City of God*, trans. Bettenson, XIV.13, XIV.28.

and with others. Therefore, technological advancement must prioritize human relationality. This theological principle finds biblical support in the concept of covenant, which frames human existence as inherently relational. Throughout Scripture, the covenant relationship between God and humanity, such as in the covenants with Abraham (Gen 12:1–3) and Israel (Exod 19:5–6), emphasizes mutual commitment, community, and responsibility. The pursuit of AI-driven technological control that isolates individuals or prioritizes efficiency over empathy violates this foundational biblical principle.

Moreover, the desire to manipulate human nature through transhumanist technologies—whether by enhancing cognitive abilities or overcoming mortality—distorts the *imago Dei* by reducing human beings to mechanical or digital entities. This reductionist view undermines the fullness of the divine image, which includes spiritual, emotional, and moral dimensions. Theological reflection grounded in Scripture resists the commodification of human life, maintaining that every individual possesses inherent dignity and worth, regardless of technological enhancements.

Divine Boundaries and Human Finitude

The Babel narrative demonstrates the theological necessity of recognizing divine boundaries and human finitude. The builders' ambition to construct a tower that would reach the heavens was a direct challenge to divine authority, reflecting a desire to establish autonomy and self-sufficiency. In response, God intervened, scattering them and confusing their language, thereby reminding them of their inherent limitations (Gen 11:7–8). This biblical story critiques human efforts to transcend divinely imposed limits, offering a vital reflection for the age of AI and transhumanism.

The doctrine of human finitude, rooted in the created order, reminds humanity that limitations are not arbitrary but divinely set to protect human dignity. Just as the prohibition against idol worship in the Decalogue safeguarded humanity from harmful practices like human sacrifice, the boundaries set by divine sovereignty protect human life from subjugation to technological idols. Modern technologies like AI, with their capacity to centralize power, risk perpetuating inequality and infringing on human dignity—seen, for instance, in AI-driven surveillance and algorithmic bias in policing. These risks echo the harmful effects of ancient idols, demanding ethical reflection.

Technological advancements in AI and biotechnology must be guided by an ethical framework that acknowledges human limitations as divinely ordained. Theological humility, as emphasized by Augustine and echoed by scholars like Westermann, urges the recognition that not all technological progress aligns with divine will.[33] Human beings are called to live in dependence on God, not to transcend their creaturely status. Whether in the construction of Babel or in modern transhumanist ambitions, the biblical narrative consistently warns against the dangers of human pride and overreach.

In conclusion, the theological boundaries set by Scripture—rooted in the *imago Dei* and the acceptance of human finitude—offer a vital framework for guiding technological progress. AI and biotechnology must be developed with the understanding that human dignity is found not in autonomy or self-sufficiency but in relationality with God and others. The Tower of Babel narrative reminds us that efforts to transcend divine boundaries inevitably lead to fragmentation and loss.

CONCLUSION: BABEL, TECHNOLOGY, AND THE PERILS OF HUBRIS

The Tower of Babel narrative offers a timeless theological critique of human ambition, particularly the pursuit of autonomy and technological transcendence. This chapter has shown how the builders of Babel sought to defy divine boundaries through collective, technological effort, much like the ambitions behind modern AI, biotechnology, and transhumanism. These contemporary technologies, while promising efficiency, enhancement, and control, mirror Babel's attempt to centralize power and bypass human limitations, ultimately challenging divine sovereignty.

The key theological lesson from Babel is that human ambition, when untethered from divine guidance, leads to fragmentation and disunity. Modern technologies, such as AI-driven smart cities or genetic manipulation, carry the same risks of idolatry and overreach. The centralization of decision-making in AI systems, the drive to transcend mortality through biotechnology, and the erosion of relationality—all reflect humanity's

---

33. Augustine, *On the Trinity*, trans. Stephen McKenna (Washington, DC: Catholic University of America Press, 1963), 84–87; Westermann, *Genesis 1–11*, 545–48.

ongoing struggle with its finitude. The pursuit of technological mastery without regard for theological boundaries risks distorting the *imago Dei*, which emphasizes human relationality, dignity, and dependence on God.

In conclusion, the Tower of Babel serves as a profound warning against technological hubris. As AI and transhumanism continue to shape society, the need for theological reflection on human limitations and divine sovereignty becomes ever more urgent. The Christian tradition calls for humility, relationality, and respect for the boundaries God has set. By keeping these values central, humanity can engage with technology in ways that preserve ethical integrity and reflect its true identity as bearers of God's image.[34]

CASE STUDY #7: AN AI-INTEGRATED SMART CITY

In 2040, the visionary "smart city" project known as Neotopia[35] launches in the Middle East. Designed as a fully AI-integrated metropolis, Neotopia incorporates AI in every aspect of urban life—from traffic control and energy management to healthcare and security. Residents live in "smart homes" that use AI to adapt to their needs and optimize energy use, while AI-driven surveillance systems monitor public spaces to ensure safety. Proponents of Neotopia praise its efficiency, environmental sustainability, and potential to improve quality of life.

However, ethical and theological concerns have emerged as Neotopia's AI systems increasingly shape daily life, often centralizing decisions once made by humans. Critics argue that the level of control exercised by AI diminishes human autonomy and moral agency. Furthermore, the surveillance infrastructure, though aimed at ensuring security, raises significant privacy concerns and challenges notions of individual freedom.

From a theological perspective, Neotopia represents a modern pursuit of perfection through technological mastery—echoing the builders of Babel, who sought to elevate their autonomy by constructing a tower "with its top in the heavens" (Gen 11:4). Like Babel, Neotopia reflects humanity's desire to transcend limitations through collective ambition,

---

34. Augustine, *City of God*, trans. Bettenson, XXII.24.

35. Neotopia is a fictional city and the "smart city" project is fictional technology created for illustrative purposes within this case study. Any resemblance to real companies, technologies, places, or individuals is purely coincidental. The case study is intended to explore ethical and theological questions related to AI-integrated smart cities and does not reference any actual existing entity.

centralizing power in AI systems that promise efficiency but risk eroding the relational and moral dimensions of human existence. The reliance on AI to solve complex urban challenges mirrors ancient idolatry, where people sought to control the divine through their own creations. In Neotopia, technology becomes a pseudodeity, providing a sense of control over life's unpredictabilities while undermining the *imago Dei*'s emphasis on relationality and human dignity.

Case Study #7: Takeaway

The Neotopia case study illustrates the ethical and theological dangers of "smart cities" that centralize decision-making power in AI systems. While efficiency and innovation are commendable, the erosion of human autonomy, privacy, and relationality poses significant risks. Christian theology emphasizes the relational aspect of the *imago Dei*, warning against the idolization of technology and the loss of personal freedom and moral responsibility.

Case Study #7: Discussion Questions

1. *Autonomy vs. Centralization:* In what ways does the centralization of AI control in Neotopia challenge individual autonomy and freedom? How does this centralization relate to theological concerns about the balance between human autonomy and divine sovereignty, as seen in the Tower of Babel narrative?

2. *Surveillance and Privacy:* What ethical and theological implications arise from AI surveillance systems like those in Neotopia? How might Christian teachings on human dignity and privacy inform responses to such technologies, particularly when they intrude on personal autonomy and relationality?

3. Imago Dei *and Relationality:* How does the use of AI in Neotopia potentially undermine the relational aspect of the *imago Dei*? Does the efficiency-driven environment foster genuine human relationships, or do AI systems inherently lead to moral disengagement and isolation? In what ways does the Babel story warn against such loss of relationality?

4. *Technological Idolatry:* How does Neotopia reflect the theological dangers of technological idolatry, similar to the ambitions of Babel? Can the reliance on AI for control and decision-making be seen as an attempt to transcend divine boundaries? How does the chapter's critique of technological ambition relate to this?

5. *Justice and Inequality:* How might Christian ethics address the potential for inequality in cities like Neotopia, where access to AI-driven infrastructure is tied to wealth and status? What biblical principles of justice, particularly from the OT's concern for the vulnerable, could be applied in such contexts?

6. *Moral Agency and Responsibility:* As AI takes over decision-making roles in Neotopia, what risks arise regarding human moral agency? How might Christian teachings on moral responsibility and divine judgment offer guidance for maintaining ethical human judgment in a highly automated environment?

CASE STUDY #8: GENE EDITING

In 2038, Genetech,[36] a leading biotech company, introduces AI-assisted gene-editing technologies designed to enhance human traits. Using CRISPR technology integrated with advanced AI algorithms, Genetech offers genetic modifications that promise to improve physical abilities, extend lifespans, and enhance cognitive function. Initially developed for curing genetic diseases, the technology quickly expands into elective services, allowing parents to select desired traits for their children, including intelligence, appearance, and even personality characteristics. While some argue that this technology could eliminate suffering and improve humanity, ethical and theological concerns arise regarding human dignity, social inequality, and tampering with God's creation.

From a theological perspective, Genetech's elective gene-editing services raise questions about human identity, autonomy, and the *imago Dei*. Like the builders of Babel, who sought to transcend divine boundaries, Genetech's technology reflects humanity's desire for autonomy and

---

36. Genetech is a fictional company created for illustrative purposes within this case study. Any resemblance to real companies, technologies, places, or individuals is purely coincidental. The case study is intended to explore ethical and theological questions related to AI-assisted gene editing for human enhancement and does not reference any actual existing entity.

control over creation. By prioritizing the ability to design or "improve" human traits, the pursuit of perfection risks undermining the relational, moral, and experiential dimensions of the *imago Dei*, as well as the acceptance of human limitations as part of God's divine design. Moreover, the potential for creating a sociogenetic divide—where only the wealthy can afford enhancements—threatens biblical principles of justice and equality.

Case Study #8: Takeaway

The Genetech case study highlights the profound ethical and theological implications of using AI for genetic engineering aimed at enhancing human abilities. This case raises concerns about the boundaries of human enhancement, the rejection of God-given limitations, and the potential distortion of the *imago Dei*. As with the Babel narrative, the desire to manipulate and improve human genetics reflects the ambition to surpass divine boundaries, leading to risks of moral degradation and the idolization of technology.

Case Study #8: Discussion Questions

1. *AI, Genetic Engineering, and Human Identity*: How does Genetech's use of AI in genetic engineering challenge the theological understanding of the *imago Dei*? In what ways might altering human genetics redefine what it means to be human, and how does this ambition parallel the Babel builders' desire to surpass natural limitations?

2. *Autonomy vs. Divine Sovereignty*: In the case of genetic enhancements, how does the desire for control over human biology challenge theological notions of divine sovereignty? How does this mirror the Babel narrative, where humanity sought autonomy through technological achievement, and how should Christian ethics respond to this challenge?

3. *Theological Boundaries and Human Finitude*: How does genetic engineering, with its potential to remove human limitations, conflict with the biblical view of human finitude as divinely ordained? In what ways does the Genetech case echo the dangers of overreaching human

ambition as seen in Babel, and how can theology reinforce the need to respect God's boundaries?

4. *Moral Responsibility and Genetic Engineering*: What ethical risks arise when AI takes control of genetic modifications that affect human life? How does the Genetech case study reflect concerns about human moral agency being undermined by technological solutions, and how might Christian teachings on moral responsibility provide guidance?

5. Imago Dei *and Relationality*: As Genetech seeks to enhance human abilities through genetic modification, how might this pursuit of perfection affect the relational aspects of the *imago Dei*? Does altering human nature for enhanced abilities promote or hinder the relationality between individuals and God, and what does the Babel narrative suggest about the risks of seeking such perfection?

6. *Technological Idolatry*: Drawing on the Tower of Babel story, how does Genetech's pursuit of genetic perfection reflect the theological danger of technological idolatry? How can Christian theology offer a counternarrative to this ambition by emphasizing human dignity, relationality, and the limitations set by divine sovereignty?

7. *Justice and Inequality*: Given that access to genetic enhancements may be limited to those with wealth and privilege, what are the potential socioeconomic inequalities that might arise from Genetech's advancements? How should Christian ethics address these concerns, using biblical principles of justice, particularly the care for the vulnerable, to inform the conversation?

CHAPTER 5

AI and the New Idolatry

The concept of idolatry has long been central to biblical theology, symbolizing the human tendency to worship created things rather than the Creator. From the graven images condemned in the Decalogue (Exod 20:4–5) to the prophetic denouncements in Isaiah (Isa 44:9–20), idolatry represents humanity's attempt to usurp divine authority through the construction of tangible or conceptual objects of worship. These idols, whether carved from wood or fashioned from precious metals, were more than religious symbols—they embodied humanity's desire to control the divine, to make gods in their own image, and to manipulate divine power for human ends. In the Hebrew Bible, this sin is repeatedly condemned as an affront to the sovereignty of Yahweh, who alone is the Creator and Sustainer of all things.[1] This theological framework highlights key elements such as divine sovereignty, the *imago Dei*, and human finitude, which form the basis for understanding modern idolatry in the age of AI.

In the modern world, idolatry has taken new forms, particularly through technological advancements. AI stands as one of the most striking examples of this new idolatry. Just as ancient idols promised access to divine power, AI promises a form of pseudo-omniscience, where vast amounts of data are centralized, processed, and used to make decisions that affect nearly every aspect of human life. AI systems have become the new gods of our digital age, promising predictive power and control.

---

1. Gerhard von Rad, *Old Testament Theology*, vol. 1, trans. D. M. G. Stalker (London: Harper and Row, 1962), 144. Von Rad's exploration of idolatry in the Hebrew Bible emphasizes that idols, whether crafted from wood or precious metals, represent humanity's desire to control the divine and create gods in their own image. This desire for manipulation, von Rad argues, is fundamentally opposed to the sovereignty of Yahweh, the Creator and Sustainer of all things.

From decision-making algorithms in governance and finance to healthcare technologies that shape patient outcomes, AI increasingly positions itself as an entity that can transcend human limitations. The theological implications are profound: AI, much like ancient idols, assumes a role of providing autonomy and control over both the present and the future, challenging the very boundaries of divine sovereignty.[2]

This chapter explores how AI reflects a new form of idolatry, and it will unfold in several key areas. First, we will examine the concept of anthropomorphism and how ancient cultures ascribed human-like characteristics to their gods in an attempt to control them. Next, we will consider reverse anthropomorphism in AI, where machines take on human capacities such as decision-making and problem-solving, leading to the divinization of technology. Following this, we will delve into specific examples such as social credit systems and predictive policing, which illustrate how AI centralizes power in ways that challenge ethical and theological boundaries. Finally, we will offer practical theological responses to these issues, rooted in the biblical themes of divine sovereignty, human finitude, and the relational nature of the *imago Dei*. Through this analysis, we will see how the rise of AI as a "new god" parallels ancient idol worship and presents unique challenges to human dignity, autonomy, and our relationship with God.

AI AS MODERN IDOLATRY

To fully grasp AI's idolatrous nature, we must reflect on biblical warnings about humanity's reliance on created things. In the Hebrew Bible, idolatry is linked to disobedience and rebellion against God's sovereignty. The Exodus narrative, for example, presents idolatry as a direct violation of the first and second commandments, where God instructs Israel to "have no other gods before me" and forbids the making of "graven images" (Exod 20:3–5). These prohibitions emphasize relational faithfulness, not just ritual obedience; they center on Israel's exclusive covenantal relationship with Yahweh. In a similar way, AI in modern contexts becomes an object of trust and reverence, gradually replacing God's role as the ultimate authority over human life and decision-making.[3]

---

2. Sherry Turkle, *The Second Self: Computers and the Human Spirit* (New York: Simon and Schuster, 1984), 212.

3. Von Rad, *Old Testament Theology*, 203–4.

Much like the ancient idols that distorted humanity's dependence on God, AI distorts our relational posture by offering a false sense of control and security. Psalm 115:8 highlights the danger of this kind of misplaced trust: "Those who make [idols] will be like them, and so will all who trust in them." In a modern context, AI has emerged as a form of technological idolatry that reflects humanity's ongoing desire for control and transcendence. Just as ancient idols were crafted to reflect human desires, ambitions, and an attempt to control the divine, AI systems mirror this dynamic by being designed to reflect and enhance human decision-making, problem-solving, and predictive capabilities.

However, AI goes beyond simple anthropomorphism. It represents reverse anthropomorphism, where human characteristics—such as reasoning, knowledge aggregation, and decision-making—are imbued into machines rather than being ascribed to divine entities. This allows AI to simulate god-like omniscience and omnipotence, centralizing vast amounts of data and using it to predict, influence, and shape human behavior. In this sense, AI functions as a modern idol, offering humanity the illusion of control and autonomy in knowledge and decision-making processes.[4]

By promising efficiency, predictive power, and control over outcomes, AI systems parallel the centralized control ancient idols provided, where people sought to manipulate the divine to ensure favorable results. As AI increasingly shapes governance, healthcare, and social systems, it becomes a pseudodeity, taking on roles once ascribed to God by offering perceived omniscience and control over human destiny. The theological implications are profound: as AI systems occupy more decision-making spaces in human life, the more they challenge divine sovereignty, just as idols of old did in the biblical narrative.

---

4. Jaron Lanier, *You Are Not a Gadget: A Manifesto* (New York: Knopf, 2010), 45. Lanier critiques the reductionist approach to human identity in the digital age, where AI and technology are imbued with human characteristics, simulating omniscience and omnipotence. This mirrors theological concerns about modern AI functioning as a "modern idol," offering the illusion of control and autonomy in decision-making and knowledge. Lanier's perspective highlights the dangers of dehumanization and the need for ethical engagement with technology, reinforcing the importance of preserving human dignity and relationality grounded in the *imago Dei*.

AI AS A "NEW GOD"

The theological critique of AI as a form of idolatry stems from its capacity to centralize human knowledge and decision-making, creating an entity that mirrors the functions traditionally ascribed to God. This is particularly evident in AI's application in governance, finance, and healthcare, where algorithms predict outcomes, assess risks, and make decisions on behalf of human beings. By placing this level of trust in AI systems, we risk granting them authority traditionally belonging to divine wisdom.[5] In relying on AI to diagnose, predict, and even "heal," AI assumes a divine-like role, wielding significant power over life and death.

Oliver O'Donovan argues that moral life must acknowledge the created order set by God, yet AI challenges this theological framework by promising transcendence over biological and natural limitations. Through machine learning and AI, AI extends human autonomy, offering digital immortality and control over unpredictable outcomes.[6] This reflects humanity's age-old desire to "become like God" (Gen 3:5), yet it undermines the human need for relationality, humility, and dependence on divine sovereignty.

Augustine's reflections in *The City of God* provide a crucial lens for viewing this phenomenon. He warns against humanity's tendency toward pride and the desire to become like God, which leads to the construction of idols offering false security.[7] In the case of AI, the idol is not a physical object but a digital entity that promises knowledge and control. However, like ancient idols, AI cannot provide the security or transcendence it promises. Instead, it risks undermining the relational and communal aspects of the *imago Dei*, reducing human beings to data points within a vast algorithmic system.[8]

As AI continues to evolve, its role as a "new god" in modern society must be critically examined. The Bible consistently warns against idolizing human creations, whether they are physical idols or digital systems. While AI has the potential to solve complex problems and enhance human life, it presents significant ethical and theological risks. Christian theology calls for engagement with AI, ensuring that human dignity and

---

5. O'Donovan, *Resurrection and Moral Order*, 111.
6. O'Donovan, *Resurrection and Moral Order*, 114.
7. Augustine, *City of God*, trans. Bettenson, XII.6.
8. Waters, *From Human to Posthuman*, 98.

relationality are preserved and warning against the temptation to place trust in human creations over the Creator.

FROM GRAVEN IMAGES TO ALGORITHMS

In ANE and Hebrew contexts, idolatry represented a profound theological rebellion against Yahweh, where human beings sought control over the divine through physical representations like graven images. These idols were anthropomorphic in nature, imbued with human traits to reflect a relational dynamic between the worshiper and the god. In these early contexts, physical idols offered a false sense of security by creating a manipulable form of the divine. As technology has advanced, however, the nature of idolatry has evolved, shifting from physical representations to abstract forms that dominate the digital age.

AI machine learning and algorithms have ushered in a new era of idolatry: one that goes beyond traditional anthropomorphism to a form of "reverse anthropomorphism." In this paradigm, rather than ascribing human characteristics to gods, human qualities and capacities are now transferred into machines. These technologies aggregate data on such a massive scale that they begin to simulate god-like powers, functioning as centralized arbiters of knowledge and decision-making. The human desire for control and transcendence, once projected onto idols, is now embodied in AI systems that promise predictive precision, enhanced decision-making, and even autonomy.

Concrete examples of this reverse anthropomorphism can be seen in technologies like facial recognition and social credit systems. Facial recognition systems, for instance, not only mimic human cognitive abilities such as identification and recognition but also exceed them, making decisions on behalf of human beings with far-reaching implications for surveillance and privacy. In China's social credit system, AI evaluates citizens' behaviors, assigns them scores, and even determines access to resources such as travel, loans, or housing. These AI-driven systems aggregate human behaviors and decisions into a centralized algorithmic authority, acting as modern idols that claim to know and judge humanity.

This shift from anthropomorphism to reverse anthropomorphism introduces significant theological and ethical implications. In traditional idolatry, the human danger was reducing the divine to human form. Today, the reverse danger lies in divinizing human creations, where machines are endowed with authority traditionally reserved for God. AI systems embody characteristics once ascribed to the divine—such as omniscience and omnipotence—by predicting future behaviors and influencing outcomes on a massive scale. As these technologies grow in influence, they challenge Christian conceptions of divine sovereignty, relationality, and human moral agency. The reliance on AI for moral and social decision-making mirrors the theological critiques of idolatry in the Bible, where trust in created things distorts humanity's relationship with God.

From Anthropomorphism to Reverse Anthropomorphism

In the ancient world, anthropomorphism was a way for humanity to relate to the divine, with deities depicted using human-like qualities—faces, hands, and emotions—to make them accessible and relatable. For example, in Babylonian religion, the ritual of *pīt pî* symbolically "breathed life" into an idol, allowing it to function as an extension of the god's presence on earth.[9] These gods were viewed as approachable yet manipulable through sacrifice and ritual. Yahweh's command in Exod 20:3–5 against the creation of idols rejected this distorted mediation, as it reduced the divine to a form that humanity could control.

In contrast, reverse anthropomorphism in AI flips this process. Rather than imposing human features on divine beings, humans now create machines that emulate human capacities—particularly decision-making, problem-solving, and data analysis—on an unprecedented scale. AI-driven systems, like facial recognition or predictive policing, simulate a form of omniscience by aggregating vast amounts of data, predicting human behavior with remarkable precision. In this sense, AI centralizes power, functioning as a pseudodivine entity, influencing decisions in areas like finance, governance, and healthcare, much like ancient idols that mediated divine power for human purposes.[10]

This new form of idolatry introduces complex theological and ethical challenges. While traditional anthropomorphism involved the humanization of the divine, reverse anthropomorphism *divinizes* human creations. AI systems, built by humans, now make autonomous decisions, functioning as "gods" that preside over crucial aspects of human

---

9. Turkle, *Second Self*, 212.
10. Lanier, *You Are Not a Gadget*, 157.

life.[11] For instance, in facial recognition technology, AI systems often determine identity and access, exerting control over public spaces and personal freedoms. Similarly, in social credit systems—like those used in China—AI-driven algorithms assess behavior, influencing individuals' social standing and access to resources, mirroring the god-like capacity to judge and reward or punish.

Isaiah's condemnation of idols (Isa 44:9–20) warns against misplaced reverence for entities that, though revered, are powerless compared to God. However, in the case of AI, these "idols" possess real power through their decision-making capabilities—they aggregate and interpret data on a scale far beyond human capacity, often lacking ethical discernment or relational concern. As AI systems increasingly assume god-like roles—predicting outcomes, controlling resources, and making judgments—they exemplify the dangers of reverse anthropomorphism and challenge core theological concepts like human dignity, autonomy, and moral responsibility.

Case Study: Predictive Policing Algorithms as AI's Centralization of Power

A vivid example of reverse anthropomorphism and the ethical implications of AI as a centralized power can be seen in predictive policing algorithms. As discussed in the predictive policing case study from chapter 2, Project Horizon, one such AI-driven system, uses machine learning to predict where crimes are likely to occur, allowing law enforcement agencies to allocate resources more efficiently. While the intention behind such technologies may be noble—preventing crime and enhancing public safety—these systems also concentrate enormous power in the hands of data-driven algorithms.

Theologically, this raises concerns similar to those found in the Tower of Babel narrative (Gen 11:1–9), where humanity's desire to centralize knowledge and power led to divine intervention. Just as the builders sought to "make a name" for themselves and transcend divine limitations, modern AI systems, by aggregating human data, seek to transcend human fallibility through centralized, algorithmic decision-making. Predictive policing technologies highlight this ambition for control and foresight. Yet, like the builders of Babel, the reliance on such

---

11. O'Donovan, *Resurrection and Moral Order*, 111.

technologies can lead to ethical and theological fragmentation, particularly when these systems perpetuate biases or dehumanize the individuals they are designed to protect.[12]

Predictive policing exemplifies the centralization of power in AI, wherein human autonomy and moral agency are increasingly diminished by algorithmic determinations. Surowiecki's insights into collective intelligence through the "wisdom of crowds" demonstrate that while the aggregation of data can lead to accurate predictions, it can also homogenize human input in ways that obscure individual nuances.[13] When algorithms make decisions based on aggregated data, they risk reducing human freedom to the binary outcomes of machine logic. This is particularly concerning in policing, where predictive algorithms have been shown to perpetuate racial biases, disproportionately targeting minority communities.[14]

The theological critique here is that reliance on AI as an all-seeing arbiter of justice echoes the idolatry of the ancient world, where idols were believed to provide divine insight but often led to injustice and moral degradation.[15] The ethical fragmentation caused by predictive policing—especially the racial and social biases it amplifies—reinforces the theological critique of human overreach. By placing trust in AI to mediate justice, society risks further moral dehumanization, reducing people to data points in a system that lacks the relational and ethical depth needed for true justice.

---

12. Gwendolyn Leick, *The Babylonians: An Introduction* (London: Routledge, 2003), 126. Leick provides historical context for the Tower of Babel narrative, noting that ancient Mesopotamian societies, such as the Babylonians, also sought to centralize power and knowledge through monumental architecture. This parallels the theological critique of human pride and the attempt to transcend divine limitations, a theme reflected in both the Babel narrative and the modern reliance on technologies like AI, which aggregate human data to control and predict behavior.

13. Surowiecki, *Wisdom of Crowds*, 37.

14. This issue has been observed in several cases. For instance, the "PredPol" system used by police departments in the United States was found to disproportionately target Black and Latino neighborhoods, perpetuating racial biases due to the data it was trained on. The feedback loop generated by such algorithms can lead to over-policing in certain communities, reinforcing existing racial disparities. Research by scholars such as Rashida Richardson, Jason Schultz, and Kate Crawford has highlighted how biased data in predictive policing algorithms can lead to discriminatory outcomes. Rashida Richardson et al., "Dirty Data, Bad Predictions: How Civil Rights Violations Impact Police Data, Predictive Policing Systems, and Justice," *New York University Law Review* 94:2 (2019) 192–98.

15. Waters, *From Human to Posthuman*, 45.

From a theological standpoint, the ethical dangers of AI's centralization of power are profound. In AI-driven systems like Project Horizon, the ability to predict and control human behavior reflects a desire for omniscience—one that mirrors ancient attempts to centralize divine power through idols. However, as Augustine warned in *The City of God*, idolatry arises when humanity places its trust in created things rather than in the Creator. By relying on algorithms to mediate justice and social order, humanity risks falling into a new form of idolatry, where machines, rather than God, become the source of moral and ethical guidance.[16] This mirrors the danger of the golden calf in Exodus, where human creation led to moral degradation.

The Next Step: Social Credit Systems as AI's Expansion of Power

Building upon the centralized power seen in predictive policing, AI's reach into social governance is exemplified by the rise of social credit systems, particularly as implemented in China. These systems represent an even more pervasive form of AI-driven surveillance and control, where algorithms assess and rate the behavior of citizens, determining their social and economic privileges. The Chinese Social Credit System uses vast amounts of data—ranging from financial transactions to social behaviors—to assign a score to each individual, which can affect their access to everything from loans to travel privileges.[17]

---

16. Augustine, *City of God*, trans. Bettenson, X.4. Augustine warns that idolatry occurs when humanity places its trust in created things rather than in the Creator. This theological insight resonates with the contemporary risk of replacing divine moral guidance with artificial intelligence and algorithms. Just as the golden calf in Exodus led to moral degradation, the overreliance on technology for justice and social order threatens to shift moral authority away from God and toward human-made systems.

17. Turgut Başer, "Artificial Intelligence and Social Credit System in China" (term project, Middle East Technical University, 2021), https://open.metu.edu.tr/bitstream/handle/11511/101891/Artificial%20Intelligence%20and%20Social%20Credit%20System%20in%20China%20-%20Turgut%20BASER%20-%202013605.pdf; Zeyi Yang, "China Just Announced a New Social Credit Law: Here's What It Means," *MIT Technology Review*, Nov. 22, 2022. https://www.technologyreview.com/2022/11/22/1063605/china-announced-a-new-social-credit-law-what-does-it-mean; Vishakha Agrawal, "Demystifying the Chinese Social Credit System: A Case Study on AI-Powered Control Systems in China," *Proceedings of the AAAI Conference on Artificial Intelligence* 36:11 (June 2022) 13124–25, https://doi.org/10.1609/aaai.v36i11.21698.

The theological implications of such systems are even more concerning than those of predictive policing. The ability of AI to monitor and judge human behavior on such a large scale mirrors the role of an omniscient god, one that is omnipresent and all-seeing. However, unlike divine omniscience, which is rooted in justice and mercy, AI-based systems like the Social Credit System operate according to human-designed algorithms that lack nuance, forgiveness, or ethical discernment. This represents a dangerous shift toward technological idolatry, where algorithmic determinations replace divine justice with cold, mechanized assessments.

As noted in our previous discussions on idolatry, the danger of such systems lies in their potential to dehumanize individuals by reducing their worth to algorithmic scores. Just as the builders of the Tower of Babel (Gen 11:1–9) sought to centralize power and knowledge to transcend divine limitations, social credit systems centralize human data to control behavior and regulate access to social privileges. In both cases, this centralization erodes the boundaries set by divine sovereignty, replacing relational justice with technological governance.

The Babylonian tradition of infusing idols with divine presence through the *pīt pî* ceremony serves as an ancient parallel to the modern faith in AI systems. Just as the Babylonians believed that their idols could mediate divine will, modern societies are increasingly entrusting AI with the authority to mediate human value and morality. The consolidation of power within AI-driven social credit systems reflects a dangerous trend toward idolatry, where technology replaces divine wisdom in guiding ethical behavior and societal order.

While the ancient *pīt pî* ritual sought to animate lifeless objects with divine breath, modern AI systems animate decision-making processes with the data of billions of people, creating a new form of "divine presence" through algorithmic judgment. The ethical and theological danger here is clear: by allowing AI to determine social value and justice, humanity risks constructing a new Tower of Babel—one that seeks to transcend divine limits through technological control, but ultimately leads to fragmentation and societal decay.

From a theological perspective, the rise of social credit systems presents a stark warning against the idolatry of technology. Just as the golden calf in Exod 32 led the Israelites away from their covenantal relationship with God, so too do AI-driven systems risk leading humanity away from the ethical and relational foundations of the *imago Dei*. As Brent Waters notes in his critique of posthumanism, the desire to transcend human limitations through technology ultimately results in the devaluation of human dignity and moral agency.[18]

In conclusion, both predictive policing and social credit systems represent modern forms of idolatry, where AI assumes the role of an omniscient, omnipotent force that governs human behavior and social order. The theological critique of these systems is rooted in the biblical warnings against idolatry, where the desire to control and manipulate divine power leads to moral and societal collapse. As AI continues to evolve, it is imperative that Christian leaders and theologians engage with these ethical challenges, offering a biblical framework that prioritizes human dignity, relationality, and the recognition of divine sovereignty.

Ethical Implications from a Theological Perspective

The rise of AI-driven technologies, such as predictive policing, presents profound ethical challenges that resonate deeply with biblical warnings against idolatry. In the ANE context, idols were more than misguided objects of worship; they represented humanity's desire to control the divine, leading to moral and spiritual corruption. This theological critique is particularly relevant in the modern age, where AI promises autonomy and predictive power but risks reducing human beings to mere data points. As AI increasingly mediates decisions about governance, justice, and healthcare, it challenges the fundamental theological principle of divine sovereignty. The biblical injunctions against idolatry—from the worship of the golden calf (Exod 32) to the centralized ambitions of Babel (Gen 11:1–9)—remind us that human attempts to centralize power apart from God lead to moral decay and societal fragmentation.[19]

In modern AI systems, this dynamic manifests in algorithmic decision-making, which assumes an almost omniscient role in society. Predictive algorithms claim to foresee outcomes with precision, yet they raise significant concerns about the erosion of human moral agency. The *imago Dei*, emphasizing the relational, moral, and spiritual aspects of human identity, becomes distorted when algorithms—not humans—become the arbiters of justice and morality.

---

18. Waters, *From Human to Posthuman*, 112–14.
19. Von Rad, *Genesis: A Commentary*, 176.

C. S. Lewis, in *The Abolition of Man*, warned against the dangers of such dehumanization, arguing that reducing individuals to mere objects of control undermines the intrinsic value of human life.[20] Lewis critiques the reduction of individuals to mere instruments of control and manipulation, where emotional depth and moral wisdom are replaced by utilitarian function. This concept is remarkably fitting in the context of AI, where decision-making is driven by cold logic and data, lacking the "chest"—the heart and moral compass—that imbues human choices with ethical and relational value. AI systems, by centralizing knowledge and power, strip away the intrinsic human elements of empathy, compassion, and moral responsibility, reducing individuals to data points. Lewis's analogy underscores the danger of AI systems that, like men without chests, operate without the ethical discernment that is central to human existence and experience. By placing trust in such systems, society risks building a technological future devoid of the qualities that give human life meaning and purpose, echoing Lewis's warnings about the spiritual and ethical consequences of dehumanization.[21]

Furthermore, the transhumanist vision of enhancing human capacities through AI and biotechnology reflects a deeper desire for control, autonomy, and self-sufficiency. This vision is rooted in the same idolatrous impulse that animated the builders of Babel, who sought to "make a name" for themselves by constructing a tower that would reach the heavens (Gen 11:4). Philosopher Jaron Lanier critiques the reductionist tendencies of AI and its implications for human freedom, noting that the centralization of data in AI systems creates a dangerous concentration of power. According to Lanier, AI systems, which aggregate human input, can reduce individuals to data points, stripping away the richness and unpredictability of human life in favor of algorithmic efficiency. This not only threatens human freedom by imposing algorithmic control over personal and societal decisions but also risks eroding the complexity of human experience, reducing it to patterns that can be quantified and manipulated.[22]

Lanier argues that the more data AI systems accumulate, the more they undermine individual agency, creating a kind of "digital feudalism," where those who control the data wield disproportionate power over those whose data is being collected. This drive for control mirrors the

20. Lewis, *Abolition of Man*, 85.
21. Lewis, *Abolition of Man*, 85.
22. Lanier, *You Are Not a Gadget*, 157.

theological dangers of idolatry, where human creations assume god-like status, distorting relationality and denying human dependence on God.²³

The ethical dangers of AI's centralization of power are evident in systems like predictive policing, which, though well-intentioned, often perpetuate systemic injustices, such as racial profiling and the over-policing of certain socioeconomic or ethnic communities. Scholars have documented how AI, when fed biased data, reinforces existing societal inequalities. This centralization of decision-making power raises critical theological questions about justice, autonomy, and moral responsibility. Augustine warned that idolatry arises when humanity places its trust in created things rather than in God.²⁴ In the case of AI, reliance on algorithms to mediate justice risks creating a new form of idolatry, where machines are revered as omniscient authorities. The theological challenge, then, is not only to critique AI as a tool but to recognize the deeper spiritual threat it poses to the integrity of human moral agency and relationality.

In conclusion, AI-driven technologies such as predictive policing highlight the profound ethical and theological dangers of centralizing power in nonhuman systems. From a theological perspective, the warnings against idolatry found in the Bible serve as a timeless critique of humanity's desire for control and autonomy. The ethical implications of these technologies must be carefully considered, not only in terms of their practical applications but in light of the deeper spiritual and relational consequences they pose for human beings made in the image of God.

DEFINING IDOLATRY IN THE CONTEXT OF AI AND BIOTECHNOLOGY

In light of rapid advancements in AI and biotechnology, the ancient theological concept of idolatry acquires new relevance. While idolatry in the biblical sense referred to physical idols crafted from wood or stone, today's "idols" emerge in the form of algorithms, machines, and bioengineered creations that challenge traditional boundaries of human agency,

---

23. Lanier, *You Are Not a Gadget*, 157.

24. Augustine, *City of God*, trans. Bettenson, X.4. Augustine warns that idolatry arises when humanity places its trust in created things rather than in God, emphasizing the dangers of relying on human-made systems instead of divine authority—a concern that is especially relevant when addressing the concentration of power in modern technological systems.

identity, and even mortality. The drive to transcend human limitations through artificial systems or biological enhancements raises deep theological questions about autonomy, divine sovereignty, and the essence of what it means to be human. As in ancient times, when idols were viewed as representations of divine power, AI and biotechnology now offer a modern pursuit of control over life, death, and human potential.

This section will explore how these technologies reflect deeper theological errors reminiscent of the idolatry criticized in Scripture, pushing the boundaries of human ambition in ways that echo the story of Babel. It will also define idolatry in light of contemporary technological advances, showing how AI and biotechnology represent a new form of theological rebellion against God's sovereignty and the relational aspects of the *imago Dei*.

Theological Definitions of Idolatry

Idolatry in the biblical tradition is profoundly tied to the rejection of divine sovereignty and the elevation of created things to the status of divinity. Scripture explicitly warns against idolatry, as seen in the Ten Commandments: "You shall have no other gods before me. You shall not make for yourself an image in the form of anything in heaven above or on the earth beneath or in the waters below" (Exod 20:3–4). Isaiah 44:9–20 further criticizes the absurdity of idol-making, pointing out that humans craft objects from wood or stone, then bow down to these inanimate creations, believing them to hold divine power.

In the context of AI and biotechnology, this ancient understanding of idolatry takes on new dimensions. Traditional idols were anthropomorphic objects designed to embody human traits and aspirations, but AI and biotechnologies function as a form of "reverse anthropomorphism." Instead of creating representations of gods in human form, human intelligence, decision-making, and creativity are now encoded into machines and biological systems. These technologies aggregate and surpass human capacities, functioning as entities that seem omniscient or omnipotent.

Theologian Dietrich Bonhoeffer's critique of idolatry is particularly relevant here: whenever human beings trust in their own creations over God, they risk moral and spiritual corruption. This principle applies directly to the development and deployment of AI and biotechnology, which are increasingly treated as authoritative sources for decisions about human life and death.[25]

Moreover, AI systems—particularly in decision-making algorithms—and biotechnology applications centralize power and knowledge in ways that mirror ancient idol worship. Walter Brueggemann extends this analysis, arguing that idolatry represents humanity's attempt to control the uncontrollable aspects of life.[26] In the digital age, AI and biotechnology give humanity the illusion of control over areas previously believed to be under divine sovereignty, including life, death, and morality. These technologies, by aggregating vast amounts of data or enabling cognitive and physical enhancements, function as modern idols that offer false promises of power, much like the idols of ancient times.

In summary, the theological definition of idolatry must expand in the modern context to include the technological manifestations of AI and biotechnology. These advancements present new challenges to divine sovereignty and human relationality within the *imago Dei*, highlighting the ethical and spiritual dangers of trusting in created things rather than in God.

AI as a Modern Tower of Babel

The Tower of Babel narrative (Gen 11:1–9) provides a vivid biblical metaphor for the theological dangers of AI and biotechnology. In Babel, human beings sought to construct a tower that would reach the heavens, symbolizing their collective ambition to transcend divine boundaries. This act represented far more than physical construction; it was an expression of humanity's desire to attain god-like power and autonomy. God's response—confusing their language and scattering the people—served as a divine reminder that human aspirations have limits and that overreach leads to fragmentation and loss of relationality.

In the same way, AI and biotechnology represent modern iterations of this ancient ambition. Technologies such as BCIs, for example, promise cognitive enhancement by allowing the brain to control external devices. China's recent advancements in BCI technology, which include systems enabling users to control robotic arms with their thoughts, exemplify the

---

25. Bonhoeffer, *Ethics*, 111.

26. Walter Brueggemann, *The Prophetic Imagination* (Philadelphia: Fortress, 1978), 24.

astonishing potential of such innovations.[27] While these advancements provide incredible benefits, particularly for those with disabilities, they also raise profound ethical and theological concerns. Like the Tower of Babel, BCIs and other AI technologies centralize human control over creation in ways that challenge divine sovereignty. By allowing humans to manipulate their own cognition and extend their abilities beyond natural limitations, BCIs blur the line between human autonomy and divine authority, pushing the boundaries of what it means to be created in the *imago Dei*.

Gerhard von Rad, in his commentary on Genesis, emphasizes that the sin of Babel lay not in the tower's construction but in the hubris of attempting to become self-sufficient and independent from divine authority.[28] The ambition to transcend human limitations through technology echoes this theological error. As AI and biotechnology increasingly mediate human decision-making, enhance cognitive abilities, and control physical functions, they offer an illusion of self-sufficiency. This technological pursuit mirrors the overreach of Babel, where humanity sought to elevate itself to divine status.

By constructing systems and technologies that mimic god-like abilities, such as predictive power or cognitive control, humanity risks falling into the same theological trap: striving for autonomy that ultimately undermines the relational and dependent nature of the *imago Dei*. The Tower of Babel narrative reminds us that attempts to transcend divine limits result not in elevation but in fragmentation and a loss of moral integrity.

In this way, AI technologies like BCIs, predictive algorithms, and other advanced systems echo the ambition of Babel, representing humanity's desire to break free from divine constraints, with the inherent risk of disintegration and ethical confusion. These modern technologies serve as new "towers" through which humanity attempts to attain god-like autonomy, yet, as in Babel, they may ultimately lead to spiritual and societal division rather than fulfillment.

---

27. Emily Mullin, "China Has a Controversial Plan for Brain-Computer Interfaces," *Wired*, Apr. 30, 2024, https://www.wired.com/story/china-brain-computer-interfaces-neuralink-neucyber-neurotech.

28. Von Rad, *Genesis: A Commentary*, 148.

Ethical Concerns in AI and Biotechnology Centralization

AI and biotechnology, by aggregating data and enhancing human capacities, create a centralization of power that mirrors the theological warnings against idolatry. Jaron Lanier critiques the reductionist tendencies of AI, arguing that when human beings are reduced to data points, they lose their moral and relational significance.[29] This concern is amplified in biotechnology, where advances such as bioengineered living tissue, used to create "living skin" for robots, raise ethical and theological concerns.[30] The ability to create biological materials that simulate human skin challenges traditional understandings of embodiment, relationality, and the boundaries between the human and the artificial.

The theological critique of these technologies must address the idolatrous centralization of power in human creations. Predictive policing algorithms, for example, delegate decisions about criminal activity to AI systems based on aggregated data, which can lead to biased outcomes and reinforce systemic inequalities. Similarly, advancements in biotechnology, such as organoid technology—miniaturized, simplified versions of organs grown in a lab—push the boundaries of what it means to create life.[31] When combined with AI, these technologies offer the potential for unprecedented control over human biology, creating ethical dilemmas around autonomy, agency, and the value of life.

The rise of social credit systems, particularly in China, further illustrates this centralization of power. These systems use AI to evaluate citizens' behaviors and assign scores that determine access to resources, jobs, and opportunities.[32] By aggregating vast amounts of data and making decisions that affect individuals' lives, social credit systems diminish human agency and outsource moral decisions to algorithms. This reflects

---

29. Lanier, *You Are Not a Gadget*, 127.

30. Irene Wang and Rocky Swift, "Say Cheese: Japanese Scientists Make Robot Face 'Smile' with Living Skin," Reuters, July 18, 2024, https://www.reuters.com/science/say-cheese-japanese-scientists-make-robot-face-smile-with-living-skin-2024-07-18.

31. Niall Byrne, "Human Brain Cells in a Dish Learn to Play Pong," Neuroscience News, Oct. 12, 2022, https://neurosciencenews.com/organoid-pong-21625. This article discusses the development of organoid technology, where lab-grown brain cells are integrated into digital systems to perform tasks like playing the game Pong. This advancement pushes the boundaries of creating life and raises ethical concerns about the extent to which humanity should replicate or interfere with natural processes.

32. Başer, "Artificial Intelligence and Social Credit," 45.

the theological concerns of idolatry, where trust is placed in human-created systems rather than in divine wisdom and justice.

Sovereignty, Human Limits, and Biotechnology

The theological concept of divine sovereignty is crucial in addressing the ethical implications of AI and biotechnology. In both Scripture and theological tradition, God alone is sovereign over creation, and human attempts to transcend divine limits are met with divine intervention. Reinhold Niebuhr's critique of human hubris is particularly relevant here, as he argues that humanity's desire to control and manipulate creation, particularly through technology, is a rejection of the finite nature of human existence.[33]

Biotechnology, particularly in the realm of cognitive enhancement through BCIs and genetic modification, represents a direct challenge to divine sovereignty. China's focus on cognitive enhancement through BCIs is a case in point, where BCIs are developed not only for medical purposes but also for augmenting the capabilities of healthy individuals.[34] This ambition reflects the theological error of Babel, where humanity sought to transcend its creaturely limitations by centralizing power in human creations. The development of BCIs for cognitive enhancement illustrates the ethical dangers of placing trust in biotechnology to "improve" human capacities rather than embracing the limits set by divine authority.

Theologically, the doctrine of the *imago Dei* asserts that human beings are created with inherent dignity, relationality, and moral agency. Biotechnology, when used to enhance or manipulate these attributes, risks undermining the very nature of humanity as created in God's image. The pursuit of cognitive enhancement through BCIs challenges the relational aspects of the *imago Dei*, as it seeks to augment individual capacities rather than foster relational interdependence. Samuel Wells warns that any technology that diminishes human agency or relationality must be critically examined through a theological lens, as it risks creating

---

33. Reinhold Niebuhr, *The Nature and Destiny of Man* (New York: Scribner's Sons, 1941), 102.

34. Mullin, "China Has a Controversial Plan."

a society where human beings are no longer viewed as moral agents but as manipulable entities.[35]

In conclusion, theologically defining idolatry in the context of AI and biotechnology reveals profound ethical and spiritual challenges. These technologies, by centralizing power and offering the illusion of control over life, death, and morality, mirror the theological warnings against idolatry found in the Bible. AI systems, BCIs, and biotechnology advancements like organoids and "living skin" push the boundaries of human autonomy in ways that challenge divine sovereignty and human finitude. Drawing from biblical critiques of idolatry and theological insights from Bonhoeffer, Niebuhr, and Wells, it becomes clear that the ambition to transcend human limitations through technology mirrors the theological error of Babel. As society continues to develop these technologies, it is essential to maintain a theological and ethical framework that respects human dignity, relationality, and the sovereignty of God.

AI'S CHALLENGE TO THE *IMAGO DEI*

The concept of the *imago Dei*—that human beings are created in the image of God—has long been a cornerstone of Christian anthropology. This theological framework not only affirms the intrinsic dignity of every human person but also emphasizes relationality, moral agency, and the embodiment of human life. However, the rise of AI and biotechnology presents significant challenges to these core aspects of the *imago Dei*, potentially eroding the relational and communal dimensions of humanity, commodifying human bodies, and distorting human dignity. This section will explore these challenges, integrating theological reflections with contemporary technological advancements, while offering Christian leaders practical guidance on addressing the ethical and spiritual dilemmas posed by AI-driven systems.

AI's Potential to Erode the Relational Aspects of the Imago Dei

At the heart of the *imago Dei* is the theological claim that human beings are relational creatures, designed for communion with God and others. The relational aspect of the *imago Dei* finds its roots in the Genesis

---

35. Samuel Wells, *Improvisation: The Drama of Christian Ethics* (Grand Rapids: Brazos, 2004), 93.

narrative, where humanity is not created in isolation but in community: "It is not good for the man to be alone" (Gen 2:18). This divine intention for human beings to live in relationship with others stands in stark contrast to the individualized, efficiency-driven focus of AI technologies, which increasingly prioritize data processing, decision-making, and productivity over human relationality.

AI systems often replace face-to-face human relationships with transactional engagements. For instance, facial recognition technologies and algorithmic decision-making tools used in public services and even the justice system may efficiently process vast amounts of data, but they do so by abstracting human individuals into data points and algorithms.[36] This abstraction fractures the communal and embodied aspects of the *imago Dei* by treating persons as disembodied sources of information rather than as relational beings with inherent dignity. As Bonhoeffer warns, reducing human life to "data" or "utility" represents a dehumanizing move away from the Christian view of the person as a living, relational soul.[37]

The emergence of advanced AI technologies also raises significant questions: How do we determine when AI becomes sentient, or if it ever does? When does AI or biotechnology alone require the attribution of personhood? These questions are no longer hypothetical, as advancements in biotechnology and AI push the boundaries of human-machine integration. The creation of organoids—miniaturized, simplified versions of organs grown in vitro using stem cells—introduces new ethical dilemmas. For example, brain organoids, while lacking the complexity of fully formed human brains, are capable of mimicking certain neural activities. Ethically, this leads to unsettling questions: If a brain organoid develops the ability to "think" or simulate consciousness, at what point do we consider it deserving of rights or protections? Can we subject these developing forms of "life" to experimentation without crossing into ethical grey areas, such as torture?

Similarly, the development of BCIs introduces another dimension to this debate. Technologies like NeuCyber's BCIs, which allow a monkey to control a robotic arm through thought alone, hint at the growing potential for machines to merge with biological elements.[38] At what point does the machine stop being a tool and start being a "person"? These

36. Turkle, *Second Self*, 212.
37. Bonhoeffer, *Life Together*, 45.
38. Mullin, "China Has a Controversial Plan."

ethical questions challenge both our theological understanding of personhood and our legal frameworks, which traditionally hinge on biological life and human experience.

Theologically, the concept of the *imago Dei*—which asserts that humans are uniquely made in the image of God—has been one of the primary criteria for distinguishing human beings from the rest of creation. However, as AI and biotechnology evolve, can these technologies possess traits like cognition or emotional processing without the embodied experiences that define human life? If brain cells can grow, learn, and act in a petri dish but lack any relational experience with other humans or the divine, can they reflect the *imago Dei*, or is their capacity for thought merely superficial mimicry? Furthermore, would allowing them to "live" in isolation constitute an act of cruelty or negligence, akin to torture?

The challenge here is navigating the fine line between developing lifesaving or life-enhancing technologies and creating forms of existence that raise ethical and theological questions about personhood, dignity, and moral responsibility. These questions are crucial as AI and biotechnology increasingly blur the lines between creation and Creator, control and autonomy, life and mimicry. The biblical vision of human dignity must engage these new challenges, questioning not only how to protect human beings from depersonalization but also how to responsibly handle the emerging forms of "life" created by these technologies.

AI and Human Dignity

Central to Christian theology is the belief that every person possesses intrinsic dignity because they are made in God's image. Theologically, this dignity is not contingent upon one's abilities, status, or contributions but is a reflection of God's creative act and the moral agency imbued in humanity. However, AI-driven systems, especially those involving biometric and facial recognition technologies, risk commodifying human bodies and reducing individuals to data points.

Facial recognition systems, for example, increasingly permeate both public and private sectors, from airport security to social media platforms. These systems do not merely recognize faces but also track and profile individuals, often for commercial or state surveillance purposes.[39]

---

39. Kate O'Neill, *Tech Humanist: How You Can Make Technology Better for Business and Better for Humans* (New York: Kogan Page, 2018), 156.

In extreme cases, like China's social credit system, these technologies merge AI with state control, monitoring and regulating the behavior of citizens based on compliance with state-defined norms of morality. This effectively reduces individuals to their biometric data and a set of evaluative metrics, dehumanizing them by reducing their worth to a score.[40] This commodification and monitoring of human life echo the theological warnings against idolatry found in the Hebrew Scriptures, where idols are critiqued for their dehumanizing impact on worshipers (Isa 44:9–20).

Moreover, "Roko's basilisk," a thought experiment conducted in 2010, introduces another extreme scenario.[41] A networked AI group, or "super-AI," has been tasked with making human life on earth more efficient. This leads the AI to make difficult decisions. Humans opposed to the use of AI impede overall efficiency and corrupt the AI's goals. Thus, the super-AI decides to eliminate resistant humans to achieve its task and torture those that do not help its growth. Roko's basilisk demonstrates another disturbing dimension of AI's dehumanizing potential. Such speculative scenarios, while not yet realized, highlight a growing fear about the control AI could exert over humanity's future, potentially turning it into a god-like entity that demands obedience. Even discussing such ideas evokes the theological caution against allowing any created thing to dominate human life, as the relationship between Creator and creation is inverted.

AI's impact on human dignity extends beyond surveillance. Technologies like AI-powered healthcare and predictive policing introduce biases that disproportionately affect marginalized communities.[42] These biases are not just theoretical; they have already manifested in real-world applications, such as algorithms that perpetuate racial profiling in policing or restrict access to healthcare based on flawed or discriminatory

---

40. Agrawal, "AI-Powered Control Systems."

41. Roko's Basilisk, a speculative thought experiment, presents a scenario in which an AI, designed to maximize efficiency, decides to eliminate those who hinder its goals—highlighting a disturbing potential for AI to exert god-like control over humanity. This scenario echoes theological concerns about the dangers of allowing any created entity, whether an idol or artificial intelligence, to dominate human agency and dictate moral direction, reinforcing the critique of AI as a modern idol. For more information see https://www.lesswrong.com/w/rokos-basilisk (last updated Nov. 30, 2022). Note: This is a speculative source rather than a formal academic citation, but it is relevant to contemporary discussions on AI ethics and the theological implications of artificial intelligence.

42. Ruha Benjamin, *Race After Technology: Abolitionist Tools for the New Jim Code* (Cambridge: Polity, 2019), 87.

data sets. When AI systems are used to determine access to healthcare, education, or law enforcement, they often perpetuate systemic injustices by relying on data sets that reflect existing social inequalities. Theologically, this violates the Christian imperative to protect the vulnerable and uphold the dignity of all people, particularly those who are marginalized. Bonhoeffer's emphasis on relationality in the *imago Dei* underscores this, as the depersonalization caused by AI distances humans from one another and from God.[43]

Augustine's critique of human pride in *The City of God* serves as a warning here: when human creations (whether idols or technologies) become the arbiters of justice, they inevitably reflect human sinfulness and bias. This is not just a moral concern but a theological one, as AI's centralization of decision-making power challenges the very foundation of human dignity by shifting moral agency from persons to machines.[44]

Practical Application for Christian Leaders

In light of these ethical concerns, Christian leaders must take a proactive role in addressing AI's potential impact on communal worship and the relational life of the church. As digital avatars, AI-driven sermons, and robot preachers increasingly integrate into worship services, these tools offer both opportunities and risks for faith communities. While AI can assist in reaching people globally, it may also lead to the depersonalization of worship. The robot priest at Kodai-ji Temple, for example, highlights the limitations of AI in replacing human authenticity and spiritual credibility.[45] While AI may efficiently deliver sermons or perform rituals, it lacks the depth of personal sacrifice, lived experience, and emotional empathy that build genuine spiritual trust.

---

43. Dietrich Bonhoeffer, *Creation and Fall: A Theological Exposition of Genesis 1–3* (Minneapolis: Fortress, 1997), 74.

44. Augustine, *City of God*, trans. Bettenson, XIX.15. Augustine's critique of human pride in *City of God* serves as a warning: when human creations (whether idols or technologies) become the arbiters of justice, they inevitably reflect human sinfulness and bias. This theological concern highlights how the centralization of decision-making power in AI challenges the foundation of human dignity by shifting moral agency from persons to machines.

45. Joshua Conrad Jackson and Kai Chi Yam, "The In-Credible Robot Priest and the Limits of Robot Workers," *Scientific American*, July 25, 2023. https://www.scientificamerican.com/article/the-in-credible-robot-priest-and-the-limits-of-robot-workers.

Human leaders engage in acts of devotion, such as pilgrimage or personal trials, that communicate authenticity in ways machines cannot. Moreover, AI's incapacity to experience or embody faith means it fails to genuinely connect with believers on a relational and spiritual level. This suggests that while AI can augment the work of ministry, the technology should not replace the role of embodied leaders who have undergone the sacrifices and experiences that build trust and spiritual authority. Worship is not merely about the transmission of information; it is a deeply relational, embodied act that involves personal engagement and spiritual leadership.[46]

In response, Christian leaders must carefully evaluate how AI technologies can enhance, rather than erode, the communal and embodied nature of Christian worship. For example, while digital avatars may enable broader participation in worship services, there is a danger that these technologies could further fragment community life, undermining the church's identity as a gathered, incarnational people of God. Leaders must ensure that AI tools are used to complement rather than replace human interaction, emphasizing face-to-face relationships, discipleship, and pastoral care.

Furthermore, Christian leaders should foster conversations around the ethical implications of technologies like facial recognition, BCIs, and AI-driven decisions in pastoral settings. These tools, if misused, risk violating human dignity by reducing individuals to data points or commodities.[47] In settings such as healthcare, or even in church communities, where BCIs might be used to monitor or influence behavior, the

---

46. Ron Hunter, "The Ethics of AI: Navigating the Moral Maze of Artificial Intelligence," *D6 Family Ministry* (blog), 2024, https://d6family.com/the-ethics-of-ai-navigating-the-moral-maze-of-artificial-intelligence. Though this is a blog and not an academic source, the author rightly discusses the ethical considerations of AI in ministry, emphasizing that while AI may enhance ministry work, it cannot replace the essential role of embodied leaders who have undergone personal sacrifices and experiences. This aligns with the argument that worship is not merely about information transmission, but involves relational engagement, spiritual leadership, and trust built through lived experience.

47. William Kilner, *Dignity and the* Imago Dei: *Theological Anthropology and Ethics* (London: Routledge, 2019). Kilner's work emphasizes the inherent dignity of every individual as made in the image of God, a principle central to Christian ethical thought. His exploration of theological anthropology underscores the importance of upholding human dignity, particularly in the face of technological advancements like AI, BCIs, and facial recognition systems. This aligns with the ethical imperative for Christian leaders to ensure that technology serves, rather than diminishes, the intrinsic worth of individuals in pastoral and healthcare settings.

Christian ethical imperative is clear: uphold the intrinsic worth of every person as made in the image of God.

Kilner's work on the *imago Dei* stresses that Christian ethics must prioritize the inherent value of human beings rather than reducing individuals to their functional or technological capabilities. He warns against the view that people's worth is based on what they can produce or achieve, emphasizing that human dignity stems from being created in God's image. In light of technological advances, Kilner argues that human identity must remain rooted in divine purpose, not in technological enhancement or functional efficiency.[48]

Lastly, pastors and theologians need to engage with the cultural narrative surrounding transhumanism, which promotes the idea that biotechnology and AI can transcend human limitations. As technologies like BCIs and genetic enhancements move closer to normalization, Christian leaders must critique the transhumanist vision of achieving a "posthuman" existence. This vision, which prioritizes autonomy and human control over the limitations of the body, stands in direct contrast to the biblical understanding of human finitude and dependence on God.[49] By emphasizing a theology of embodiment, relationality, and moral responsibility, Christian leaders can offer a robust counternarrative that challenges the transhumanist pursuit of self-deification and technological immortality.[50]

As AI and biotechnology become more integrated into various aspects of human life—governance, healthcare, and worship—Christian leaders must thoughtfully engage with the ethical implications of these developments. By maintaining a strong theological focus on the *imago Dei*, they can ensure that technological advancements serve to support human dignity rather than undermine it. In doing so, the church can provide a crucial ethical framework for navigating the challenges of the digital age, upholding a vision of human flourishing grounded in relationality, embodiment, and moral integrity.

---

48. Kilner, *Dignity and the* Imago Dei.

49. Lanier, *You Are Not a Gadget*, 219. Lanier critiques the transhumanist vision of achieving a "posthuman" existence, emphasizing the importance of preserving human dignity and the limitations of the body. He argues that prioritizing autonomy and human control over the body's limitations can lead to a dehumanizing perspective.

50. Turkle, *Second Self*.

ETHICAL AND SPIRITUAL DANGERS: AI AS A TOOL OF CONTROL

The rapid rise of AI-driven technologies presents profound ethical challenges, especially as they are increasingly used as instruments of control in both public and private sectors. AI's ability to surveil, predict, and manage human behavior introduces questions that intersect with both Christian ethics and theological anthropology. This section will explore how these emerging technologies not only threaten human autonomy but also mirror the dynamics of idolatry, where humans are subjugated by what they create.

Surveillance Capitalism and Algorithmic Bias

At the heart of the ethical dilemma posed by AI is the way it enables surveillance capitalism. Pioneered by tech giants, this economic model thrives on the commodification of personal data, using AI to predict and influence behavior. Shoshana Zuboff describes this as a new form of capitalism, where human experience becomes the raw material for commercial practices, fundamentally shifting the nature of freedom.[51] This transformation in economic practices is particularly visible in the Chinese social credit system, where facial recognition technologies and behavioral algorithms determine a citizen's access to services and freedoms.[52] The system rewards compliance with state norms while punishing those deemed noncompliant. Such systems align with the theological critique of idolatry found in the Hebrew Scriptures, where idols represent false power structures that manipulate and control (Isa 44:9–20). Like ancient idols, AI promises efficiency and order while subjugating individuals through dehumanizing processes.

The Christian ethical tradition, rooted in the *imago Dei*, upholds the intrinsic dignity of every person. Surveillance systems and commodification run contrary to this dignity, reducing human beings to their behavioral patterns and treating them as mere data points. For theologians like Jacques Ellul, technological society, by its nature, strips individuals of their moral agency, transforming human beings into objects of control.[53]

---

51. Shoshana Zuboff, *The Age of Surveillance Capitalism: The Fight for a Human Future at the New Frontier of Power* (New York: PublicAffairs, 2019), 34.

52. Başer, "Artificial Intelligence and Social Credit," 56.

53. Ellul, *Technological Society*, 85.

Ellul's insights align with the current function of AI as an all-encompassing system of oversight, curtailing moral agency and freedom through algorithmic governance.

AI's Disconnection from Human Moral Agency

The dehumanization that AI fosters is deeply connected to its capacity to disconnect human moral agency from decision-making. Ancient idol worship similarly dehumanized individuals by entrusting their fate to the will of lifeless, human-made objects, which could neither see, hear, nor feel (Ps 115:4–7). The theological warning against idolatry, as expressed in texts like Exod 20:3–5, critiques this very dynamic: placing trust in things that, by their nature, cannot reflect divine will or human moral consciousness. Similarly, AI systems that replace human judgment in law enforcement and healthcare create an ethical void where decisions are made without the requisite human empathy or moral reflection.

In governance, for example, predictive policing algorithms such as Project Horizon have been implemented to determine crime hot spots based on historical data. While these systems claim to enhance efficiency, they often perpetuate racial biases, disproportionately targeting minority communities. This disconnect between algorithmic judgment and moral responsibility mirrors the idol-centric systems of the ANE, where the worship of false gods often justified societal inequalities and oppression.[54] By prioritizing data-driven decision-making over human moral agency, AI risks fostering a society where accountability and justice are reduced into binary processes, devoid of the relational and ethical nuances central to Christian anthropology.

Biotechnology, Transhumanism, and the Control of the Body

Biotechnology, particularly BCIs, introduces a new dimension to the ethical concerns surrounding AI. Recent developments in BCIs that allow users to control machines through thought alone challenge our understanding of human personhood and autonomy.[55] The integration of biotechnology and AI raises the question of where the boundaries of human control and divine sovereignty lie. Technologies like BCIs

---

54. Lanier, *You Are Not a Gadget*, 157.
55. Mullin, "China Has a Controversial Plan."

represent humanity's desire to transcend its natural limitations, echoing the ambitions of the builders of the Tower of Babel, who sought to make a name for themselves and challenge divine order (Gen 11:4). Just as the Babel narrative critiques human hubris and the desire for control, so too does the Christian tradition caution against transhumanist ambitions that seek to bypass the embodied nature of human life in pursuit of technological perfection.

The ethical challenge presented by transhumanism is that it places ultimate trust in human innovation, reducing human bodies to substrates for enhancement. As Jaron Lanier critiques in *You Are Not a Gadget*, this technological mindset risks commodifying human life, turning individuals into programmable entities whose value is determined by their functional capacity.[56] In theological terms, this represents a distortion of the *imago Dei*, where humanity is no longer seen as a reflection of divine image and purpose but as a project to be optimized through technological intervention. The biblical narrative affirms the goodness of human finitude and dependence on God, a reality that transhumanist ideologies seek to overcome through the augmentation of human biology. The quest for immortality, often advanced by transhumanist advocates, undermines the Christian hope in the resurrection, where the body is not abandoned but transformed through divine action (1 Cor 15:42–44).

AI and the Ethics of Control

The increasing use of AI and biotechnology to exert control over individuals not only challenges Christian ethical principles but also reshapes our understanding of autonomy. AI's capacity to monitor, predict, and influence behavior places unprecedented power in the hands of those who control these technologies. This centralized power reflects Augustine's critique of human pride, where humanity's desire for control becomes a form of idolatry.[57] When AI systems govern human behavior, they usurp

---

56. Lanier, *You Are Not a Gadget*, 142.

57. Augustine, *City of God*, trans. Bettenson, XIV.28. Augustine critiques human pride and the desire for control, warning that when humanity seeks to dominate creation, it mirrors the sin of idolatry. This critique is particularly relevant in the context of modern technologies like AI and biotechnology, which centralize power and influence human behavior. As humanity relies increasingly on these technologies, there is a risk of elevating human-made systems to a position of authority, akin to the idolatry Augustine warns against, where the desire for control becomes an end in itself, overriding divine order and moral responsibility.

the role of moral agents—deciding who is rewarded or punished, and whose actions are deemed worthy or unworthy. This violates the Christian understanding of justice, which is rooted in relationality and the respect for individual moral agency.

The ethical dangers of AI, particularly in its capacity to control, are compounded by the rise of algorithmic bias. AI systems, when built on flawed data sets, often reinforce existing social prejudices. Theologically, this reflects the biblical warnings against unjust systems of power that exploit the vulnerable (Amos 5:24). As AI becomes an arbiter of justice, it risks perpetuating the very injustices it was designed to eliminate, creating a society where moral agency is outsourced to machines that lack the capacity for empathy, forgiveness, or moral reasoning.

In conclusion, the ethical and spiritual dangers posed by AI as a tool of control demand careful reflection within the Christian tradition. AI's capacity to surveil, predict, and govern behavior raises profound questions about freedom, justice, and the nature of human dignity. While AI technologies offer efficiency, they also echo ancient forms of idolatry, where human creations subjugate their makers. By engaging deeply with these challenges, Christian ethics can offer a robust framework for navigating the digital age, one that upholds the dignity and moral agency of every person as a reflection of the *imago Dei*.

PRACTICAL RESPONSES

As we have explored the ethical and spiritual dangers posed by AI as a tool of control, it is now essential to shift our focus toward specific practical responses for Christian leaders. Engaging with these technologies from a theological perspective, pastors, theologians, and worship leaders must develop frameworks that both honor human dignity and resist the pull of technological idolatry. This section provides guidance on how Christian leaders can responsibly integrate AI into ministry while upholding core biblical principles and fostering ethical discernment within their communities.

Developing Theological and Ethical Frameworks

As AI and related technologies become more integral to society, Christian leaders are tasked with forming clear and robust theological and ethical frameworks to engage these advancements. Grounding these frameworks in the Bible and early church traditions is essential to navigate the ethical complexities without succumbing to technological idolatry. The doctrine of the *imago Dei*, which emphasizes human dignity, relationality, and moral agency, offers a key lens for assessing AI's depersonalizing effects.

Jürgen Moltmann's *The Ethics of Hope* also provides valuable insights for integrating technology with Christian ethics. Moltmann critiques human pride in creating systems that undermine God's design for creation and calls for an eschatological hope that resists attempts to transcend human finitude.[58] For Moltmann, technological advancements, including AI, should be oriented toward God's redemptive purposes, avoiding the temptation to replace divine sovereignty with human innovation. Augustine similarly warns in *The City of God* that placing trust in human constructs over God risks corrupting moral agency.[59] Such warnings are crucial in an age when AI increasingly takes on decision-making roles that shape society.

The *exitus-reditus* framework, drawn from Augustine and later adopted by Aquinas, provides another theological tool for understanding AI's place in creation. This concept describes creation's departure from God (*exitus*) and its return to God (*reditus*), offering a model for human engagement with the world. In this framework, AI, when ethically aligned with divine purpose, can participate in this return, but it must remain within the bounds of human finitude and moral responsibility. Christian leaders can thus articulate a theology that encourages responsible AI usage without succumbing to the illusion of technological omnipotence.

N. T. Wright's *Surprised by Hope* reinforces this eschatological perspective by emphasizing Christian hope in resurrection and the transformation of creation.[60] Rather than seeking transcendence through technology, Wright argues that Christian engagement with AI should focus on the renewal of creation through God's redemptive plan. His work challenges transhumanist ideologies that view AI and biotechnology as

---

58. Moltmann, *Ethics of Hope*.

59. Augustine, *City of God*, trans. Bettenson, XIV.28. Augustine warns that placing trust in human creations rather than in God risks corrupting moral agency. This critique resonates with the theological concerns raised by technological advancements like AI, which, if not aligned with divine purposes, could usurp divine sovereignty and diminish humanity's reliance on God's redemptive plan.

60. Wright, *Surprised by Hope*.

means to escape mortality, offering a counternarrative of hope grounded in God's promises for creation's renewal.

Practical Advice for Engaging AI in Church and Society

Christian leaders must not only develop theological frameworks but also offer practical guidance for integrating AI into ministry while safeguarding human dignity. The first step is educating congregations and theological institutions about AI's capabilities and limitations. Leaders can foster critical thinking about the potential dangers of algorithmic bias, surveillance, and transhumanism while also acknowledging AI's potential to enhance ministry.

One practical approach is for local church boards to consider AI-driven tools for decision-making in nonessential matters, such as administrative tasks, scheduling, or membership management. However, it is crucial that such technologies never replace the human discernment necessary for pastoral care, governance, or spiritual leadership. AI may provide valuable insights, but decisions should always be mediated through human decision-makers who are grounded in theological and ethical considerations. *Resurrection and Moral Order* by Oliver O'Donovan provides a useful guide for such discernment, emphasizing that human decisions must be shaped by a moral order that reflects creation's inherent goodness and God's purposes.[61]

AI technologies may also be employed in outreach efforts, particularly through digital platforms and virtual worship environments. For example, chatbots and AI-driven content recommendation systems can assist in evangelism and discipleship, but their use must be ethically managed. It is vital that AI never replaces the relational and embodied aspects of worship. The Kodai-ji Temple's use of the robot priest "Mindar" highlights this, as, despite its technological prowess, it lacked the credibility and spiritual depth required for authentic religious leadership.[62]

---

61. O'Donovan, *Resurrection and Moral Order*.

62. Jackson and Yam, "In-Credible Robot Priest." This article discusses the use of the robot priest "Mindar" at Kodai-ji Temple, illustrating the limitations of AI in religious leadership. Despite its technological advancements, the robot priest lacks the authenticity, emotional empathy, and spiritual depth necessary for genuine religious leadership, highlighting the dangers of replacing the relational and embodied aspects of worship with artificial systems.

In pastoral care, AI may assist with logistical tasks, but the core act of pastoral care—listening, guiding, praying—must remain a deeply relational, human-centered practice. The pastoral act embodies Christ's love for the church, where relational and empathetic engagement cannot be replicated by AI systems.

Worship leaders, too, can incorporate AI into their services in ways that enhance creativity without compromising theological integrity. AI-powered tools can assist in crafting meaningful worship experiences, but care should be taken to avoid depersonalizing worship. Worship is a communal, embodied act that mirrors Christ's incarnational ministry, where the church represents the body of Christ (1 Cor 12:27). This underscores the necessity of physical presence and relational connection in worship, where AI's virtual representations cannot substitute for embodied community. In 1 Cor 12:27, Paul emphasizes that each believer contributes to the church's overall health and function, mirroring the unity and diversity within a physical body. The Hebrew understanding of *kavod* (glory) as God's manifested presence among his people underscores the importance of physical, relational worship, where AI's virtual representations cannot substitute for embodied community. The communal act of worship brings the glory of God into tangible presence, emphasizing relationality and shared spiritual experience.

Christian educators and theologians should also engage AI in academic settings, ensuring that students are equipped to critically analyze technological advancements from a biblical worldview. This involves fostering interdisciplinary collaboration between theology, ethics, and technology studies, encouraging future leaders to navigate the ethical complexities of AI. The Christian academy has a vital role in shaping the conversation about AI, developing curricula that address both its potential benefits and risks. Courses on theological ethics, for example, can integrate case studies on AI, exploring how technologies like BCIs and facial recognition challenge Christian conceptions of human dignity and freedom.

Ethical Use of AI in Governance and Pastoral Decision-Making

In governance contexts, AI can be usefully integrated into decision-making processes where it enhances human judgment without replacing it. For example, AI can assist church boards with community trend analysis, financial management, or membership data, but decisions involving pastoral care or doctrinal matters must always remain under human discernment. AI, though efficient, lacks the spiritual and moral insight required for such decisions. O'Donovan's work in *Resurrection and Moral Order* highlights the need for human agency to reflect divine moral order, ensuring that decisions align with God's purposes.[63]

When it comes to pastoral care, AI tools can assist with tasks such as tracking prayer requests or scheduling visitations. However, the relational and empathetic nature of pastoral care requires personal engagement that AI cannot replicate. In 1 Pet 5:2–3, to "shepherd" means to guide, protect, and nurture the spiritual well-being of the flock with genuine care, patience, and humility. The Bible's call for shepherds to care for their flocks implies a level of intimacy and responsibility that cannot be automated. Shepherding involves leading by example, not domineering but showing Christ-like compassion. Church leaders must be vigilant in ensuring that AI's use in ministry enhances, rather than erodes, these vital human connections.

Resisting Technological Idolatry

A crucial task for Christian leaders is to resist the subtle idolatry of placing ultimate trust in technological systems over divine authority. Paul's warnings against idolatry in Rom 1:21–23 highlight the spiritual degradation that occurs when humanity replaces God's sovereignty with lesser creations. Just as early Christians resisted the idolatrous practices of the Roman Empire, modern Christians must resist the idolization of AI technologies that promise control, autonomy, or immortality.

Christian leaders must embrace a countercultural stance on AI by prioritizing human dignity, relational depth, and moral responsibility over technological efficiency. This involves making practical choices that reflect the intrinsic worth of every person as made in God's image. Leaders can model the stewardship of technology by upholding the *imago Dei*, affirming each person's intrinsic worth and fostering community-centered ministry practices. In doing so, they resist the idolization of technology, providing a theological framework that upholds divine sovereignty and ethical use of AI. Leaders can model the stewardship of technology by

---

63. O'Donovan, *Resurrection and Moral Order*.

upholding the *imago Dei*, ensuring that AI is used ethically and responsibly in ways that support human flourishing.

This is not a call to reject technology or its advancements; rather, Christians, as bearers of the *imago Dei*, should lead in responsibly advancing technology. Reflecting God's creative nature, we are tasked with using our ingenuity for the good of creation. God, the ultimate Creator, imbued humanity with creativity and stewardship, meaning that technological progress should align with the values of human dignity, relationality, and divine purpose. Our engagement with AI and other technologies should be marked by both innovation and reverence for God's creation.

As AI continues to reshape society, Christian leaders, pastors, teachers, worship leaders, and theologians must engage deeply with its ethical and theological implications. By developing robust frameworks rooted in the Bible and early church traditions, they can ensure that AI is used in ways that promote human dignity, relationality, and moral agency rather than undermining these core tenets of Christian anthropology. Christian leaders stand at a pivotal moment, where technological advancements offer both potential and ethical challenges. While AI can enhance ministry, decision-making, and outreach, it also poses risks of depersonalization, idolatry, and loss of moral agency. By developing theological frameworks rooted in Scripture and early church traditions, Christian leaders can ensure that AI is used in ways that honor human dignity and uphold divine sovereignty. Through this approach, Christian leaders can guide responsible innovation that supports relationality, moral responsibility, and embodied community in the digital age.

CONCLUSION: PRESERVING HUMAN DIGNITY

AI's rapid ascent as a dominant force in shaping human life raises pressing theological and ethical questions about the nature of control, autonomy, and identity. This chapter has explored how AI, much like the idols of ancient cultures, offers humanity a dangerous illusion of power. By mirroring human desires for mastery and immortality, AI systems centralize decision-making, create biases, and dehumanize individuals—all while promising a future free from limitations. Yet, as we have seen, these technologies distort the *imago Dei* by eroding the relational and moral dimensions that are central to human existence.

IDOLATRY AND TECHNOLOGY   157

The concept of reverse anthropomorphism, where machines take on human-like roles, further complicates this idolatry. From AI-driven predictive policing to digital avatars, the line between human authority and machine control becomes increasingly blurred. This reflects a modern-day Babel, where humanity seeks to transcend its divinely ordained boundaries through technological means, risking fragmentation and the loss of relationality.

At the heart of the Christian response to these developments lies a call to humility, ethical discernment, and theological grounding. Like ancient idols, AI may promise security and efficiency, but it cannot replace the relational, embodied nature of human life designed by God.

In conclusion, as AI continues to evolve, Christian leaders must engage with these technologies thoughtfully, resisting the lure of technological idolatry. By affirming the limits of human power and the centrality of God's sovereignty, the church can lead the way in preserving human dignity and relationality in a world increasingly shaped by algorithms. Only by grounding our engagement with technology in a robust theological framework can we ensure that AI serves humanity rather than becoming its master.

CASE STUDY #9: AI-DRIVEN WORSHIP

In 2027, a popular megachurch in Texas implements an AI-driven worship system called SpiritVerse,[64] which uses digital avatars to lead its services. The church's leadership views the technology as a means to expand their reach, allowing congregants to interact with virtual preachers, musicians, and pastoral staff from anywhere in the world. The avatars can simulate emotions, adjust sermon content based on real-time data analytics, and even perform pastoral care via AI-generated conversations. While initially this innovation appears to strengthen the church's online presence, especially for those unable to attend physically, concerns soon emerge.

Critics begin to question whether relying on AI avatars undermines the relational, embodied nature of Christian worship. The theological concern is that digital avatars, however sophisticated, may dehumanize

---

64. SpiritVerse is fictional technology created for illustrative purposes within this case study. Any resemblance to real companies, technologies, places, or individuals is purely coincidental. The case study is intended to explore ethical and theological questions related to AI-driven worship and does not reference any actual existing entity.

worship participants and shift the focus away from the incarnational nature of Christ. Some theologians argue that the use of AI in worship risks losing the essential human element that mirrors the *imago Dei* and reflects the relational and communal aspects of the body of Christ (1 Cor 12:27). They worry that avatars, no matter how advanced, cannot fully represent the presence, empathy, and moral agency required for authentic pastoral care.

Supporters of SpiritVerse, however, argue that the technology helps bridge geographical and physical limitations, allowing people to engage in worship who might otherwise be excluded. For those isolated due to health or distance, AI-driven worship offers an accessible means to participate in the life of the church. They believe that this technological innovation represents a natural progression in the church's mission to reach more individuals globally.

As the debate intensifies, the leadership must decide how to balance technological innovation with the core values of human dignity, relationality, and embodied worship. The central question becomes: How can the church responsibly integrate these advancements while maintaining the integrity of its mission and the theological principles that ground Christian worship?

Case Study #9: Takeaway

The SpiritVerse case study highlights the ethical and theological concerns associated with AI-driven worship, particularly the use of digital avatars in place of human spiritual leaders. The central challenge revolves around the potential depersonalization of worship and the erosion of relationality and embodiment within the Christian faith. This case emphasizes the need for careful discernment in how AI is integrated into church practices, ensuring that technology does not replace the relational, communal, and incarnational aspects of worship. The risk of reducing worship to a performance or digital interaction, detached from genuine spiritual leadership, reflects a broader tension between technological innovation and maintaining theological integrity.

Case Study #9: Discussion Questions:

1. *Theological Perspective:* How does the incarnational theology of Christ (John 1:14) challenge or support the use of AI-driven avatars in worship? How might these technologies impact the understanding of the *imago Dei*, particularly in a worship context where physical presence and relationality are crucial?

2. *Embodiment and Relationality:* In what ways does the digitalization of worship potentially undermine the relational and communal aspects of faith, particularly the idea of the gathered body of Christ (1 Cor 12:27)? Conversely, how might AI-driven worship facilitate connections among isolated individuals? How does this change the church's mission of fostering relationships and community?

3. *Technological Boundaries:* What are the ethical limits of AI in worship? Should AI be used for logistical support or extend to more profound aspects of ministry, such as delivering sermons or providing pastoral care? At what point does AI risk supplanting human leadership and relationality in ways that compromise the theological integrity of worship?

4. *Spiritual Leadership and Authority:* In 1 Pet 5:2–3, spiritual leadership is described as shepherding the flock with humility and care. Can AI avatars ever fulfill the relational and pastoral responsibilities required of human leaders? How might they fall short in modeling Christ-like leadership, particularly in their inability to embody the lived experience that undergirds pastoral authority?

5. Imago Dei *and Digital Representation:* Can digital avatars, which lack the capacity for moral agency and true relationality, embody the *imago Dei*? How does their use in worship challenge or enhance the church's understanding of human dignity? What are the implications of replacing human leaders with virtual representations in light of Christian anthropology?

6. *Worship and Authenticity:* How important is the authenticity of worship leaders in shaping a congregation's spiritual experience? Does the use of AI risk reducing worship to an engineered performance, manipulating emotions through data analytics rather than fostering a genuine spiritual encounter?

7. *Practical Ministry Applications:* Could AI-driven avatars serve beneficial roles in certain aspects of church life, such as outreach or online ministry, without replacing embodied worship? How might churches responsibly integrate AI while maintaining the integrity of the gathered community and prioritizing in-person relational engagement?

CASE STUDY #10: AI-GENERATED ORGANOIDS

In 2042, LifeQuant,[65] a biotechnology company, introduces AI-generated brain organoids—miniaturized and simplified versions of human brains grown in vitro. These organoids are developed to study neurological diseases, improve cognitive function, and test new pharmaceuticals without the need for human or animal trials. AI algorithms are integrated into the development process, allowing these brain organoids to grow rapidly, simulate neural activity, and even mimic basic cognitive functions.

However, as these organoids exhibit signs of learning and adapting to stimuli, ethical concerns arise. Some researchers suggest that these organoids could, in the future, simulate consciousness or thought. LifeQuant's CEO argues that these organoids offer unparalleled opportunities for medical breakthroughs. Still, she acknowledges the growing discomfort surrounding the treatment of organoids and their potential personhood. The question of when an organoid can be considered "alive" or sentient complicates the ethical landscape.

Religious and ethical debates intensify. Theologians question whether the organoids, though devoid of human experiences and relationships, might reflect a distorted image of the *imago Dei*. Some worry that allowing AI-driven organoids to develop into more advanced states without ethical boundaries risks crossing into territory where "life" is artificially created and quantified, raising questions about the sanctity of human life.

As LifeQuant prepares to commercialize its technology for broader use, governments, religious leaders, and the public grapple with how to regulate this new frontier in biotechnology. Is the company advancing the bounds of medical science, or are they playing God with life itself?

---

65. LifeQuant is a fictional company created for illustrative purposes within this case study. Any resemblance to real companies, technologies, places, or individuals is purely coincidental. The case study is intended to explore ethical and theological questions related to AI-generated organoids and does not reference any actual existing entity.

Case Study #10: Takeaway

The LifeQuant case study underscores the complex ethical and theological issues surrounding AI-driven organoid development. The use of AI to create and simulate neural activity in brain organoids introduces profound questions about the nature of life, sentience, and the *imago Dei*. As AI allows for the rapid growth and potential learning capacities of these organoids, society must consider at what point these creations might cross the boundary into personhood or sentience. The risk of quantifying life through AI raises theological concerns about human attempts to create and control life in ways that may conflict with divine sovereignty and the natural order of creation. This case highlights the need for ethical boundaries in the development of technologies that blur the line between human life and artificial creation.

Case Study #10: Discussion Questions

1. Imago Dei *and Artificial Life*: How does the development of AI-driven brain organoids challenge traditional Christian understandings of the *imago Dei*? At what point, if any, could artificially grown organoids reflect the image of God, and what are the theological implications of this possibility?

2. *Quantifying Life and Sentience*: What are the ethical and theological risks of quantifying "life" through AI, particularly when brain organoids show signs of neural activity or learning? How do these developments parallel or deviate from biblical teachings on the sanctity of life and creation?

3. *Divine Sovereignty vs. Human Innovation*: In what ways does the creation of AI-driven organoids reflect humanity's desire to control or manipulate life? How does this ambition compare to the theological warnings found in the Babel narrative (Gen 11:1–9) about human overreach and the rejection of divine boundaries?

4. *Ethical Boundaries and Medical Advancements*: How should Christian ethics respond to the potential medical benefits of AI-driven organoids while also ensuring that ethical boundaries regarding life and personhood are respected? At what point does medical innovation cross into territory that undermines the theological principles of creation?

5. *Moral Responsibility and AI-Created Entities:* If brain organoids begin to demonstrate cognitive capabilities or consciousness, what moral responsibilities do humans have toward these creations? How might this shift the theological understanding of stewardship, creation, and the role of humanity in God's world?

6. *Playing God vs. Advancing Science:* How does the commercialization of AI-driven organoids reflect a desire to "play God" in manipulating life? Can this technology be used responsibly, or does it inherently challenge theological principles of divine sovereignty and human limitation?

7. *Legal and Theological Definitions of Life:* As AI continues to advance, how should governments and religious institutions collaborate to define and regulate what constitutes "life" in an ethical manner? What role should the church play in guiding society's engagement with such complex technologies?

CHAPTER 6

Transhumanism and the Quest for Immortality

TRANSHUMANISM PROPOSES A RADICALLY alternative vision of salvation, one that not only contrasts but directly conflicts with the theological conceptions central to Christian soteriology. At its core, transhumanism refers to a movement that seeks to replace the need for divine intervention with human achievement, striving to transcend bodily limitations and mortality through technological innovations such as cognitive enhancements, genetic engineering, and the pursuit of digital or biological immortality. This vision of "salvation" is rooted in human autonomy and technological progress, diverging sharply from Christian teachings that emphasize grace, resurrection, and the relational aspects of the *imago Dei*.

By emphasizing human control over life and death, this vision of "salvation" represents a modern, technocratic reimagining of ancient human aspirations, echoing the myth of the Tower of Babel, where humanity sought to transcend divine limits. However, it distorts key theological tenets of Christian soteriology, particularly in the areas of redemption, grace, and transformation in Christ. Christian salvation, grounded in the death and resurrection of Jesus, offers a transformative redemption that is both bodily and relational, rooted in God's sovereign grace.

This chapter critiques transhumanism's approach to salvation, highlighting the theological inconsistencies and ethical dangers that arise when technology attempts to replace divine grace. We will explore how the transhumanist promise of immortality through technology fails to address the deeper spiritual needs that only divine grace can fulfill, positioning itself as a false alternative to Christian hope.

TRANSHUMANISM AS A MODERN MOVEMENT

Transhumanism is a contemporary philosophical and technological movement that advocates for transcending the biological limits of the human condition through science and innovation. It is driven by the idea that death, aging, and even human intelligence are not inevitable boundaries but technological obstacles to be overcome. Proponents like Nick Bostrom envision a future where humanity evolves into a "posthuman" species, a new form of existence that no longer shares the biological and cognitive limitations of present-day humans.[1] This posthuman species would possess enhanced cognitive and physical abilities, and even the capacity to conquer mortality.[2]

At the heart of transhumanism is the concept of the "singularity," a theoretical point in the future when AI will surpass human intelligence, leading to exponential technological growth. Advocates believe this will usher in an era when human consciousness can be uploaded into machines, allowing for "digital immortality." Technologies such as BCIs, genetic modifications, and cybernetic enhancements are seen as tools that can eventually facilitate this radical transformation of the human species.

Transhumanism presents death not as an inevitable reality but as a problem to be solved through human innovation. Many in the movement believe that technology can "fix" death, turning it from an irreversible condition into a solvable challenge. In this framework, science and technology assume the role traditionally held by religion, offering salvation through human ingenuity rather than divine intervention.

While this techno-optimism aligns with modernity's faith in progress, it also poses a direct challenge to traditional theological views on mortality. In Christian theology, death is understood as an essential part of the human condition—an entry point into a transformed and redeemed existence through God's grace. Mortality, rather than being something to overcome through technological means, requires redemption through Christ and participation in the hope of bodily resurrection.

1. Nick Bostrom, *Superintelligence: Paths, Dangers, Strategies* (Oxford: Oxford University Press, 2014), 3.

2. Ray Kurzweil, *The Singularity Is Near: When Humans Transcend Biology* (New York: Penguin, 2006), 15.

Transhumanism, by rejecting the theological significance of death, reflects a secular worldview that denies the need for divine grace and resurrection. Where transhumanists place their hope in technological immortality, Christianity places its hope in the transformative power of resurrection, a hope rooted in God's redemptive plan for humanity.

A Brief History of Humanity's Fascination with Immortality: From the ANE to Modern Times

Humanity's desire to overcome death is ancient, manifesting in myths, rituals, and theological traditions across history. In the ANE, immortality was often pursued through mythological narratives and religious practices. For example, the *Epic of Gilgamesh*, one of the earliest known literary texts, recounts the Sumerian king's quest for eternal life after witnessing the death of his friend Enkidu.[3] The epic reflects the universal human preoccupation with mortality and the desire to transcend death, yet it concludes with Gilgamesh's realization that immortality is beyond human grasp, reinforcing the idea that death is an intrinsic part of the human condition.

Ancient Egypt offers another significant example. Pharaohs constructed elaborate tombs, such as the pyramids, to ensure their preservation and continued existence in the afterlife. Immortality in Egyptian traditions was not only a desire for continued physical existence but also symbolized participation in divine eternity.[4] Here, eternal life was intertwined with religious rituals, where alignment with divine order, through moral living and offerings to the gods, could secure a place in the afterlife.

In the Hebrew Bible, reflections on mortality and the fleeting nature of life are central themes. Psalm 90:10 starkly expresses the brevity of human life: "The days of our years are seventy, or perhaps eighty, if we are strong; even then their span is only toil and trouble; they are soon gone, and we fly away." This psalm emphasizes the inevitability of death and the futility of human efforts to control or extend life, while simultaneously affirming divine sovereignty over human existence.[5]

---

3. Andrew R. George, *The Epic of Gilgamesh* (London: Penguin, 2003), 67.

4. Richard H. Wilkinson, *The Complete Gods and Goddesses of Ancient Egypt* (London: Thames and Hudson, 2003), 89.

5. Walter Brueggemann, *The Message of the Psalms* (Minneapolis: Augsburg Fortress, 1984), 54.

Genesis 3:22–24 offers a theological reflection on death as a consequence of human sin. After Adam and Eve eat from the tree of knowledge, they are expelled from the garden of Eden, and access to the tree of life is barred. This narrative introduces mortality as part of the human condition, with eternal life reserved for those in perfect communion with God, not something that can be seized by human initiative. The flaming sword guarding the way to the tree of life serves as a symbolic barrier between fallen humanity and immortality, underscoring that eternal life is a divine gift, not a human achievement.[6]

Throughout history, from the ANE to the present day, humanity has wrestled with its mortality. Ancient myths often framed immortality as a divine gift—one that could be granted by the gods but was beyond human reach. In contrast, modern transhumanism proposes a radically different vision: that death can be conquered not through divine intervention but through human technological innovation. This shift marks a significant departure from the religious and theological traditions that have historically shaped human understanding of life and death.

Framing the Question: Age-Old Aspirations or New Theological Challenge?

Transhumanism may appear as a continuation of humanity's ancient desire to overcome death, but it introduces a fundamentally new approach to achieving this goal. Whereas ancient traditions placed the hope for immortality in the hands of the divine, transhumanism places that hope in human hands. In doing so, transhumanism reframes humanity's relationship with death and salvation, challenging core aspects of Christian theological anthropology.

In Christian thought, death is not merely a biological cessation but a theological reality—one that is intertwined with sin, grace, and redemption. In Gen 3, death enters the world as a result of humanity's rebellion against God. Yet, through the death and resurrection of Christ, Christians believe that death has been defeated and eternal life is offered as a gift of grace (1 Cor 15:54). This eschatological hope for immortality stands in stark contrast to the transhumanist vision, which is rooted in technological mastery rather than divine grace.

---

6. John H. Sailhamer, *Genesis Unbound: A New Reading of the Early Chapters of Genesis* (Colorado Springs: Multnomah, 1996), 116.

Overview Exegesis of Key Biblical Passages

To fully grasp the theological implications of mortality and immortality within the biblical narrative, it is essential to explore key passages that underscore the limitations of human life in contrast to divine eternity. Psalm 90:10 and Gen 3:22–24 offer profound insights into the nature of human existence, especially in light of humanity's desire for immortality. These texts reveal an ancient understanding that life is finite, shaped by God's sovereignty, and draw boundaries around human attempts to transcend death, offering critical theological boundaries against transhumanism's technological pursuit of immortality.

The following sections will examine the linguistic and theological depth of these passages, offering a framework for understanding human mortality in contrast to the promises of eternal life. In doing so, they challenge transhumanism's attempt to achieve immortality through human innovation, illustrating that life and death remain within the sovereign domain of God's authority.

Psalm 90:10

> The days of our life are seventy years,
> or perhaps eighty, if we are strong;
> even then their span is only toil and trouble;
> they are soon gone, and we fly away.

The Hebrew text uses the term *gevurah* for "strength," which conveys not merely physical ability but resilience, often linked to divine empowerment. Even for those who reach "eighty years," this *gevurah* is limited, emphasizing human frailty before God. The term *amal*, translated as "toil," suggests burdensome labor and hardship, reinforcing the biblical theme that human life, particularly in later years, is marked by difficulty and suffering. The phrase "they are soon gone" is represented by the verb *chish*, which carries the connotation of swiftness or suddenness, underscoring the brevity of human life. Additionally, the phrase "we fly away" metaphorically illustrates the ephemeral nature of existence, akin to a fleeting shadow.

The wisdom tradition in this psalm instructs humanity to live within the boundaries established by divine sovereignty, recognizing that eternal life is a gift from God, not something to be seized through technological means. This perspective stands in stark contrast to transhumanism's aspiration to conquer death through human effort. Transhumanism's innovation-based pursuit of immortality defies the theological boundaries set by God's created order, where mortality serves as both a humbling reminder of human limitations and an invitation to trust in divine providence. As William P. Brown observes, the psalmist employs rich metaphorical language to emphasize mortality's inescapable reality, urging the reader to embrace a perspective of humility and dependence on divine wisdom.[7]

Genesis 3:22–24

> Then the Lord God said, "See, the man has become like one of us, knowing good and evil; and now, he might reach out his hand and take also from the tree of life, and eat, and live forever"—therefore the Lord God sent him forth from the garden of Eden, to till the ground from which he was taken. He drove out the man; and at the east of the garden of Eden he placed the cherubim, and a sword flaming and turning to guard the way to the tree of life.

Genesis 3:22–24 offers profound theological and linguistic significance in the context of mortality and divine sovereignty. The phrase "live forever" (*ḥay lə' ōlām*) emphasizes the divine prerogative over eternal life. The root word for life (*ḥay*) combined with *l'olam* (forever) indicates that immortality is not inherent to humanity post-fall but a gift reserved for those within God's divine favor.

The verb *shalach* (sent) reflects God's decisive action in removing Adam and Eve from the garden of Eden, preventing them from accessing the tree of life. This was not a passive act but a protective measure against humanity grasping at immortality on their own terms, a direct theological rejection of the transhumanist vision.[8]

---

7. William P. Brown, *Seeing the Psalms: A Theology of Metaphor* (Louisville: Westminster John Knox, 2002), 58–60. See also James L. Mays, *Psalms*, Interpretation: A Bible Commentary for Teaching and Preaching (Louisville: Westminster John Knox, 1994), 295–98. Mays examines Ps 90's wisdom tradition, emphasizing how its reflection on human transience serves as a theological counterpoint to human pride and self-sufficiency, a theme particularly relevant to critiques of transhumanist aspirations.

8. Wenham, *Genesis 1–15*, 85.

The images of the "flaming sword" and the cherubim reinforce this divine boundary. In ANE contexts, cherubim were often seen as guardians of sacred spaces, suggesting that eternal life is a holy realm, distinct from mortal experience. The flaming sword (*laḥat ḥerev*), a unique phrase in Hebrew, adds an element of divine power and impenetrability, ensuring that humanity could not reclaim access to the tree of life. This narrative draws a clear theological line: eternal life is a divine gift, bestowed through God's grace, not something that can be seized by human effort or technology.[9]

In contrast to the transhumanist aspiration for immortality through innovation, Gen 3 asserts that immortality lies beyond the grasp of fallen humanity. Just as Adam and Eve were barred from the tree of life, human beings today cannot achieve eternal life through technological means— only through divine redemption.

Transhumanism in Theological Perspective

Transhumanism, while tapping into ancient human desires for immortality, introduces a radically different paradigm. By seeking to conquer death through technology, transhumanism offers a vision that fundamentally opposes Christian teachings on mortality and resurrection. While the pursuit of life beyond death has been a central theme throughout history, Christian theology maintains that eternal life is not achieved through human means but is a gift of divine grace (Eph 2:8–9). This theological distinction challenges the very foundation of transhumanism, which envisions technology as the vehicle for immortality, often in the form of disembodied consciousness or "digital immortality."

"Digital immortality"—the idea that human consciousness can be uploaded into a machine or virtual environment—presents a significant theological conflict with the Christian hope of the bodily resurrection. Scripture teaches that eternal life is not merely a continuation of consciousness but involves the full restoration of body and soul, as seen in Christ's resurrection (1 Cor 15:42–44). Christian theology affirms the inherent goodness of the body, which will be transformed and glorified in the eschaton. By contrast, transhumanism's vision of disembodied

---

9. John H. Walton, *Genesis*, NIV Application Commentary (Grand Rapids: Zondervan, 2001), 229–32.

immortality undermines the embodied relationality central to Christian anthropology.

Human beings, created *imago Dei*, are not merely minds or data points but embodied, relational creatures. The transhumanist notion of consciousness existing apart from the body devalues the relational and communal dimensions of human life. Christian theology asserts that human dignity is not based on cognitive capacity or technological enhancement but on the holistic nature of human existence—body, mind, and spirit, united in relationality with God and others (Gen 2:7, Matt 22:37–39).

The implications of transhumanism's disembodied consciousness for theological anthropology are profound. By focusing on individual autonomy and technological control, transhumanism threatens to reduce human identity to mere data, detaching individuals from the communal and embodied experience of life. In Christian thought, the resurrection is not an escape from the body but a transformation of the entire person—a redemptive restoration that transcends physical death without severing the relational ties inherent to human existence. This sharply contrasts with the transhumanist vision, which bypasses the relational and communal nature of human life in pursuit of digital immortality.

Ultimately, transhumanism presents a fundamentally different vision of salvation—one that replaces divine grace with technological achievement. In doing so, it distorts the Christian understanding of human dignity, relationality, and the nature of eternal life. The pursuit of immortality apart from God not only risks dehumanizing the person but also denies the transformative hope offered in the bodily resurrection, where true restoration is found in Christ.

OVERCOMING MORTALITY THROUGH TECHNOLOGY

The quest for immortality has long been an intrinsic part of human aspiration, and the transhumanist movement seeks to actualize this dream by leveraging technological advancements. Transhumanism posits that through AI, genetic engineering, and biotechnology, humanity can transcend its biological limitations, including mortality. By advocating for mind uploading, cybernetic enhancements, and gene editing, proponents believe that death can be transformed from an inevitable part of human existence into a problem to be solved. This section explores the visions of key transhumanist figures, the strategies they advocate for overcoming death, and the ethical implications from a theological perspective.

One of the central promises of transhumanism is *digital immortality*—the belief that human consciousness can be uploaded and preserved indefinitely in a digital format. This view assumes that personhood and identity can be reduced to patterns of information, which can be transferred to machines or cloud systems, thus bypassing the need for a physical body. Similarly, gene-editing technologies such as CRISPR hold out the hope of eliminating diseases, enhancing physical and cognitive traits, and extending lifespans far beyond natural human limits.

However, these ambitions raise profound theological concerns. The concept of mind uploading reflects a disembodied notion of the self, one that disregards the intrinsic unity of body, mind, and soul affirmed in Christian anthropology. In the Christian understanding, humans are not merely data to be preserved but embodied souls who experience life in relationship with God and others. The promise of digital immortality ignores the significance of the body in this relational existence, ultimately reducing human dignity to an algorithmic existence.

From a theological perspective, the Christian hope is not grounded in escaping the body but in the resurrection of the body—where mortality is overcome not through human innovation but through divine grace. Cybernetic enhancement and gene editing also pose ethical questions, as they shift the focus away from accepting the God-given nature of human finitude and toward a desire for control over creation. Theologically, the drive to overcome death through technological means echoes the temptation of Adam and Eve in the garden of Eden, seeking autonomy from God rather than trusting in divine wisdom and redemption.

Christian theology asserts that eternal life is a gift from God, experienced in the full restoration of the person—body and soul—through the resurrection in Christ. In contrast, transhumanist visions of immortality, whether digital or biological, fall short of this hope, offering instead a distorted version of eternal life that severs human beings from their embodied, relational existence and their dependence on God.

Key Figures in Transhumanism: Ray Kurzweil and Nick Bostrom

Among the leading proponents of transhumanism, Ray Kurzweil stands as a central figure. Known for his prediction of the singularity, a future moment when machine intelligence will surpass human intelligence, Kurzweil envisions a world where technology allows humans to merge with AI. This merging would grant individuals the ability to upload their consciousness into digital substrates, achieving a form of digital immortality. Kurzweil's focus on AI and its potential to extend human life is framed as a solution to the limitations imposed by biological death.[10] Nick Bostrom, in *Superintelligence*, further elaborates on this vision, presenting AI as a force that will eventually possess cognitive capabilities far beyond human capacity. Bostrom believes that this superintelligence could lead to advancements that effectively grant immortality, not only by extending physical life but by preserving and even enhancing human consciousness.[11]

These ideas reflect a dramatic shift from traditional humanist ideals to a transhumanist future, where technological enhancements allow humans to transcend mortality. However, as N. T. Wright critiques in *Surprised by Hope*, these aspirations present a fundamental misunderstanding of human nature. Wright emphasizes that Christian hope lies not in transcending the body but in the promise of bodily resurrection through Christ. He suggests that the transhumanist desire for immortality through technology is a misplaced trust in human ingenuity over divine sovereignty.[12]

AI, Genetic Engineering, and Biotechnology in the Transhumanist Quest

Transhumanism envisions several pathways for overcoming mortality, including the use of AI, genetic engineering, and biotechnology. Through AI, the most futuristic promise is the uploading of consciousness, where the mind is transferred to a digital platform, potentially ensuring eternal life as long as the technology is maintained. Genetic engineering and biotechnology, on the other hand, offer more immediate possibilities, such as gene therapy to eliminate disease or CRISPR technology to edit DNA, allowing humans to live longer, healthier lives.

One of the most ambitious projects in the transhumanist quest for immortality is Neuralink, a company founded by Elon Musk, which

---

10. Kurzweil, *Singularity Is Near*, 203.
11. Bostrom, *Superintelligence*, 89.
12. Wright, *Surprised by Hope*, 182.

seeks to develop BCIs. These interfaces are designed to integrate human brains with AI, allowing for the enhancement of cognitive functions and, theoretically, enabling the possibility of mind uploading. While this technology is still in its infancy, proponents see it as a vital step toward overcoming the limitations of the human body and achieving a form of immortality.[13]

Cryogenic preservation, as practiced by companies like Alcor, offers another approach. Cryonics is the practice of freezing a human body or brain at the point of death, with the hope that future technologies will allow for reanimation. Though it remains speculative and unproven, this strategy underscores the transhumanist belief in the eventual triumph of technology over death.[14]

Human Cloning as a Version of Immortality

Another avenue of transhumanist exploration is human cloning. While not often framed as a form of direct immortality, human cloning presents a unique pathway toward what might be termed a version of virtual immortality. Cloning allows for the creation of a genetic replica of an individual, potentially continuing their biological essence, even if not their consciousness.

Human cloning, as explored by Klotzko and other scholars, raises profound ethical and theological questions. In therapeutic contexts, cloning could alleviate suffering by regenerating tissues or organs, but organismic cloning—cloning to replicate entire individuals—introduces issues related to the Christian doctrine of *imago Dei*. The process of human cloning risks reducing the uniqueness of personhood to genetic material, bypassing the inherent dignity that God has imbued in every soul. Is a cloned individual a fully distinct person, or merely a reflection

---

13. Elon Musk's Neuralink is developing brain-computer interfaces (BCIs) to merge human brains with AI, with the goal of enhancing cognitive functions and potentially enabling mind uploading. Information on their ongoing research and updates on developments can be found in the "Technology" section of the official Neuralink website www.neuralink.com.

14. Alcor is one of the leading organizations practicing cryonics, which involves freezing the body or brain at the time of death with the hope that future technology may allow for reanimation. The concept underscores transhumanist beliefs in the eventual triumph of technology over mortality, although cryonics remains speculative and unproven. Additional details on the practice and Alcor's research can be found on their official website www.alcor.org.

of another? Does cloning attempt to bypass the uniqueness that God has imbued in each human soul?[15]

From a transhumanist perspective, cloning is seen as a way to defy death, allowing for the physical continuation of a person. However, as Klotzko argues, even if genetic replication is achieved, it fails to reproduce the "social and historical copying" that makes a person truly unique.[16] Theologically, this points to a deeper issue: true immortality cannot be achieved through technological or biological replication. The *imago Dei* entails not only the physical aspects of human existence but the spiritual and relational dimensions, which cannot be cloned or digitally replicated.

Cloning also presents a profound challenge to Christian anthropology, which views each person as relationally and spiritually unique. The relationality inherent in the *imago Dei*—our capacity to engage in meaningful relationships with God and others—cannot be recreated in a clone. The biblical narrative, particularly in Genesis, emphasizes that human life is unique and divinely appointed. Cloning, while offering a potential biological replication, remains inadequate in addressing the theological dimensions of human life, death, and immortality. This raises the question of whether the cloned individual, devoid of the original's social and historical context, truly embodies the relational and moral aspects of personhood. As Frank Tipler suggests in *The Physics of Immortality*, even if science could replicate bodies or preserve minds, it would fall short of the true resurrection life promised in Christian eschatology.[17]

Projects and Strategies: Overcoming Biological Death

Beyond cloning, transhumanists are exploring various strategies to bypass biological death. Cryonics and consciousness uploading represent the pinnacle of transhumanist innovation, aimed at preserving human identity beyond physical demise. Alcor, the leading cryonics institute, freezes bodies and brains with the hope that future medical advancements will allow these individuals to be revived, cured of their diseases, and possibly granted extended or eternal life.[18]

15. Arlene Judith Klotzko, *The Ethics of Cloning* (London: Routledge, 2004), 57.

16. Klotzko, *Ethics of Cloning*, 62.

17. Frank J. Tipler, *The Physics of Immortality: Modern Cosmology, God, and the Resurrection of the Dead* (New York: Doubleday, 1994).

18. Alcor is the leading cryonics institute, freezing bodies and brains with the hope that future advancements in medical technology will allow for revival, healing, and

However, theological critiques of these technologies, as articulated by scholars such as Wright and Bonhoeffer, suggest that this approach fundamentally misunderstands the nature of human existence. The transhumanist emphasis on control—whether through cryogenic preservation or mind uploading—reveals a desire to escape the limitations of mortality. Yet Christian theology insists that life and death are in God's hands, and that the true hope for eternal life lies not in technological advances but in the resurrection of the body.[19]

While transhumanism offers the tantalizing prospect of artificial immortality, it often fails to grapple with the spiritual and ethical dimensions of human life. As Kurzweil and others envision a future where humans merge with machines, the question remains: What does it mean to be human if we no longer inhabit our physical bodies? The promise of immortality through technology risks reducing human identity to mere data, ignoring the deeper aspects of human relationality, embodiment, and the soul.

Conclusion: The Limits of Technology in the Quest for Immortality

The transhumanist vision, whether through AI, genetic engineering, or cloning, presents a bold attempt to overcome mortality. Yet, as we have seen, these approaches raise profound ethical and theological questions. The transhumanist promise of immortality, while technologically ambitious, remains deeply flawed from a Christian perspective. The doctrine of the *imago Dei* asserts that human life is not merely biological but spiritual, relational, and ultimately dependent on God. In Christian theology, bodily resurrection, not technological enhancement, offers the true hope for eternal life.

The transhumanist quest for immortality ultimately reflects humanity's ancient desire to transcend death—a desire rooted in the very fabric of creation. However, as the biblical narrative reminds us, eternal life is a gift from God, not something that can be engineered or achieved through human innovation. In contrast to transhumanism's reliance on human autonomy, Christian hope is rooted in divine grace and the transformative power of the resurrection. In pursuing this quest, transhumanists

---

potentially extended or eternal life. More details on their cryonics practices and research are available on their official website www.alcor.org.

19. Bonhoeffer, *Ethics*, 143.

may unwittingly be repeating the mistakes of Babel, seeking to reach the heavens by their own power rather than trusting in the divine promise of resurrection and new creation.

Ultimately, the limits of technology in addressing the deepest human longings—life, meaning, and relationship with God—reveal that no amount of scientific progress can substitute for the hope found in Christ's resurrection. Christian theology offers a vision of immortality that transcends biological enhancement, pointing instead to the restoration of all creation through God's redemptive work. In this light, the pursuit of technological immortality, while fascinating, cannot replace the eschatological promise of new life in Christ, a promise that encompasses both the body and the soul in perfect communion with God.

DEATH AND IMMORTALITY IN ANTIQUITY

The pursuit of immortality has deep roots in human history, particularly within ANE cultures, where death was often viewed as a boundary that only gods could transcend. These cultural conceptions shaped how the Hebrew Bible approached mortality and the afterlife, positioning the Israelite understanding of death as distinct yet conversant with the surrounding Mesopotamian and Egyptian views. The Hebrew Bible offers a theological reflection on mortality that, while acknowledging the inevitability of death, ultimately points toward divine sovereignty over life and death.

Death and Afterlife in Hittite and Ugaritic Cultures

Hittite culture, while lesser-known compared to Mesopotamian or Egyptian civilizations, offers intriguing insights into ancient beliefs surrounding death and the afterlife. The Hittites, a powerful Anatolian civilization, had a concept of the underworld governed by deities like Lelwani, the goddess of the dead. Unlike Mesopotamian myths, the Hittites seemed to emphasize the inevitability of death but offered little in the way of a hopeful afterlife. Their rituals, including the royal burial customs, suggest an attempt to placate the gods of the underworld rather than seek eternal life, reflecting a pragmatic acceptance of mortality. However, Hittite texts, such as those in the "Plague Prayers of Mursili II," invoke divine protection against death and seek healing from deities, hinting at the hope that human beings could negotiate a better fate in life but not necessarily in the afterlife.[20]

In contrast, Ugaritic culture, originating from the ancient city of Ugarit on the Mediterranean coast, offers another unique perspective on death and immortality. Ugaritic texts, particularly the *Baal Cycle*, illustrate a strong preoccupation with death through the character of Mot, the god of death. In this mythology, Baal, the storm god, is temporarily overcome by Mot, symbolizing the cyclical nature of life, death, and rebirth. The conflict between Baal and Mot echoes themes of renewal and fertility, central to Ugaritic religion. However, the Ugaritic view of death did not entail personal immortality for mortals. Instead, it reinforced the idea of the gods' power over life and death, underscoring human mortality as a fixed reality.[21] This portrayal further solidifies the ANE perspective that while gods could embody cycles of death and rebirth, human beings remained bound to their mortal fates without the possibility of personal resurrection or eternal life.

These examples reveal how ancient Near Eastern cultures grappled with the finality of death and sought to express these realities through their myths and rituals. The Hittites and Ugarites, though differing in their mythologies, both ultimately reaffirmed the boundary between the divine realm and human mortality, setting the stage for later developments in Hebrew theology that emphasized the hope of resurrection and redemption in contrast to the fatalism of their neighbors.

Hebrew Concepts of Mortality and the Afterlife

The Hebrew Bible, in contrast to ANE traditions, presents a more restrained view of immortality, focusing on the reality of human mortality and the sovereignty of Yahweh. Death, in the Hebrew understanding, is an inevitable part of the human experience, and, while there are reflections on the afterlife, they are not central to Israelite religion in the same way as in Egyptian, Mesopotamian, Hittite, or Ugaritic thought. Instead, the Hebrew Scriptures emphasize life in the present, under God's covenant.

20. Mark W. Chavalas, "Hittite Rituals and Religious Beliefs in Mursili's Plague Prayers," in *The Context of Scripture: Canonical Compositions from the Biblical World*, vol. 1, ed. William W. Hallo, 160–64 (Leiden: Brill, 2003).

21. John H. Walton, *Ancient Near Eastern Thought and the Old Testament: Introducing the Conceptual World of the Hebrew Bible* (Grand Rapids: Baker Academic, 2006), 233–36.

The concept of Sheol serves as the primary depiction of the afterlife in the Hebrew Bible. Sheol is often portrayed as a shadowy, indistinct place where the dead reside, but it lacks the clear judgment and afterlife system found in Egyptian beliefs. Sheol is depicted as a place of silence and inactivity, where the dead no longer have any influence over the living or interaction with God. Job 14:10–12 offers a poignant reflection on human mortality and Sheol: "But mortals die and are laid low; humans expire, and where are they? As waters fail from a lake and a river wastes away and dries up, so mortals lie down and do not rise again; until the heavens are no more, they will not awake or be roused out of their sleep." In this passage, Job laments the reality of death, comparing human life to a river that dries up. The Hebrew word בָּכַשׁ (*shakhav*)—translated here as "is laid low"—conveys the finality of death, suggesting that death is an irreversible state until divine intervention. The image of the heavens passing away conveys an almost apocalyptic scope, indicating that resurrection or revival from death is beyond human capacity. Here, death is understood as the great equalizer, a point beyond which no human effort or strength can alter one's fate.

In Ps 6:5, the psalmist also reflects this somber view of Sheol: "For in death there is no remembrance of you; in Sheol who will give you praise?" The Hebrew term *Sheol* is used here to describe the abode of the dead, and it is depicted as a place where the dead cannot praise God. The phrase "no remembrance" (זֵכֶר, *zeker*) emphasizes the finality and isolation of Sheol, where the dead are cut off from the living and from active participation in God's world. This view of Sheol reflects the Hebrew understanding that death represents separation, both from earthly life and from the relational experience of worshiping God. Death, in this sense, is a state of profound loss and detachment.

Theological Shift from Sheol to Resurrection

While the early Hebrew Scriptures largely reflect this view of Sheol as a final, neutral resting place for the dead, later Jewish thought introduces the hope of bodily resurrection. This shift is most notably present in Dan 12:2: "Many of those who sleep in the dust of the earth shall awake, some to everlasting life, and some to shame and everlasting contempt." Here, the Hebrew term *yaqitzu* (shall awake) reflects a radical development in Israelite eschatology. Unlike the earlier view of Sheol as a place of final rest, this passage speaks of an awakening—a bodily resurrection. The phrase "sleep in the dust" (*yishenai admat afar*) carries the connotation of death, but with the promise of future restoration. This passage represents a major theological shift, where death is no longer viewed solely as the end, but as a transition to a new reality—either to "everlasting life" (*chayei olam*) or "everlasting contempt." The resurrection hope in Daniel reflects the growing influence of eschatological thought within late Jewish theology, which would later be fully developed in early Christian beliefs regarding bodily resurrection. This theological shift from Sheol to resurrection also sets the stage for understanding death and immortality within a broader redemptive framework, where the ultimate defeat of death comes through divine intervention rather than human striving.

Hebrew Thought vs. ANE Concepts

In contrast to the mythologies of surrounding ANE cultures, where immortality was often depicted as something reserved for the gods, the Hebrew Bible presents a God who exercises sovereign control over life and death. While Mesopotamian myths, such as the *Epic of Gilgamesh*, illustrate the human pursuit of immortality, they ultimately underscore the limitations of human life, depicting immortality as a privilege that only the gods can access.[22] Similarly, in Egyptian religion, the myth of Osiris reflects the possibility of resurrection, though this hope was largely tied to elaborate rituals, mummification processes, and the judgment of the gods.[23] In both traditions, immortality is a guarded gift of the divine, inaccessible to ordinary humans without special intervention.

The Hittites, though less concerned with immortality per se, reflected a deeply ritualized acceptance of mortality. Their religious texts, such as the "Plague Prayers of Mursili II," show an emphasis on divine intervention in life and death but offer little in the way of afterlife hope beyond placating the gods of the underworld.[24] Ugaritic mythology, with its portrayal of Baal's conflict with Mot, the god of death, echoes the

---

22. Stephanie Dalley, *Myths from Mesopotamia* (Oxford: Oxford University Press, 2000), 77–100.

23. Erik Hornung, *The Ancient Egyptian Books of the Afterlife* (Ithaca, NY: Cornell University Press, 1999), 129–35.

24. Author, "Hittite Rituals and Religious Beliefs," 160–64.

cyclical nature of life and death but again reaffirms the human position of subservience to the divine order.[25]

Against this backdrop, the Hebrew Scriptures present a unique and contrasting theological perspective. The God of Israel is not one among many competing deities but is sovereign over all life and death. Passages such as Gen 3:22–24 emphasize that immortality is not an inherent right of humanity but is safeguarded by God. The expulsion of Adam and Eve from Eden, away from the tree of life, underscores that eternal life remains under divine control, granted only through God's grace.[26] This theological boundary establishes that human mortality is a part of the created order and cannot be bypassed through human effort or manipulation.

Whereas Egyptian and Mesopotamian cultures sought to secure an afterlife through meticulous burial rituals and divine favor, the Hebrew Bible emphasizes the transient nature of human life and the importance of cultivating a present relationship with God. In passages such as Ps 90:10, the brevity of human life is accepted, not as a tragedy, but as part of the divine plan. The emphasis shifts from the human pursuit of immortality through ritual to a reliance on God's promise of eternal life, revealed progressively through the Hebrew prophets and culminating in the NT doctrine of resurrection.

The transhumanist vision of conquering death through technology mirrors these ancient myths in many ways. Like Gilgamesh or Osiris, transhumanism presents a human-driven path to overcoming death, whether through genetic manipulation, mind uploading, or other technological advancements. However, the Hebrew Scriptures caution against these human attempts to circumvent death, emphasizing that life and death remain in God's hands. Ultimately, any hope of overcoming death is not found in human achievement or technology, but in the divine promise of resurrection and the gift of eternal life through God's grace.

CHRISTIAN THEOLOGY: DEATH AND RESURRECTION

The Christian theology of death and resurrection stands at the heart of the faith's response to the universal reality of human mortality. While ancient cultures, including those in the Greco-Roman world, pursued various paths to immortality—whether through mythological deification,

---

25. Walton, *Ancient Near Eastern Thought*, 233–36.
26. Wenham, *Genesis 1–15*, 87.

the afterlife of the soul, or mystical transcendence—Christianity presents a profoundly distinct vision: the bodily resurrection of the whole person through Christ. This belief is not merely a continuation of ancient aspirations for eternal life but represents a theological revolution: a redemption of both body and soul through divine grace. Rooted in the death and resurrection of Jesus, this doctrine forms the foundation of Christian eschatology and offers a unique response to human suffering, sin, and death.

Rather than escape the physical world, Christian theology affirms the ultimate redemption and transformation of both body and soul. Where transhumanism seeks to avoid or overcome death through technological means, Christian theology sees death not only as a consequence of sin but also as the gateway to resurrection and new creation. The resurrection is not a rejection of the body, but the promise of its transformation, sanctified by God's power. This concept directly counters the transhumanist desire for "digital immortality," which disconnects personhood from embodiment, stripping away the relational, spiritual, and sacramental significance of the human body.

Central to this theology is Paul's extensive treatment of death and resurrection, particularly in 1 Cor 15 and Rom 6, where the apostle addresses not only the hope of bodily resurrection but also its implications for Christian life and ethics. Paul's theology of resurrection contrasts sharply with the transhumanist quest for immortality, as it frames death and resurrection within the context of sin and divine grace. In Rom 6:23, Paul famously writes, "For the wages of sin is death, but the free gift of God is eternal life in Christ Jesus our Lord." This verse encapsulates the Christian understanding that death is the result of human sin, and resurrection is the ultimate act of divine redemption, not a technological achievement.

In 1 Cor 15:53, Paul emphasizes, "For this perishable body must put on imperishability, and this mortal body must put on immortality." This passage underscores that Christian immortality is not a continuation of fallen human existence but a complete transformation of the body and soul into a glorified state. Unlike the transhumanist vision, which seeks to prolong human life through technological means, Paul insists that the resurrection body is something fundamentally different from the mortal body—a new creation, perfected through Christ.

Theologically, sin and death are intrinsically linked in Christian thought, and only through Christ's resurrection can this bond be broken.

The transhumanist quest to bypass mortality, however, fails to address the deeper issue of sin and its consequences. It presents a flawed view of immortality, one based on human effort and technological mastery rather than the grace of God. Where transhumanism offers a temporary extension of life, Christian resurrection promises a transformed and eternal existence—one that fully restores humanity's relational and spiritual dimensions, grounded in the love and grace of God.

Pauline Theology of Death and Resurrection (1 Corinthians 15:12–58; Romans 6:5–9)

In the NT Paul's theology of death and resurrection offers the most robust Christian response to human mortality. Unlike the transhumanist quest for technological immortality, which seeks to bypass the limitations of the human body through AI, biotechnology, or other scientific means, Paul's view affirms the goodness of the created body and anticipates its redemption through resurrection. This sharply contrasts with transhumanist aspirations, where human consciousness is disembodied or uploaded, focusing instead on transformation rather than escape from the body.

Paul's exposition in 1 Cor 15:12–58 is critical for understanding the Christian doctrine of resurrection, while Rom 6:5–9 offers theological insight into how the believer's participation in Christ's death and resurrection transforms the Christian approach to mortality. Together, these passages articulate a theology that celebrates the resurrection of the body and affirms the ultimate defeat of death through the work of Christ, rejecting the idea that immortality can be achieved by human effort or technological advancement.

Detailed Exegesis of Key New Testament Passages

This section will explore two key NT texts that shape the Christian understanding of death and resurrection: 1 Cor 15:12–58 and Rom 6:5–9. In 1 Cor 15, Paul addresses concerns about bodily resurrection, contrasting the natural and spiritual bodies and emphasizing the future hope of bodily transformation. Through a close examination of key Greek terms such as ἀνάστασις (*anastasis*, "resurrection"), σῶμα πνευματικόν (*sōma pneumatikon*, "spiritual body"), and ψυχικόν (*psychikon*, "natural body"), we will see how Paul refutes the idea of disembodied immortality and affirms the Christian hope of a glorified, resurrected body.

In Rom 6:5–9, Paul connects believers' participation in Christ's death and resurrection through baptism, using the metaphor of ὁμοίωμα (*homoiōma*, "likeness"). This analysis will highlight how baptism symbolizes the believer's participation in both death and resurrection, providing a theological foundation for Christian hope in bodily resurrection. Both passages will be contextualized within the Greco-Roman worldview, contrasting Paul's resurrection theology with contemporary views on immortality, thus deepening our understanding of how these texts speak against the transhumanist quest for disembodied immortality.

1 Corinthians 15:12–58:
The Resurrection Body and Christian Hope

In 1 Cor 15, Paul addresses concerns about the resurrection, particularly refuting those in the Corinthian church who doubted the bodily resurrection of believers. The passage offers a detailed account of Paul's resurrection theology, making it one of the most significant biblical texts for understanding Christian eschatology. Paul opens with a defense of the resurrection by appealing to Christ's own resurrection as the "firstfruits" (ἀπαρχή, *aparchē*) of those who have died (1 Cor 15:20), affirming that Christ's resurrection guarantees the resurrection of believers.[27]

The Greek term for resurrection, *anastasis* (ἀνάστασις), used in verse 12, carries the meaning of "rising up" or "standing again," specifically in reference to the body being raised from death. Paul's use of this term directly counters disembodied visions of immortality—whether in gnostic thought or modern transhumanism—by affirming that resurrection involves the transformation of the body itself, not the abandonment of it.[28] His distinction between the ψυχικόν (*psychikon*, "natural body") and the πνευματικόν (*pneumatikon*, "spiritual body") in verse 44 must be understood within this context. Paul is not suggesting that the "spiritual body" is immaterial or nonphysical; rather, it is a transformed, glorified

---

27. Wright, *Resurrection of the Son of God*, 212–18.

28. Ben Witherington III, *Paul's Narrative Thought World* (Louisville: Westminster John Knox, 1994), 67–68.

body, animated by the Holy Spirit rather than by the fallen world's limitations.[29]

Paul's argument challenges gnostic tendencies that favored a disembodied view of immortality, which would have been prevalent in Corinth at the time. The gnostic worldview, often seeing the material world as corrupt or evil, would seek salvation through escape from the physical realm. Paul, however, reaffirms the goodness of creation and the body by emphasizing that resurrection does not discard the physical but transforms it. The term *sōma pneumatikon* (σῶμα πνευματικόν) does not mean "immaterial" but "empowered by the Spirit," reflecting the continuity between the current body and the resurrected body, which will be incorruptible and imperishable (1 Cor 15:42–43).[30]

Furthermore, Paul's use of *anastasis* underscores the hope of bodily resurrection, rooted in the Jewish understanding of the term but expanded in light of Christ's resurrection. In Jewish thought, resurrection was primarily a corporate hope for Israel, as seen in texts like Dan 12:2. Paul, however, extends this hope to all believers, emphasizing that the resurrection is both individual and cosmic in scope. The body sown in corruption will be raised in incorruption, thus signifying not an escape from creation but its ultimate renewal.

Paul's emphasis on the transformation of the body directly critiques any vision of immortality that seeks to separate human identity from the physical body, such as the transhumanist concept of uploading consciousness into machines. The body, according to Paul, is essential to human identity and is included in God's redemptive plan. By using σῶμα πνευματικόν (*sōma pneumatikon*, "spiritual body") and contrasting it with σῶμα ψυχικόν (*sōma psychikon*, "natural body"), Paul highlights that the resurrected body is still a body, albeit one transformed by the Spirit and no longer subject to decay, sin, or death. The resurrection body, for Paul, is the completion of God's creative work, not its abandonment.[31]

---

29. Gordon D. Fee, *The First Epistle to the Corinthians* (Grand Rapids: Eerdmans, 1987), 774–78.

30. Richard Bauckham, *The Jewish World Around the New Testament* (Grand Rapids: Baker Academic, 2010), 217–20.

31. Wright, *Resurrection of the Son of God*, 343.

Romans 6:5–9: Baptism, Death, and Resurrection

Romans 6:5–9 deepens Paul's theology of resurrection by linking it to the believer's participation in Christ's death and resurrection through baptism. Paul writes, "For if we have been united with him in a death like his, we shall certainly be united with him in a resurrection like his" (Rom 6:5). The Greek word ὁμοίωμα (*homoiōma*, "likeness") conveys the idea of a profound unity between Christ's death and the believer's participation in it. This identification with Christ's death and resurrection shapes the Christian understanding of bodily resurrection as something inseparable from Christ's own victory over death.[32]

Through baptism, believers symbolically die and are raised to new life, prefiguring the bodily resurrection to come. Yet, for Paul, this baptismal imagery is far more than a symbolic act; it is participatory. The use of *homoiōma* emphasizes that just as Christ's resurrection was bodily and real, so too will the believer's resurrection involve the body's transformation and restoration, not its replacement or transcendence through technological means. The believer's hope for bodily resurrection is grounded in their union with Christ, who has conquered death and risen from the dead. This connection between Christ's resurrection and the believer's bodily transformation directly challenges transhumanist ideas, which often frame immortality as a disembodied or purely mental experience.[33]

Paul's theology here stands in stark contrast to the Greco-Roman fascination with immortality, which often envisioned a disembodied existence in the afterlife. Greek thought, heavily influenced by Platonic dualism, tended to view the body as a prison for the soul, with death being the release of the soul into a higher, spiritual realm. In this context, Paul's emphasis on bodily resurrection was radical. Rather than seeing salvation as an escape from the body, Paul preached that salvation involves the transformation and glorification of the body itself, bringing it into a new, redeemed state.[34]

This contrast between the Christian doctrine of bodily resurrection and the Greco-Roman view of immortality provides important insights into contemporary debates surrounding transhumanism. Like the

---

32. Witherington, *Paul's Narrative Thought World*, 55.

33. C. E. B. Cranfield, *Romans: A Shorter Commentary* (Grand Rapids: Eerdmans, 1985), 153–55.

34. Anthony C. Thiselton, *The First Epistle to the Corinthians*, New International Greek Testament Commentary (Grand Rapids: Eerdmans, 2000), 1281–84.

Greeks, transhumanism seeks to transcend the limitations of the body, often viewing it as a hindrance to true freedom. Yet Paul's message in Rom 6, grounded in the death and resurrection of Christ, rejects this disembodiment. For Paul, the body is not something to be discarded or transcended; it is an essential part of human identity that will be redeemed and restored by God in the resurrection. Transhumanism, by proposing the preservation of consciousness while discarding the body, fails to grasp the profound significance of the body in Christian anthropology and eschatology.

Paul's Theology vs. Greco-Roman Fascinations with Immortality

In Greco-Roman thought, influenced by Platonic dualism, the body was often seen as a temporary vessel for the soul. Plato, in works like *Phaedo*, argued that true freedom and immortality came when the soul was liberated from the body.[35] In this worldview, the body was viewed as corruptible and something to be escaped in order to reach higher, spiritual realms. The afterlife, according to this tradition, could involve either a shadowy existence in Hades, or, in some variations, the soul's transcendence to the Elysian Fields, where the worthy lived in blissful eternity apart from the physical body. This stands in stark contrast to Paul's message, which rejects any notion of salvation as the soul's escape from the body. Paul's teaching of bodily resurrection in 1 Cor 15 would have presented a radical departure from this thinking.

The imperial cult of Rome further complicated notions of immortality by promoting the idea that emperors could attain a form of divine immortality through deification. This blurring of human and divine identity through status and achievement stands opposed to Paul's teaching, where resurrection is solely a gift of God, not something attained through human power or merit. This critique of Roman imperial ideology can be extended to modern transhumanism, where the quest for immortality through human effort (whether through genetic engineering, consciousness uploading, or AI) reflects a similar hubris, seeking to grasp at divinity through technological achievement.

---

35. Plato, *Phaedo*, trans. David Gallop (Oxford: Oxford University Press, 1993), 64c–67b. Plato argues that the soul is immortal and only truly free when it is separated from the body, which is seen as a temporary, limiting vessel for the soul. This dualistic view influenced much of Greco-Roman thought concerning life, death, and immortality.

The Doctrine of the Resurrection of the Body vs. Transhumanist Immortality

Christian theology asserts that the resurrection of the body is a divine act, distinct from transhumanist concepts of technological immortality. While transhumanism seeks to extend life indefinitely through genetic manipulation or consciousness preservation, Paul's theology promises a resurrection body that is imperishable, glorified, and transformed by God (1 Cor 15:53). This transformation is achieved not through human hands but by God's grace. The Greek term χάρισμα (*charisma*, "gift" or "grace") underscores the core difference: immortality in Christianity is a divine gift, not something earned by human means.

Paul's insistence on the σῶμα πνευματικόν reflects this theological conviction. The body is not discarded or transcended but transformed and redeemed. Christian hope is grounded not in the escape from the physical body but in its full redemption and restoration through God's redemptive work.[36] This stands in direct opposition to the transhumanist drive to conquer mortality through technology—a human attempt to achieve control over what only God can truly redeem.

In the transhumanist vision, the quest for immortality expresses a desire for mastery over death, attempting to bypass mortality through technological prowess. Yet Paul's theology reorients this drive toward control, calling believers to trust in God's ultimate victory over death through Christ's resurrection. The Greek concept of *charisma* (χάρισμα), meaning "gift" or "grace," highlights the stark theological divide: eternal life is a divine gift, not something achieved by human effort or technological prowess. Paul's vision of the resurrection emphasizes that the body is not to be transcended or replaced by technological means, but

---

36. While Pauline theology emphasizes the bodily resurrection, scholars have addressed concerns about cases where the body may be unrecoverable, as in situations involving cremation, accidents, or decomposition. Paul's focus is on the transformed, glorified body rather than on the preservation of the physical body as it is now. As N. T. Wright notes, "the God who made heaven and earth can also remake bodies, regardless of their current state." Wright, *Surprised by Hope*, 153–56. Similarly, Richard B. Hays emphasizes that the promise of resurrection is not contingent on the condition of the earthly body at death, but on the transformative power of God's grace. Richard B. Hays, *The Moral Vision of the New Testament: Community, Cross, New Creation: A Contemporary Introduction to New Testament Ethics* (New York: HarperCollins, 1996), 298–301. These scholars remind us that the doctrine of resurrection reflects God's sovereignty and ability to restore life from any state of physical decay, affirming the eschatological hope that transcends the current limitations of human understanding.

rather redeemed and glorified in God's new creation. Far from advocating a disembodied or purely spiritual existence, Paul affirms the goodness of the created body, promising its renewal rather than its disposal. The Christian doctrine of bodily resurrection places the focus on God's redemptive power, in contrast to transhumanism's belief in technology as a means of self-salvation.

Furthermore, Christian theology shows that the hope for resurrection is deeply relational, rooted in the covenantal love of God for his creation. In contrast, transhumanist ideals, which seek to prolong life at any cost, often reduce the human body to an object of manipulation. In Christian thought, the body is an integral part of God's creation, designed for relationality with both God and others. Eternal life, in the Christian sense, is not merely the indefinite extension of biological existence but the transformation of human life into perfect communion with God. Paul's teachings point to this eschatological hope: the resurrection is an act of divine love, a transformation that surpasses the limitations of human nature, in contrast to a technological solution to death.

In summary, Pauline theology offers a profound counterpoint to the transhumanist pursuit of immortality. While transhumanism seeks to overcome death through technological advances, the Christian hope in bodily resurrection rests entirely on the grace and power of God. Paul's insistence on the bodily resurrection—opposing both gnostic and transhumanist visions of disembodiment—upholds the integrity of creation, promising its ultimate renewal through Christ. In this sense, the resurrection is not merely an answer to death; it is the ultimate affirmation of God's creative purpose and the fulfillment of his redemptive plan for humanity.

TECHNOLOGICAL SALVATION?

Transhumanism proposes a radically alternative vision of salvation that contrasts sharply with the theological conceptions central to Christian soteriology. At its core, transhumanism seeks to transcend bodily limitations and mortality through technological innovations such as cognitive enhancements, genetic engineering, and the pursuit of biological immortality. This vision of "salvation" represents a modern, technocratic reimagining of ancient human aspirations, yet it distorts key theological tenets of Christian soteriology, particularly in the areas of redemption, grace, and transformation in Christ. By attempting to replace divine grace with human achievement, transhumanism undermines the foundational Christian belief that salvation is solely a gift from God. This section aims to critique transhumanism's approach to salvation, highlighting the theological inconsistencies and ethical dangers that arise when technology attempts to replace divine grace.

Transhumanism and Technological Salvation: Overcoming Bodily Limitations

Transhumanism offers a future where human limitations—aging, disease, and death—are seen not as inherent aspects of life but as problems to be solved through technological means. Figures like Ray Kurzweil envision a future where biological immortality is achieved by merging the human body with machines, allowing for consciousness to persist indefinitely.[37] His notion of overcoming death through technology offers a "salvation" in which human beings are not bound by the constraints of their biological makeup but are instead liberated by the mastery of nature through science. In this vision, the pursuit of salvation becomes a project of human effort and control, not an act of divine grace. However, this version of salvation misinterprets the nature of human existence and misses the theological depth of human limitation.

In the context of ANE thought, particularly in Mesopotamian and Egyptian cultures, human mortality was understood as an inescapable reality, even for kings and heroes. Myths such as the "Epic of Gilgamesh" demonstrate the deep awareness of human finitude, where immortality was the prerogative of the gods and not something to be grasped by human effort.[38] In contrast, transhumanism presents immortality as achievable through technology, reflecting a secular reinterpretation of these ancient longings for eternal life. The difference, however, is that ANE cultures, while lamenting death, accepted it as part of the divine order. Transhumanism, by contrast, sees death as an obstacle to be conquered, often neglecting the ethical and theological implications of such conquest. This technological reimagining of immortality turns salvation into a problem to be solved rather than a relationship to be restored through God's grace.

37. Kurzweil, *Singularity Is Near*, 137.
38. Walton, *Ancient Near Eastern Thought*, 87–89.

Christian Soteriology and the Nature of Redemption

Theologically, transhumanism presents a distorted view of salvation, particularly when compared to Christian soteriology. In Christian theology, salvation is a divine act rooted in grace, not human effort. As Paul teaches, "By grace you have been saved, through faith—it is the gift of God, not by works" (Eph 2:8–9). Redemption comes through the transformative work of Christ, who conquers sin and death, not by circumventing death but by entering into it and rising victorious through resurrection. This salvific act is not achieved by human innovation but through Christ's obedience and divine power. The apostle Paul's declaration in Rom 6:5–9 that believers are united with Christ in both his death and his resurrection establishes that true life—eternal life—comes through participation in Christ's death, not through the avoidance of mortality.[39] The Greek term *homoiōma* (ὁμοίωμα), meaning "likeness," emphasizes that believers are not merely saved *from* death but are saved *through* their participation in Christ's redemptive death, a theological concept fundamentally opposed to the transhumanist promise of biological immortality.[40]

Transhumanism's attempt to prolong life through enhancements, such as Neuralink's brain-computer interface or cryogenic preservation by companies like Alcor, is a form of self-salvation that echoes the ancient Pelagian and gnostic desire to escape the material world.[41] However, Paul's theology in 1 Cor 15:12–58 refutes any notion that salvation comes through separation from the body. Instead, the Christian hope lies in the transformation of the body, which is sown perishable but raised imperishable.[42] This Pauline eschatology reflects the biblical view that the body, while subject to decay and death, is part of God's good creation and will be redeemed, not discarded.

Grace and Transformation: The Theological Critique of Technological Immortality

Theologically, transhumanism replaces divine grace with human innovation. Christian soteriology teaches that salvation is a gift from God,

---

39. Wright, *Resurrection of the Son of God*, 279–82.

40. Witherington, *Paul's Narrative Thought World*, 119.

41. David Noble, *The Religion of Technology: The Divinity of Man and the Spirit of Invention* (New York: Knopf, 1997), 83–85.

42. Bauckham, *Jewish World Around the New Testament*, 225–27.

not a human achievement. The term *charisma* (χάρισμα), used by Paul to describe the gift of grace, underscores the idea that eternal life cannot be attained through effort, technology, or human ingenuity.[43] Paul consistently points to grace as the decisive element in salvation, teaching that the believer's hope is grounded in God's unmerited favor, not human effort (Rom 5:17). Salvation is the result of God's grace in Christ, not the result of human conquest over nature or the body. In contrast, transhumanism seeks to establish a form of "grace" through science, in which the human condition is improved, perfected, and ultimately made immortal by technological means.

Yet this technological form of salvation cannot address the deeper issues of sin, brokenness, and human relationality that are central to Christian soteriology. The doctrine of the *imago Dei* in Gen 1:26–27 affirms that human dignity is grounded in relationship—with God and with others.[44] Technological immortality, by separating consciousness from the body, distorts the image of God by undermining the relational and embodied aspects of human life. Transhumanist technologies, such as mind uploading, which aim to preserve individual consciousness apart from the body, inherently distort this relational understanding of the human person. In doing so, they echo gnostic tendencies to escape the material world, ignoring the importance of the body in God's redemptive plan. Salvation in Christian theology is communal and relational, as reflected in Paul's vision of the resurrection of the body, which emphasizes continuity between the present and the future creation rather than a disembodied escape.[45]

Furthermore, the Christian doctrine of resurrection speaks to the transformation of the whole person, body and soul, into a new creation. As N. T. Wright explains, Christian eschatology does not envision salvation as the preservation of disembodied souls but the transformation of the entire creation, including the body, into a state of incorruptibility and glory.[46] This transformation is not something that can be technologically engineered; it is a work of divine grace that goes beyond the limitations of human power. In contrast, transhumanism offers only a mechanical extension of life, which, while delaying death, cannot offer the true transformation that Christian theology envisions.

43. Wright, *Resurrection of the Son of God*, 375.
44. Kilner, *Dignity and Destiny*, 63.
45. Wright, *Resurrection of the Son of God*, 382–84.
46. Wright, *Resurrection of the Son of God*, 388.

As transhumanism promises a future of endless life through technology, it bypasses the deeper theological understanding of salvation, which is grounded in the relational, grace-filled act of God. This raises an important contrast that the next section will explore in greater depth: the limits of transhumanist salvation in light of the gospel's promise of resurrection and divine grace.

CONCLUSION: TRANSHUMANIST SALVATION VS. CHRISTIAN HOPE

Transhumanism offers a vision of salvation that is fundamentally at odds with the core principles of Christian theology. While transhumanism promises to overcome death through technological means, it overlooks the deeper spiritual and relational dimensions of salvation. By placing human control at the center of life and death, it distorts the Christian understanding of true salvation as a grace-filled act of God, not a human achievement. In Christian soteriology, eternal life is not something we engineer; it is a divine gift, realized through the bodily resurrection and the transformation of all creation. Paul's profound theology in 1 Cor 15 and Rom 6 shows that death is not the final word. Through Christ's death and resurrection, believers find the true hope of eternal life—not through the mastery of nature but through the unfathomable grace of God.

Where transhumanism seeks to transcend human limitations, Christian theology invites us to embrace these limitations as part of God's divine design. Humanity's worth is not tied to its ability to conquer mortality but to its intrinsic dignity as bearers of the *imago Dei*. Christian eschatology, rooted in the resurrection of the body and the renewal of creation, stands in direct contrast to the fragmented, techno-optimistic vision of salvation proposed by transhumanism—one that ultimately falls short of addressing the full reality of death.

For Christian leaders, theologians, and communities, engaging with the promises of transhumanism requires a response grounded in both theological critique and pastoral wisdom. Churches can offer a compelling alternative to the transhumanist vision by proclaiming the power of the resurrection, addressing humanity's deepest fears not with technological fixes but with the transformative hope found in the gospel. Rather than framing death as an enemy to be conquered by human innovation, Christians are called to witness to the ultimate victory of Christ's resurrection, pointing the world to a hope that rests not in human hands but in the redeeming power of God.

CASE STUDY #11: TRANSHUMANIST IMMORTALITY

In 2030, a leading transhumanist corporation, BioTranscend, announces its newest breakthrough: the EternalMind[47] program, which promises to upload human consciousness into digital systems, ensuring immortality. Initially, the program is marketed as a way to preserve the minds of terminally ill patients, offering them a chance to live on beyond their physical death. As the technology becomes more refined, it is made available to the broader public, especially appealing to the wealthy elite who seek not only life extension but permanent escape from the limitations of the human body.

Many who participate in the EternalMind program see it as a form of technological salvation, allowing their consciousness to live in virtual environments, free from physical ailments or death. However, Christian theologians and ethicists express deep concern over the theological and ethical implications of such a development. They argue that this quest for digital immortality mirrors ancient human attempts to grasp divine power, echoing the story of the Tower of Babel or Adam and Eve's desire for the fruit of the tree of life.

Theologians further assert that this technological vision of immortality distorts the Christian doctrine of bodily resurrection, which teaches that eternal life is a gift from God, granted through the resurrection of the body, not through human achievement. EternalMind, they argue, reflects an underlying transhumanist belief that humanity can conquer death through its own means, bypassing the need for divine grace. This raises significant theological questions: What is the nature of human identity? Can immortality truly be achieved apart from the body? Does this technology threaten to blur the boundaries between human and divine roles in salvation?

In response, BioTranscend defends its innovation, claiming that technological advancements such as EternalMind represent the next

---

47. BioTranscend is a fictional company and EternalMind is fictional technology created for illustrative purposes within this case study. Any resemblance to real companies, technologies, places, or individuals is purely coincidental. The case study is intended to explore ethical and theological questions related to transhumanist immortality and does not reference any actual existing entity.

phase in human evolution. They argue that by expanding human capacities and offering freedom from physical limitations, EternalMind fulfills humanity's mandate to exercise dominion over creation (Gen 1:28) and to "improve" the human condition. Supporters suggest that EternalMind is not merely about escaping death but about human flourishing—transcending the biological limitations that have restricted human potential throughout history.

As this debate unfolds, the tension between transhumanist aspirations and Christian eschatology deepens. Both sides wrestle with profound questions about human mortality, the meaning of eternal life, and the role of technology in shaping the future of humanity.

Case Study #11: Takeaway

The EternalMind case study highlights the profound theological and ethical tensions between transhumanist aspirations for digital immortality and the Christian doctrines of bodily resurrection and salvation by grace. Transhumanism's quest to overcome death through technological means, while offering an enticing vision of freedom from human limitations, ultimately misunderstands the nature of human existence and divine salvation. The Christian hope of resurrection is not about escaping the body or mastering death through human effort but is rooted in the grace-filled act of God transforming both body and soul through the resurrection of Christ. As Christian leaders and theologians engage with the promises of transhumanism, they must offer a clear articulation of how true eternal life is a divine gift, intimately tied to the resurrection of the body and the relational aspects of human identity that technology cannot replace.

Case Study #11: Discussion Questions

1. *Theological Reflection on Death and Resurrection:* How does the Christian doctrine of bodily resurrection, as articulated in 1 Cor 15 and Rom 6:5–9, challenge the transhumanist pursuit of digital immortality? Can human consciousness ever be fully preserved apart from the body in a way that aligns with Christian eschatology?

2. *The* Imago Dei *and Human Identity:* How does the concept of the *imago Dei*—the belief that humans are created in the image of

God—inform our understanding of human identity in the face of technological advancements like EternalMind? Does the attempt to separate consciousness from the body compromise this theological principle, and, if so, how?

3. *Salvation and Grace vs. Technological Achievement:* How does the Christian concept of salvation, rooted in divine grace and the resurrection of Christ, differ from the transhumanist vision of immortality through human innovation? Is there a place for technological advances in extending life within Christian theology, or do such efforts inherently conflict with the nature of Christian soteriology?

4. *Ethical Implications of Digital Immortality:* What ethical challenges arise from the possibility of uploading human consciousness into a digital system? Should there be limitations on who can access EternalMind, and how should society regulate the pursuit of technological immortality? How does the potential for a social divide between those who can afford immortality and those who cannot reflect broader questions of justice and equity?

5. *Mortality and Human Flourishing:* From a Christian theological standpoint, how does embracing human mortality contribute to a meaningful life? Does the transhumanist desire to overcome death diminish the importance of human finitude, suffering, and the relational aspects of life that are shaped by the limitations of the human body?

6. *The Tower of Babel and Transhumanism:* Theologically, does the transhumanist quest for immortality parallel the biblical story of the Tower of Babel, where humanity sought to reach the heavens through its own efforts, ultimately leading to divine judgment? How can this analogy help frame an ethical and theological critique of transhumanist ideals, particularly the desire for human control over life and death?

CASE STUDY #12: CYBERNETIC SUPER SOLDIERS

In 2032, the United States Department of Defense unveils the Sentinel Program, a pioneering defense initiative in partnership with NeuroTech Defense Systems.[48] This program aims to create an elite force of cyberneti-

---

48. NeuroTech Defense Systems is a fictional company and the Sentinel Program is fictional technology created for illustrative purposes within this case study. Any

cally enhanced soldiers through advanced brain-computer interfaces, genetic enhancements, and biomechanical augmentations. These super soldiers possess significantly enhanced physical strength, cognitive speed, and near-instantaneous access to battlefield data through neural implants connected to military command systems. The Sentinel Program claims that such enhancements will reduce the human error typically present in combat situations, decrease casualties, and provide unparalleled military superiority on the global stage.

From a strategic standpoint, the Sentinel Program seems like a breakthrough in defense technology. However, it sparks intense debate within ethical, religious, and philosophical circles. The technology transforms human soldiers into something far beyond their natural capabilities, raising concerns about human dignity, moral agency, and the nature of warfare. Christian ethicists voice particular concern, arguing that the Sentinel Program fundamentally challenges the *imago Dei* (the image of God), which upholds human beings as inherently valuable and relational beings, not merely instruments of war.

The primary ethical concern arises from the potential dehumanization of soldiers. By augmenting humans with technology, the military risks reducing these individuals to mere tools—perfecting their physical form but compromising their humanity. What happens to human dignity when soldiers are turned into weapons of war, optimized for efficiency rather than recognized for their relational and moral worth? The cybernetic implants and AI-driven enhancements that connect soldiers to military commands raise further concerns about the erosion of free will. If a soldier's thoughts, actions, and reflexes can be remotely monitored or influenced, what does this mean for their moral agency and accountability?

Theologically, the pursuit of superhuman soldiers mirrors historical attempts to transcend human limitations, such as the Tower of Babel or humanity's temptation to "become like gods" in Genesis. Some Christian leaders see the Sentinel Program as the latest manifestation of humanity's ongoing struggle with pride and autonomy, echoing the ancient Pelagian heresy, which claimed that humans could achieve salvation and perfection through their own effort, without divine grace. In creating soldiers who can seemingly surpass human limitations, the program reflects a

---

resemblance to real companies, technologies, places, or individuals is purely coincidental. The case study is intended to explore ethical and theological questions related to cybernetic super soldiers and does not reference any actual existing entity.

dangerous ambition to perfect and control human nature through technology, bypassing the need for dependence on God.

Moreover, the program threatens to introduce new forms of inequality within society. Augmented soldiers, equipped with superhuman abilities, may become a distinct class of individuals who, through their enhancements, wield immense power and authority. The program's focus on military elites could have ripple effects, challenging not only Christian ethics around equality but also the traditional concept of just war theory. If wars are fought using enhanced soldiers with unparalleled abilities, does this challenge the ethical norms of warfare, particularly around proportionality and the value of life?

The Sentinel Program exemplifies the theological and ethical crisis raised by transhumanism's drive to transcend human limitations, especially in the context of warfare. As militaries around the world consider the potential of cybernetic enhancements, questions surrounding human dignity, moral agency, and the proper use of technology in conflict continue to intensify.

Case Study #12: Takeaway

The Sentinel Program raises profound ethical and theological concerns regarding the military use of cybernetic enhancements. By augmenting human soldiers to superhuman levels, the program risks dehumanizing individuals, reducing them to tools of warfare, and undermining their moral agency through brain-computer interfaces. Theologically, the program mirrors humanity's ancient desire to transcend its limitations, reflecting a modern version of the Pelagian heresy, which sought self-salvation without divine grace. From a Christian perspective, human dignity is rooted in the *imago Dei*—inherent worth that cannot be enhanced or diminished through technological means. The Sentinel Program further challenges the Christian understanding of moral responsibility, free will, and just war ethics. As society advances toward the age of augmented humans, Christian leaders must grapple with these pressing questions, offering a theological critique that emphasizes human dignity, moral accountability, and the limitations of technological salvation.

Case Study #12: Discussion Questions

1. *Human Identity and the* Imago Dei: How does the enhancement of soldiers through cybernetic augmentation challenge the Christian understanding of human dignity and the *imago Dei*? Does transforming soldiers into superhuman entities compromise their inherent worth as image-bearers of God?

2. *Moral Agency and Free Will:* What ethical and theological concerns arise from the potential for augmented soldiers to be controlled through brain-computer interfaces? Does this technology compromise their moral agency, and how does this align with Christian views of free will?

3. *The Ethics of Warfare:* How does the creation of cybernetically enhanced soldiers affect the traditional Christian view of just war theory? Can the use of such technology be morally justified in warfare, or does it create new ethical dilemmas regarding the value of life and the ethics of violence?

4. *Transcending Human Limits:* Theologically, does the pursuit of superhuman capabilities in soldiers parallel humanity's ancient attempts at self-deification, such as in the Tower of Babel narrative? How can Christian theology critique the drive to transcend human limitations through technological augmentation in warfare?

5. *Social Justice and Inequality:* What are the ethical implications of creating an elite class of soldiers with capabilities far beyond those of the average human? How does this reflect broader concerns about inequality, justice, and the distribution of power in society? Does the creation of super soldiers threaten the common good?

CHAPTER 7

Salvation, Grace, and the Limits of Technology

THE PURSUIT OF SALVATION has always been at the heart of human existence, as people seek ways to transcend mortality, suffering, and imperfection. In our contemporary era, technological advancements, particularly within the fields of AI, biotechnology, and transhumanism, have introduced what seem to be new solutions to these age-old dilemmas. Proponents envision a future where humanity can overcome its biological and cognitive limitations, offering promises of immortality, enhanced intelligence, and physical perfection. Figures like Ray Kurzweil have popularized this vision, suggesting that the singularity—an event where machine intelligence surpasses human intelligence—will mark a new phase in human evolution, where death and suffering are mere technical problems to be solved by advanced technology.[1]

However, these promises of technological salvation come with profound ethical and theological implications. While AI and transhumanism promise an almost utopian future where human beings are free from the constraints of mortality, Christian theology offers a radically different vision of salvation. In contrast to the human quest for immortality through technology, Christian theology grounds salvation in divine grace, redemption, and resurrection. Instead of seeking to overcome death through human achievement, Christianity teaches that true salvation lies in God's redemptive work through Christ, as articulated in Pauline theology.[2] These promises of technological transcendence, as seen

---

1. Kurzweil, *Singularity Is Near*.
2. Wright, *Surprised by Hope*.

in transhumanist narratives, fail to address the deeper spiritual needs of humanity, particularly the issues of sin, moral failure, and the inherent brokenness of the human condition.

The central question at hand is not simply whether technology can improve human life but whether it can offer true salvation. While transhumanism envisions a future where humans might avoid death and suffering through technological advancements, Christian theology asserts that salvation lies beyond human achievement and is instead anchored in divine grace and the promise of redemption through Christ. This chapter will explore this tension, asking whether technology can offer more than a fleeting respite from mortality and whether it ultimately confronts or obscures humanity's deepest spiritual needs. Through this exploration, we will critique the assumption that human perfection can be engineered, contrasting it with the Christian understanding of grace and the limits of human power.

N. T. Wright, in *Surprised by Hope*, critiques the idea that humanity can engineer their own salvation, especially through technological means. For Wright, the Christian hope is not found in the avoidance of death or the prolongation of life through science, but in the promise of bodily resurrection and the renewal of creation.[3] This theological vision stands in stark contrast to the transhumanist notion of escaping mortality through digital immortality or genetic enhancement. In Christian eschatology, eternal life is a divine gift, received through faith and grace rather than something earned or created through human innovation. Paul's depiction of the resurrection body in 1 Cor 15 underscores that it is not the result of human achievement but the transformative work of God. The Christian hope is not an escape from the physical world but the transformation and redemption of it, including the human body.

This theological counternarrative becomes crucial in the face of the modern technological optimism promoted by figures like Kurzweil. His vision of the singularity, where humans can transcend biological limits by merging with AI, is rooted in a fundamentally different understanding of human nature.[4] Transhumanism views human limitations as obstacles to be overcome through cognitive enhancement and the fusion of human minds with machines. Kurzweil's framework treats death as a technical problem, solvable through progress, and human perfection as achievable

---

3. Wright, *Surprised by Hope*, 34–36.
4. Kurzweil, *Singularity Is Near*, 127.

through science. Yet this vision fails to engage with the moral, relational, and spiritual dimensions of the human experience, focusing narrowly on physical and intellectual enhancement.

Stanley Hauerwas, in *God, Medicine, and Suffering*, offers a sharp critique of this perspective, addressing the limitations of medical and technological solutions to human suffering. For Hauerwas, suffering and mortality cannot be adequately addressed through technology because such solutions fail to engage with deeper questions of meaning, morality, and the need for divine grace. Christian tradition teaches that suffering is not something to be avoided at all costs but can be a means of spiritual growth and transformation.[5] While transhumanism seeks to eliminate suffering through enhancement, the Christian narrative emphasizes that suffering and death are not the final word. Instead, they are part of the human condition, ultimately redeemed through Christ's resurrection. As Hauerwas notes, the desire to overcome suffering through technology often reflects a deeper unwillingness to confront the realities of human vulnerability and dependence on God.

In this chapter, we will explore these theological tensions in greater depth, demonstrating how the Christian doctrines of grace and redemption challenge the promises of technological salvation. While transhumanism offers an attractive vision of human perfection, it ultimately falls short of addressing the core issues of sin, mortality, and the need for divine intervention. Christian theology asserts that human beings, created in the image of God but marred by sin, cannot achieve salvation through their own efforts. Instead, salvation is a gift, granted through the redemptive work of Christ, who conquers sin and death on behalf of humanity. The grace of God, as revealed in the NT, offers a transformative hope that transcends the limits of human technology.

As we examine these contrasting visions throughout this chapter, we will explore case studies that demonstrate how the promises of AI and transhumanism reflect humanity's ancient desire to transcend death and suffering. However, these technological solutions, while offering temporary alleviation of physical limitations, cannot address the deeper, existential realities of the human condition. Christian theology, rooted in the doctrines of grace and redemption, provides a more robust response to questions of mortality and human limitation, pointing to the ultimate hope found in the resurrection and the renewal of all things. Through the

---

5. Stanley Hauerwas, *God, Medicine, and Suffering* (Grand Rapids: Eerdmans, 1990), 45.

lens of Christian grace, we will see that the true promise of salvation lies not in human technological mastery but in the grace of God that redeems and transforms all of creation.

DIVINE GRACE: A THEOLOGICAL FOUNDATION

This section delves into the profound theological concept of grace, examining its significance both linguistically and doctrinally. By focusing on the Greek term *charis* (χάρις) and the Aramaic *ḥenā* (חֲנָא), we will explore how these terms provide a foundation for understanding divine grace as articulated by Paul and other NT authors. Through an analysis of key biblical passages—such as Eph 2:8–9, Rom 3:23–24, and 2 Cor 12:9—this section will contrast grace with the prevalent merit-based systems in the first-century Mediterranean world.

The overarching aim is to illuminate how grace functions not merely as an abstract gift but as a transformative force that redefines the human relationship with God. In this sense, Paul's theology of grace challenges both ancient religious practices and modern ideologies that prioritize human achievement. This understanding of grace, as a divine initiative rather than human merit, forms the basis for a deeper critique of technological aspirations. Transhumanism's drive to overcome human limitations mirrors the ancient merit-based systems, but Paul's emphasis on grace reveals the inadequacy of human efforts—whether in first-century religion or twenty-first-century technology.

As this section unfolds, it will demonstrate how divine grace transcends human effort, offering a redemptive vision that technology alone cannot achieve, ultimately restoring the *imago Dei* through Christ's work. This exploration will unfold in several key parts. We begin with an analysis of the linguistic dimensions of grace, first in Greek and Aramaic, revealing how these ancient terms take on new theological depth in Paul's writings. Then, we will expand on biblical texts like Rom 9:16 and Eph 2:4–5 to emphasize the limits of human achievement versus divine grace. We will then examine how grace operates within key NT passages, emphasizing its unmerited and relational nature. Through this, we will critique technological mastery as a means of salvation, contrasting it with the Christian understanding of divine grace as relational, redemptive, and empowering.

The Meaning of Grace in Greek and Aramaic

The concept of grace (*charis*, in Greek, *ḥenā* in Aramaic) forms the foundation of Christian soteriology, emphasizing the unearned and divine nature of salvation. In this section, we will explore the linguistic and theological dimensions of grace, as expressed in key biblical passages, and compare these with Greco-Roman understandings of divine favor.[6]

Exegesis of *Charis* (χάρις) in Greek and *Ḥenā* (חֲנָא) in Aramaic

The Greek term *charis* (χάρις) and the Aramaic *ḥenā* (חֲנָא) both connote favor, kindness, and grace. However, in the NT, *charis* assumes a deeper theological significance that reshapes its classical usage. In Greco-Roman culture, *charis* often referred to reciprocal gifts, a kind of favor granted based on one's worth or societal standing. This notion contrasts with the Christian understanding of *charis*, which denotes unmerited favor from God, freely given without regard to human effort or achievement.[7]

In Aramaic, *ḥenā* similarly reflects divine favor, often associated with compassion and mercy, drawing from its use in the Hebrew Bible. Both terms are integral to understanding Paul's articulation of salvation through grace, especially as he reframes these concepts in a theological context that emphasizes God's initiative rather than human merit. In essence, the biblical concepts of grace, unlike technological attempts to "earn" or "create" salvation, cannot be replicated or manufactured.[8]

Grace in Ephesians 2:8–9: "By Grace You Have Been Saved"

In Eph 2:8–9, Paul encapsulates the Christian doctrine of salvation by grace with the phrase "For by grace you have been saved through faith" (τῇ γὰρ χάριτί ἐστε σεσῳσμένοι). This declaration is critical for understanding the nature of salvation in Christian theology as completely unearned and reliant on divine initiative. The term *charis* underscores the

---

6. Stanley E. Porter, *The Apostle Paul: His Life, Thought, and Letters* (Grand Rapids: Eerdmans, 2016), 319–20.

7. Markus Barth, *Ephesians: Introduction, Translation, and Commentary on Chapters 1–3*, Anchor Yale Bible 34 (New Haven: Yale University Press, 2008), 224–26.

8. Brown et al., *Acts–Revelation*, 368.

gratuitous nature of God's gift—human beings, who were dead in sin, are made alive not through any action of their own but by the favor of God.[9]

The grammatical structure of the phrase in verse 8—σεσῳσμένοι (*sesōsmenoi*), the perfect passive participle of σῴζω (*sōzō*)—indicates that salvation is an act completed by God in the past, with continuing effects into the present. The passive voice further emphasizes that human beings are not the actors in their salvation; rather, God is the one who saves, making this action complete and ongoing through his grace.[10]

Paul's emphasis here stands in direct opposition to the merit-based systems of Greco-Roman religious and philosophical practices, where divine favor was often thought to be earned through piety, sacrifice, or moral excellence. This rejection of merit-based salvation parallels today's critique of transhumanism's reliance on technological achievement as a pathway to perfection. Just as no moral or ritual act could earn salvation, no technological feat can bring about human transcendence. The *charis* (χάρις) in Eph 2:8–9 dismantles the idea of self-salvation—whether through ancient works or modern technological prowess.[11]

Grace and Justification in Romans 3:23–24: "Justified Freely by His Grace"

In Rom 3:23–24, Paul's argument reaches a climax when he writes: "For all have sinned and fall short of the glory of God, and are justified by his grace as a gift, through the redemption that is in Christ Jesus" (τῇ γὰρ χάριτι ἐστε σεσῳσμένοι, *dikaioumenoi dōrean tē autou chariti*). Here, *charis* (χάρις) is linked to the act of justification, the legal declaration of righteousness before God. Paul's use of *dikaioumenoi* (δικαιούμενοι)—the present passive participle of *dikaioō* (δικαιόω)—underscores the ongoing nature of this justification: it is an act performed by God, freely bestowed.[12] In contrast to the Greco-Roman view, where favor or righteousness might be secured through ethical conduct or the fulfillment of religious duties, Paul asserts that human beings are justified purely as an act of God's grace. This doctrine dismantles the idea that salvation can be earned or negotiated, placing all hope of righteousness solely in

---

9. Porter, *Apostle Paul*, 285–86.
10. Porter, *Apostle Paul*, 400–401.
11. Porter, *Apostle Paul*, 400.
12. Barth, *Ephesians*, 217–18.

the hands of God.¹³ This passage further illustrates how human effort, whether in first-century moral or religious contexts or through modern technological advancement, cannot justify humanity. Paul contrasts human insufficiency with divine sufficiency, a dichotomy that directly critiques transhumanism's confidence in human mastery.¹⁴

Grace Perfected in Weakness: 2 Corinthians 12:9

In 2 Cor 12:9, Paul reflects on a deeply personal experience, recounting his struggle with what he calls a "thorn in the flesh." In response to his plea for relief, Christ replies: "My grace is sufficient for you, for my power is made perfect in weakness" (ἡ χάρις μου ἀρκεῖ σοι, ἡ γὰρ δύναμις ἐν ἀσθενείᾳ τελεῖται, hē charis mou arkei soi, hē gar dynamis en astheneia teleitai). This passage further develops the theme of grace as the sustaining force in the life of the believer.¹⁵

The phrase ἡ χάρις μου ἀρκεῖ σοι (hē charis mou arkei soi)—"My grace is sufficient for you"—points to the sufficiency of God's grace in all circumstances, especially in human weakness. Paul's understanding of grace here moves beyond the initial moment of salvation to encompass the ongoing, daily experience of the believer. In this case, grace is not merely a past event or a theological concept; it is an active, empowering reality that sustains Paul in the midst of his trials.¹⁶

The term *astheneia* (ἀσθενείᾳ, weakness) becomes the very context in which God's *dynamis* (δύναμις, power) is manifested. Here, grace is not merely an abstract theological construct but is intricately tied to divine power, which is revealed not in human strength but in human vulnerability. This passage serves as a corrective to the Greco-Roman ethos of self-sufficiency and human achievement.¹⁷ Just as human limitations and suffering are spaces where divine grace operates, technological solutions, which aim to bypass or eliminate weakness, cannot grasp the transformative potential of God's grace. Paul's notion of grace perfected in weakness critiques the transhumanist drive to eliminate weakness through

---

13. Porter, *Apostle Paul*, 319.
14. Porter, *Apostle Paul*, 319–20.
15. Brown et al., *Acts–Revelation*, 368.
16. Barth, *Ephesians*, 225.
17. Barth, *Ephesians*, 224–25.

enhancement, revealing instead that it is precisely in weakness that divine grace becomes most effective.

Grace in the First-Century Mediterranean World: Contrasting Models of Salvation

To fully understand the radical nature of Paul's theology of grace, it is essential to place it within the broader context of the first-century Mediterranean world. The prevailing religious and philosophical systems often emphasized works-based salvation, where divine favor was contingent upon human action, moral virtue, or ritual observance.[18]

In Greco-Roman religion, divine favor was often tied to sacrifice, ritual, and reciprocity. Gods were believed to grant favor in exchange for piety and offerings. This transactional model of divine-human relations stood in stark contrast to Paul's proclamation of salvation by grace through faith, which rejected any notion of human merit. Paul's theology subverts this system by presenting a God who gives unmerited favor, a gift that cannot be earned, only received.[19]

Transhumanism presents an advanced version of this works-based system, where technological mastery is seen as a means of salvation. Paul's critique of first-century merit-based salvation, then, directly applies to the modern mindset of achieving human transcendence through scientific and technological advancement.

The Radical Nature of Divine Grace

Paul's use of *charis* and *ḥenā* represents a radical departure from the prevailing views of his day. In place of a transactional system of divine favor, Paul offers a vision of grace that is entirely unmerited and freely given. The passages examined—Eph 2:8–9, Rom 3:23–24, and 2 Cor 12:9—collectively articulate a theology of grace that denies any human ability to earn salvation. Instead, grace is the sole means by which salvation, justification, and strength are given, transforming the believer's relationship with God from one of striving to one of trust and dependence.[20]

---

18. Porter, *Apostle Paul*, 285.
19. Barth, *Ephesians*, 226.
20. Barth, *Ephesians*, 217–18.

Through this theology of grace, Paul calls his readers to recognize their own weakness and need, not as deficiencies to be overcome but as the very conditions in which God's grace can be made manifest. This message continues to challenge modern notions of self-sufficiency and technological salvation, pointing instead to a deeper, more enduring source of hope—God's unmerited favor, offered through Christ.[21]

Grace as Relational and Redemptive

In the NT, *charis* is not simply an abstract or transactional concept but deeply relational and redemptive, reflecting God's initiative in reconciling humanity to himself This relational dimension of grace contrasts sharply with the individualistic and impersonal promises of transhumanism. Grace involves relational reconciliation with God, something that no technological innovation can accomplish. In this section, we will explore how grace is portrayed in key biblical texts as God's redemptive work through Christ, contrasting this with the impersonal and mechanistic advancements of technological mastery, which seek only functional improvement without addressing the relational fracture between humanity and God.

The Initiative of Grace in Reconciliation

At the heart of Pauline theology is the portrayal of grace as God's initiating action in the reconciliation of humanity. This theology directly challenges the transhumanist view that humans can master their fate. Instead, Paul insists that grace is not about what humans can achieve but about what God has already accomplished.

John Barclay emphasizes this in his work *Paul and the Gift*, where he argues that *charis* in Paul's writings carries an element of incongruity—the grace is given without regard to the worth of its recipient.[22] This notion runs counter to the transactional models prevalent in the Greco-Roman world, where gifts and favors were exchanged based on merit or social status. In the Christian framework, God's grace is extended without condition, particularly through the redemptive work of Christ. This is evident in passages such as Rom 5:8: "But God shows his love for us

---

21. Porter, *Apostle Paul*, 320.
22. John M. G. Barclay, *Paul and the Gift* (Grand Rapids: Eerdmans, 2015), 567.

in that while we were still sinners, Christ died for us." Here, Paul underscores that grace is neither deserved nor earned; rather, it is given freely to those who are estranged from God.

In contrast to the mechanistic progress of technology, which often focuses on enhancing human capabilities, divine grace addresses the fundamental rupture in human relationality with God. Technological mastery can improve aspects of human life—extending lifespan, augmenting abilities, or solving specific problems—but it cannot heal the relational and spiritual alienation that sin creates. As C. F. D. Moule points out in *The Origin of Christology*, grace in early Christian theology was always seen as a restorative force, aimed at mending the broken relationship between God and humanity.[23] Grace is not about enhancing human capacity for autonomy or self-mastery, but about bringing humanity back into communion with its Creator.

The Contrast with Technological Mastery

The redemptive aspect of grace also sets it apart from the impersonal nature of technological solutions to human suffering. While technology might offer temporary relief from physical limitations or extend human life, it does not address the deeper spiritual and relational needs that define the human condition. This is evident in how Paul contrasts the works of the law—human attempts at self-righteousness and control—with the unmerited gift of grace (Gal 2:21; Rom 11:6). Where human systems, including technological advancements, strive to achieve perfection through mastery and control, grace acknowledges human weakness and dependency, offering relational restoration instead.

Paul's words in 2 Cor 5:18–19 reflect this relational restoration: "All this is from God, who through Christ reconciled us to himself and gave us the ministry of reconciliation." Grace, therefore, is fundamentally about restoring right relationships, both between God and humanity and within the human community. It is through grace that humanity is called back into its intended role as God's image-bearers, living in relationship with him and with others.

---

23. C. F. D. Moule, *The Origin of Christology* (Cambridge: Cambridge University Press, 1977), 105.

Grace as Relational Empowerment

Grace does not merely restore; it also empowers. This empowerment, however, is not about human mastery or technological control over nature. Instead, it empowers believers to live in accordance with God's will, depending on God's sufficiency rather than their own self-sufficiency. In transhumanism, empowerment comes from human enhancement, but in Christianity, empowerment comes through submission to God's grace.

While technological mastery aims to enhance human autonomy and power over the environment, grace empowers humanity to live in accordance with God's will. It redefines power in terms of dependence on God rather than independence from him. As Barclay notes, grace in Paul's theology transforms recipients into active participants in God's work of reconciliation.[24] This participation is not about achieving perfection through human effort but about being transformed by divine love and empowered by the Spirit to live in the fullness of God's purposes.

In this way, grace calls humanity into a relational dynamic where dependence on God becomes the source of true empowerment. This is vividly seen in 2 Cor 12:9, where Paul declares that God's power is made perfect in weakness: "My grace is sufficient for you, for my power is made perfect in weakness." Here, grace is portrayed as not only redemptive but also sustaining and empowering in the midst of human frailty.[25]

The relational and redemptive dimensions of grace present a profound theological counternarrative to the promises of technological salvation. While technological advancements seek to overcome human weakness through mastery and control, divine grace meets humanity in its weakness, offering reconciliation with God and empowering believers to live in relationship with him. This relational aspect of grace is what makes it fundamentally different from technological improvement—it does not seek to bypass human frailty but redeems and transforms it through the love of God.

Redemption through Christ

The resurrection of Christ is central to Christian soteriology and informs the understanding of redemption throughout the NT. This section will

---

24. Barclay, *Paul and the Gift*, 574.
25. Barth, *Ephesians*, 226.

explore the biblical and theological dimensions of redemption as it relates to Christ's atoning sacrifice and resurrection. We will investigate the Greek term *apolytrōsis* (ἀπολύτρωσις, redemption) as used in key NT texts, focusing on its implications for human salvation and freedom from sin. By examining texts such as Rom 3:24, Eph 1:7, and Col 1:14, we will uncover the richness of the redemptive narrative as it contrasts with contemporary ideals of self-perfection and technological transcendence, such as those found in transhumanist thought.

This section is divided into two parts. The first, "Redemption in the Greek New Testament," will involve a detailed exegesis of key passages that utilize *apolytrōsis*. These texts emphasize the cost of redemption and the necessity of divine intervention through Christ's sacrificial death. In contrast to transhumanism's vision of human-driven salvation, these passages underscore that redemption is beyond human capacity—it requires God's grace and Christ's intervention.

The second part, "The Role of Christ's Resurrection in Redemption," will focus on how Christ's resurrection brings about not just deliverance from sin but also restoration to new life in God's eternal plan. This part will highlight the eschatological implications of Christ's resurrection as a divine act that renews and restores all creation, a reality that technological advancement alone cannot achieve.

Redemption in the Greek New Testament

The concept of *apolytrōsis* (ἀπολύτρωσις), translated as "redemption" in the NT, reflects a rich theological understanding of salvation that is rooted in the sacrificial work of Christ. The term carries significant weight, as it encapsulates the idea of ransom, deliverance, and release from bondage—specifically, the bondage of sin and its consequences. This section will examine the use of *apolytrōsis* in three key passages: Rom 3:24, Eph 1:7, and Col 1:14, each of which stresses the redemptive work of Christ as freeing humanity from the enslavement of sin.

This exploration of *apolytrōsis* contrasts with modern transhumanist ideals, which often view human perfection as achievable through technological innovation. While transhumanism focuses on individual enhancement and the elimination of limitations, biblical redemption emphasizes that true freedom and restoration can only come through divine grace and not human effort.

Romans 3:24: Redemption as Deliverance

In Rom 3:24, Paul writes, "They are now justified by his grace as a gift, through the redemption [ἀπολύτρωσις, *apolytrōsis*] that is in Christ Jesus." This passage reveals the core of Paul's soteriological argument: that justification comes not through human effort but through divine grace and redemption. The term *apolytrōsis* here conveys the idea of a price paid to set captives free.[26] In the context of first-century Greco-Roman society, *apolytrōsis* often referred to the buying back of a slave's freedom, a concept that Paul reinterprets theologically as the redemption of humanity from the bondage of sin.

Paul's use of *apolytrōsis* emphasizes that salvation is both a gift and a costly act of grace. The idea of redemption as a ransom points to the sacrificial death of Christ, who offers his life in exchange for human liberation.[27] This act of deliverance not only absolves humanity from the penalty of sin but also restores them to a right relationship with God. As NT scholar John Barclay notes in *Paul and the Gift*, this aspect of grace—given without regard for human merit—upends conventional religious expectations of reciprocity and worth.[28] The contrast with transhumanist ideologies of self-perfection is stark: while transhumanism seeks to overcome human limitations through technology, Paul insists that humanity's deepest need is not technological advancement but divine redemption. Human efforts to achieve perfection, whether through gene editing or mind uploading, cannot replicate the radical transformation that grace offers through Christ.

Ephesians 1:7: Redemption Through Christ's Blood

In Eph 1:7, Paul further develops the theme of redemption, stating, "In him we have redemption [*apolytrōsis*] through his blood, the forgiveness of our trespasses, according to the riches of his grace." Here, the phrase "through his blood" (διὰ τοῦ αἵματος αὐτοῦ, *dia tou haimatos autou*) explicitly ties redemption to Christ's sacrificial death on the cross.[29] The

---

26. Brown et al., *Acts–Revelation*, 208.
27. Brown et al., *Acts–Revelation*, 208.
28. Barclay, *Paul and the Gift*, 231.
29. Barclay, *Paul and the Gift*, 399. Barclay discusses how redemption (*apolytrōsis*) in Eph 1:7 is explicitly tied to Christ's sacrificial death on the cross ("through his blood"). This connection underscores the theological significance of Christ's atoning sacrifice,

blood of Christ serves as the means by which the debt of sin is paid, fulfilling the requirement for atonement.

The mention of "blood" invokes the sacrificial system of the OT, particularly the Day of Atonement (Lev 16), where the shedding of blood was necessary for the forgiveness of sins.[30] In this context, *apolytrōsis* signifies not only the cancellation of sin's penalty but also the establishment of a new covenant relationship with God. As Richard Bauckham emphasizes in his exploration of NT theology, this relational aspect of redemption is essential—salvation through Christ is not merely a transactional or legal event but an invitation into restored relationship with God.[31] Redemption is not simply a legal transaction but a relational restoration between God and humanity, brought about by the self-giving love of Christ.

This emphasis on Christ's blood contrasts sharply with transhumanist aspirations, which often focus on enhancing human life through technological means. While transhumanism seeks to prolong life and potentially conquer death through human ingenuity, Paul's theology points to the necessity of Christ's death and resurrection for true redemption. Theologically, this challenges the idea that technological solutions—however advanced—can address the core human issues of sin and mortality. In the Christian worldview, it is not technology but the sacrificial love of God that redeems and transforms human life.

Colossians 1:14: Redemption as Freedom from Sin

Colossians 1:14 continues this theme of redemption, stating, "In whom we have redemption, the forgiveness of sins." The use of *apolytrōsis* here, as in Ephesians, emphasizes both deliverance and forgiveness. Paul's wording draws attention to the freedom that believers have already received through Christ's death, a freedom that is not future but present.[32]

---

highlighting that redemption is not just a general concept but one that is rooted in the sacrificial gift that Christ offered for humanity's sins. The gift of grace in Ephesians is thus framed by Christ's death, marking it as the means by which believers receive forgiveness and redemption.

30. Max Anders, *Galatians, Ephesians, Philippians and Colossians*, Holman New Testament Commentary 8 (Nashville: Broadman and Holman, 1999), 92–93.

31. Richard Bauckham, *Jesus and the God of Israel: God Crucified and Other Studies on the New Testament's Christology of Divine Identity* (Grand Rapids: Eerdmans, 2008), 182.

32. Wright, *Colossians and Philemon*, 67–75.

The phrase "forgiveness of sins" underscores the relational aspect of redemption. In Christ, believers are not only freed from the penalty of sin but are also reconciled to God. This redemption is a decisive act of divine grace, one that redefines the believer's identity and relationship with God.[33] Unlike transhumanist ideals, which focus on self-enhancement, Christian redemption is fundamentally communal and relational. As Bauckham argues in *Bible and Mission*, the biblical concept of salvation is not merely individualistic but includes the restoration of humanity's collective relationship with God.[34] Transhumanism's emphasis on individual enhancement through technology often neglects the communal nature of redemption.

The contrast between this biblical view of redemption and modern technological aspirations is again evident. While transhumanist visions often promise liberation from physical and mental limitations through artificial means, Paul's understanding of redemption emphasizes liberation from the deeper bondage of sin and death. In this sense, redemption is not merely about human flourishing in this life but about being restored to the fullness of life in God. Transhumanist promises of immortality through technology fail to address the deeper spiritual reality of sin, which requires divine redemption rather than human innovation.

Through the exegesis of *apolytrōsis* in these key NT passages, we see a consistent theme: redemption is a costly act of divine grace that frees humanity from the enslavement of sin. This redemption is achieved not through human effort or technological mastery but through the sacrificial death of Christ. In the Christian understanding, redemption is both relational and restorative, offering not just freedom from sin but reconciliation with God.

This stands in direct opposition to transhumanist ideals, which often place human achievement and technological advancement at the center of human flourishing. By focusing on self-perfection and individual enhancement, transhumanism misses the communal and relational aspects of salvation that are central to the Christian narrative. For Paul, the true path to freedom and fulfillment lies not in human innovation but in the redeeming work of Christ—a work that is grounded in divine grace and accomplished through the cross.

---

33. Wright, *Colossians and Philemon*, 67–75.

34. Richard Bauckham, *Bible and Mission: Christian Witness in a Postmodern World* (Grand Rapids: Baker Academic, 2003), 85–86.

The Role of Christ's Resurrection in Redemption

Paul's theology of redemption hinges on the resurrection of Christ, which serves as the foundation for humanity's future resurrection and ultimate redemption. In contrast to the transhumanist pursuit of immortality through technological means, Paul presents the resurrection not just as a return to life but as the transformative act that reconciles humanity with God, defeating death and restoring creation. In 1 Cor 15:20–22, Paul argues that Christ's resurrection marks the beginning of the eschatological redemption of all believers, a radical counterpoint to any reliance on human mastery over life and death.

This section focuses on the significance of Christ's resurrection as the "firstfruits" of those who have died, setting the stage for the redemption of all who are united with him. The theological implications of the resurrection, as explored in key texts such as Rom 5 and 1 Cor 15, reveal the relational and communal dimensions of grace, distinguishing it from any notion of individual enhancement or technological perfection.

Resurrection as Firstfruits: 1 Corinthians 15:20–22

Paul opens this passage by affirming the reality of Christ's resurrection: "But Christ has indeed been raised from the dead, the firstfruits of those who have fallen asleep" (1 Cor 15:20). The term *firstfruits* (ἀπαρχή, *aparche*) invokes imagery from Israel's agricultural practices, where the first portion of the harvest was consecrated to God (Lev 23:10). This offering was not only a sign of gratitude but also a pledge of the future harvest to come. In this context, Paul uses firstfruits to signify that Christ's resurrection is not an isolated event; it is a precursor and guarantee of the resurrection of all believers.

According to Thomas Schreiner, this concept points to Christ as the beginning of a larger redemptive plan, wherein his resurrection certifies the future resurrection of believers.[35] This metaphor signals that Christ's victory over death is not an event confined to the past; it is the initiation of a new eschatological reality in which death will be fully defeated for all who are "in Christ."

This understanding is deeply rooted in Paul's broader theology of creation and new creation. N. T. Wright argues that the resurrection

---

35. Thomas R. Schreiner, *1 Corinthians: An Introduction and Commentary*, Tyndale New Testament Commentaries 7 (London: InterVarsity, 2018), 311–12.

serves as a pivotal moment in God's plan to renew creation.[36] Just as Adam's sin brought death into the world, Christ's resurrection ushers in the possibility of new life, reversing the effects of sin and death. This perspective directly contrasts with transhumanist ideals, which often seek to circumvent death through human ingenuity rather than accepting the necessity of divine intervention.

The Theological Contrast: Adam and Christ

Paul further develops his argument by contrasting the roles of Adam and Christ in 1 Cor 15:21–22: "For since death came through a man, the resurrection of the dead comes also through a man. For as in Adam all die, so in Christ all will be made alive." Here, Paul identifies two key figures—Adam and Christ—as representatives of humanity's past and future. Adam, as the first man, brought death into the world through sin, while Christ, as the second Adam, brings life through his resurrection.

The comparison between Adam and Christ, also developed in Rom 5, highlights the cosmic implications of Christ's resurrection. Adam's disobedience led to the universal experience of death, while Christ's obedience and resurrection offer the possibility of eternal life. Leon Morris explains that Paul's use of Adam in this context underscores the corporate nature of both sin and salvation.[37] Just as all humanity is implicated in Adam's fall, so too can all who are "in Christ" share in his resurrection.

In contrast to the transhumanist vision, which seeks to achieve immortality through self-perfection and technological mastery, Paul's theology insists that true life can only be received through union with Christ. Richard Hays emphasizes that, for Paul, the resurrection is not simply an individual event but a relational and communal reality.[38] Those who are united with Christ through faith participate in his resurrection, sharing in the life that he has inaugurated.

---

36. Wright, *Resurrection of the Son of God*, 568.

37. Leon Morris, *1 Corinthians: An Introduction and Commentary*, Tyndale New Testament Commentaries 7 (Downers Grove, IL: InterVarsity, 1985), 205–6.

38. Richard B. Hays, *The Faith of Jesus Christ: The Narrative Substructure of Galatians 3:1–4:11*, 2nd ed. (Grand Rapids: Eerdmans, 2002), 45–49.

Resurrection vs. Technological Immortality: A Theological Critique

Paul's vision of resurrection as *anastasis* (ἀνάστασις), a physical and transformative event, stands in direct opposition to both Hellenistic and modern technological visions of immortality. In Hellenistic thought, immortality was often conceived as the liberation of the soul from the body, a dualistic understanding that devalued the material world.[39] In contrast, Paul affirms the goodness of creation and the body by insisting that resurrection involves the restoration and transformation of the physical self.

This theological emphasis poses a significant challenge to transhumanist ideologies, which seek to extend life through technological means such as mind uploading, genetic manipulation, or cybernetic enhancement. These efforts often rest on the assumption that human perfection can be achieved through mastery over the physical body and natural processes. However, Paul's theology of resurrection reminds us that true life—eternal and transformative—comes only through the grace of God, not through human achievement.

N. T. Wright argues that the resurrection is the decisive moment in God's plan to redeem creation, not through abandonment but through transformation.[40] This transformation is not something humans can achieve on their own; it is the result of God's gracious intervention in history through Christ's death and resurrection. The contrast with transhumanism is clear: while technology may offer temporary enhancements, it cannot provide the ultimate solution to death or restore the brokenness of creation. Only the resurrection can do that.

HUMAN LIMITATION AND DIVINE GRACE

This section examines the theological significance of human mortality in the Christian tradition, tying it into the larger discussion of how transhumanism seeks to transcend human limitations. In this context, mortality is not viewed as a defect to be corrected by technological means but rather as a boundary that defines humanity's relationship to God. By exploring biblical texts such as Gen 3:22–24 and 2 Cor 12:7–10, we will highlight how divine grace operates within the limits of human frailty,

---

39. Wright, *Resurrection of the Son of God*, 90–91.
40. Wright, *Resurrection of the Son of God*, 570.

contrasting this with the transhumanist desire for immortality and self-perfection. This exploration aligns with the book's broader thesis, which critiques the transhumanist vision of technological salvation and emphasizes the theological necessity of embracing human limitation as a part of God's redemptive plan. Through grace, human weakness becomes the very space where divine power is most fully revealed, offering a counter-narrative to the modern drive toward mastery over death and decay.

Mortality as a Theological Boundary

Human mortality, a fundamental aspect of Christian theology, is a boundary that cannot be transcended by human means. In contrast to the transhumanist ideal of using technology to overcome human limitation, Christian doctrine views mortality as an intrinsic feature of the created order, shaped by divine intention. Within this framework, death is not merely a biological reality but a theological one, woven into the fabric of what it means to be human in relation to God.

The account in Gen 3:22–24 provides the cornerstone for this understanding, where humanity, having fallen from grace through sin, is expelled from Eden. In this passage, God recognizes that humanity has "become like one of us, knowing good and evil" (Gen 3:22). The expulsion from the garden of Eden is not a punishment for curiosity but a merciful act to prevent eternal life in a state of corruption. By barring access to the tree of life, God ensures that mortality serves as a boundary between humanity's fallen state and the possibility of eternal life outside his redemptive plan.[41]

Dietrich Bonhoeffer, in *Ethics*, highlights how mortality is inseparable from the limits God has placed on human existence. For Bonhoeffer, the human attempt to transcend these limits represents a fundamental rebellion against God's will, mirroring Adam and Eve's original sin. This rebellion is not only futile but tragic, as it seeks to bypass the divine plan of redemption that can only be fully realized within the context of human limitation.[42]

---

41. Brown et al., *Acts–Revelation*, 208.
42. Bonhoeffer, *Ethics*, 67.

The Divine Imposition of Mortality: Genesis 3:22–24

The story of humanity's fall, as depicted in Gen 3:22–24, emphasizes the inextricable link between sin and mortality. Upon eating from the tree of knowledge of good and evil, Adam and Eve gain an experiential knowledge of evil, a knowledge previously unknown to them. God's decision to bar them from the tree of life is laden with theological significance, for, in this state of sin, eternal life would result in an eternity separated from divine grace. Stanley Hauerwas, in *Suffering Presence*, argues that this expulsion was an act of divine mercy, establishing mortality as a boundary within which humanity could seek redemption rather than perpetuate its rebellion against God.[43] Hauerwas sees this limitation not as punitive but as a space in which grace can work to bring about restoration.

In contrast to the Christian understanding of mortality as a boundary that facilitates divine grace, transhumanism seeks to eliminate death altogether, viewing it as an obstacle to human flourishing. Transhumanists propose that technological advancements could eventually eradicate the biological limitations that lead to death, offering a form of technological immortality. However, this perspective fails to recognize that mortality is not merely a biological constraint but a theological necessity—one that safeguards humanity from eternal estrangement from God.

Bonhoeffer addresses this tension, asserting that human attempts to transcend their divinely imposed limits invariably lead to destruction. For him, the transhumanist project of overcoming mortality mirrors the hubris of Babel—an effort to ascend to heaven through human ingenuity, thereby usurping God's sovereignty. In doing so, humanity seeks to remake itself in its own image rather than the image of God.[44]

Paul's Thorn and the Sufficiency of Grace: 2 Corinthians 12:7–10

The apostle Paul's reflections in 2 Cor 12:7–10 amplify this theme of human limitation. In his description of the "thorn in the flesh," Paul reveals how human weakness is not something to be overcome through strength or technology but through the sufficiency of divine grace. The phrase "My grace is sufficient for you, for my power is made perfect in

---

43. Stanley Hauerwas, *Suffering Presence: Theological Reflections on Medicine, the Mentally Handicapped, and the Church* (Notre Dame: University of Notre Dame Press, 1986), 87–88.

44. Bonhoeffer, *Ethics*, 75–76.

weakness" (2 Cor 12:9) underscores the paradox of divine power manifesting through human frailty. Paul's acceptance of this thorn reflects his recognition that human limitations are opportunities for God's grace to work most powerfully.[45]

The precise nature of Paul's thorn has been widely debated, ranging from physical ailment to spiritual torment.[46] Colin Kruse notes that the thorn, described as "a messenger of Satan," is something that continuously torments Paul. Rather than removing the thorn, God allows it to remain as a means of keeping Paul grounded in his dependence on divine grace.[47] Paul's acceptance of this weakness is a stark contrast to the transhumanist ideal of self-sufficiency, where human enhancement is pursued as a means of transcending physical and cognitive limitations.

Stanley Hauerwas offers a compelling critique of modern attempts to bypass suffering and weakness, arguing that such efforts are fundamentally at odds with the Christian understanding of grace. For Hauerwas, the acceptance of weakness is not a capitulation to despair but a recognition of the way God works in the world through human vulnerability. In this sense, Paul's thorn becomes a model for Christian discipleship, where weakness becomes a conduit for the transformative power of grace.[48]

N. T. Wright, in *The Resurrection of the Son of God*, further explores how Paul's theology of resurrection is intimately connected to this understanding of human limitation. Paul's confidence in the resurrection is not merely a hope for life after death but a declaration that God's power will ultimately defeat all forms of death and weakness. The resurrection is the final vindication of God's grace working through human frailty.[49] Wright argues that, for Paul, resurrection life is not the negation of the body's limitations but the transformation of those limitations into the fullness of life in Christ.

---

45. Richard L. Pratt Jr., *I and II Corinthians*, Holman New Testament Commentary 7 (Nashville: Broadman and Holman, 2000), 427–28.

46. Colin G. Kruse, *2 Corinthians: An Introduction and Commentary*, 2nd ed., Tyndale New Testament Commentaries 8 (Nottingham, England: InterVarsity, 2015), 264–67.

47. Kruse, *2 Corinthians*, 266.

48. Hauerwas, *Suffering Presence*, 93–94.

49. Wright, *Resurrection of the Son of God*, 220–21.

Divine Grace in the Face of Human Mortality

The contrast between divine grace and technological mastery is perhaps most apparent in the way grace functions relationally, whereas transhumanism views enhancement as a purely functional process. John Barclay, in *Paul and the Gift*, emphasizes that grace in Pauline theology is not a transaction or compensation for weakness but a gift that restores relationships between humanity and God.[50] Transhumanism, on the other hand, focuses on extending human life as a means of overcoming death, viewing it as a problem to be solved rather than a condition through which grace might flow.

Bonhoeffer's insight into human limitation and divine will is equally crucial here. In his view, the desire to transcend human limits through technology ultimately leads to alienation from God's will. The Christian embrace of mortality is, therefore, an acknowledgment of one's dependence on God—a reliance that transhumanism seeks to eradicate in favor of self-reliance and autonomy.

In sum, human mortality, rather than being a limitation to be transcended, serves as the necessary framework within which divine grace operates. Paul's thorn, the expulsion from Eden, and the theology of resurrection all point to the same truth: it is in human weakness that God's grace is most fully realized. Any attempt to transcend these limits through human ingenuity risks bypassing the very means by which God brings redemption.

THE LIMITS OF TECHNOLOGY: A THEOLOGICAL CRITIQUE

In examining the limitations of technology, particularly in the context of AI and transhumanism, it becomes clear that the promises these movements make—to eliminate human suffering, overcome mortality, and enhance human capabilities—fail to address humanity's deeper spiritual needs. Transhumanism, driven by a reliance on human innovation, offers what can only be considered superficial solutions to existential crises. While these movements promise transcendence, they are rooted in the same hubris seen in biblical narratives like the Tower of Babel, where humanity sought to rival God through technological overreach. In contrast,

---

50. Barclay, *Paul and the Gift*, 93–95.

Christian theology asserts that true redemption and reconciliation can only be achieved through the divine action of God in Christ, not through technological mastery. This section will analyze how AI and transhumanism, despite their lofty ambitions, remain fundamentally inadequate as responses to human suffering, and we will explore the theological critique of such ambitions by drawing explicit parallels with the Babel narrative and modern technological hubris.

Technological Solutions vs. Divine Redemption

The transhumanist quest to transcend human limitations is primarily aimed at offering technological solutions to human suffering and mortality. Whether through AI advancements, gene editing, or attempts at digital immortality, the movement aspires to a form of salvation rooted in human ingenuity.[51] However, these efforts ultimately fall short of addressing humanity's deeper spiritual and relational needs. Transhumanism focuses on the external—the enhancement of the body and mind—while neglecting the internal need for reconciliation with God and transformation through Christ.

In contrast, Christian theology emphasizes that redemption is a work of divine grace. Salvation cannot be engineered, nor can human beings redeem themselves through technological effort. As Bonhoeffer notes, human beings, in their sinfulness, cannot redeem themselves.[52] Transhumanism's desire for self-salvation stands in direct opposition to the Christian doctrine that only God can restore what has been broken by sin. Stanley Hauerwas similarly critiques the modern obsession with technological solutions as a reflection of humanity's desire to escape suffering rather than confront it in the light of Christ's suffering on the cross.[53] For Hauerwas, the very weakness and vulnerability that transhumanism seeks to eliminate are the avenues through which God's grace becomes most apparent. The apostle Paul's declaration that God's power is made perfect in weakness (2 Cor 12:9) underscores this theological principle.

This critique also challenges the hubris of technological determinism—the belief that technological progress will inevitably lead to human

---

51. Ellul, *Technological Society*, 51.
52. Dietrich Bonhoeffer, *The Cost of Discipleship* (New York: Macmillan, 1959), 53.
53. Hauerwas, *Suffering Presence*, 67.

betterment. Theologians like Jacques Ellul have argued that modern technology, while providing material benefits, often leads to a loss of freedom and a deeper entanglement in systems of control.[54] Transhumanism, with its promises of transcendence through technology, mirrors this dynamic, offering not liberation but further enslavement to the idea that human beings must constantly improve themselves. As Ellul suggests, the failure to acknowledge the limits of human power leads to spiritual impoverishment and a failure to recognize the true source of redemption in God.[55]

Ultimately, technological solutions can only ever address the symptoms of human suffering, not its root cause. Christian theology holds that suffering is a result of the fall, and that salvation—both in this life and in the next—comes not through human mastery over the material world but through the grace of God. Transhumanism's failure to recognize this truth renders its promises of salvation hollow, as it seeks to bypass the necessary reality of divine intervention and redemption.

Technology as Babel: Human Hubris in the Face of Divine Sovereignty

The story of the Tower of Babel (Gen 11:1–9) provides a powerful allegory for the transhumanist pursuit of technological transcendence. In the Babel narrative, humanity's desire to build a tower that reaches to the heavens represents an attempt to rival God, to achieve autonomy and self-sufficiency through human effort alone. Similarly, the transhumanist ambition to transcend the limitations of the human condition through technology echoes the same hubris—a desire to become like gods, independent of divine authority. Both Babel and transhumanism reveal a fundamental rejection of human dependence on God and an overreach that seeks to seize control over life and death.

While the Babel narrative has been explored in previous chapters of this book, its thematic relevance here cannot be overstated. The central sin of Babel was not merely technological ambition but the rejection of human limitation and dependence on God. The builders of Babel sought to create a name for themselves and to avoid being scattered across the earth, which mirrors transhumanism's desire to overcome mortality and suffering through human achievement. Yet, as the story illustrates, God's

---

54. Ellul, *Technological Society*, 35.
55. Ellul, *Technological Society*, 108.

sovereignty cannot be thwarted. In the same way that God scattered the nations at Babel, he will ultimately frustrate any human effort to achieve immortality apart from his redemptive plan. The scattering of the nations at Babel demonstrates the futility of human attempts to transcend the boundaries set by God.

Scholars such as Brent Waters have drawn parallels between Babel and modern technological culture, noting that both are driven by a desire for control and mastery over creation.[56] Waters critiques the transhumanist vision as one that seeks to eliminate all forms of dependence and vulnerability—whether physical, mental, or even spiritual. Yet, in doing so, transhumanism ironically undermines the very relationships and communal bonds that give life meaning. By attempting to "reach the heavens" through technological advancement, transhumanism risks repeating the mistake of Babel: seeking autonomy from God and refusing to acknowledge the limits of human power.

Moreover, the Babel narrative warns of the consequences of such hubris. Just as God intervened to disrupt the plans of the Babel builders, so too will any human attempt to achieve salvation apart from God's grace ultimately fail. Ellul's critique of modern technological culture echoes this biblical warning, as he argues that the unchecked pursuit of technological progress often leads to unintended consequences—spiritual alienation, environmental degradation, and social fragmentation.[57] Like Babel, the technological city we are building today may ultimately be a monument to our own limitations rather than to our triumphs.

The Christian response to this hubris is not to reject technology outright, but to recognize its limits and place it in the proper context of divine sovereignty. Technology can be a gift, but when it is used to replace God's role in human flourishing, it becomes idolatrous. As Bonhoeffer argues, true freedom is found not in the rejection of human limitation but in submission to God's will.[58] The theological critique of transhumanism, therefore, is not merely a rejection of its technological ambitions but a call to embrace the truth that human beings are created for relationship with God and that redemption is found in Christ alone.

---

56. Waters, *Christian Moral Theology*, 89.
57. Ellul, *Technological Society*, 129.
58. Bonhoeffer, *Ethics*, 202.

GRACE, REDEMPTION, AND RESURRECTION

In the face of transhumanism's promise of technological immortality and human self-perfection, Christianity offers a radically different vision of redemption and eternal life. The Christian eschatological hope is firmly grounded in the resurrection of Jesus Christ and the transformative power of divine grace, which serves as the ultimate foundation for human salvation. This section contrasts the finality of Christ's work with the transhumanist ambition to overcome human limitations through technology. In doing so, it emphasizes that Christian salvation is not dependent on human advancement but on the grace of God, manifest in Christ's resurrection and the future hope for believers.

The Finality of Christ's Work

The Christian doctrine of resurrection stands in direct contrast to the transhumanist quest for immortality. While transhumanism seeks to extend life indefinitely through artificial means, the Christian narrative asserts that immortality is a gift received through the resurrection of Christ. The texts of Phil 3:20–21 and Rom 8:23–24 present this theological truth with powerful clarity, pointing toward an eschatological transformation that is divinely initiated, not humanly engineered.

In Phil 3:20–21, Paul asserts, "Our citizenship is in heaven" (τὸ πολίτευμα ἡμῶν ἐν οὐρανοῖς), highlighting that the Christian's true allegiance and hope reside not in earthly efforts but in the coming of the Savior, Jesus Christ. The Greek term *politeuma* evokes the imagery of a colony, reminding the Philippians—residents of a Roman colony—that their ultimate identity lies with Christ in the heavenly kingdom.[59] This heavenly citizenship, however, does not detach believers from the present world; rather, it calls them to live in expectation of a future transformation. As Ralph P. Martin notes, the idea of citizenship here draws a sharp distinction between the earthly and the heavenly, framing the believer's

---

59. Ralph P. Martin, *Philippians: An Introduction and Commentary*, Tyndale New Testament Commentaries 11 (Downers Grove, IL: InterVarsity, 1987), 167. Martin emphasizes that Phil 3:21 presents a theological contrast between earthly existence and the heavenly transformation that believers anticipate at Christ's return. He notes that the "transformation" described in this verse is not merely a physical upgrade, as envisioned by transhumanists, but rather a complete recreation of the believer's body to be like Christ's glorious body. This theological distinction reinforces the idea of a new existence that transcends human limitations.

life as one of eager anticipation of Christ's return, when "He will transform the body of our humiliation that it may be conformed to the body of his glory, by the power that also enables him to make all things subject to himself" (Phil 3:21).⁶⁰ This transformation is not a mere upgrade or enhancement, as transhumanists envision through technology, but a complete re-creation, a new existence conformed to the risen Christ.

Paul's focus on transformation, rather than enhancement, critiques the transhumanist ambition to transcend human limitations through AI and biotechnology. The Christian hope rests not in human ingenuity but in the transformative power of Christ, who "will transform the body of our humiliation" (τὸ σῶμα τῆς ταπεινώσεως ἡμῶν) to be conformed to his own resurrection body (Phil 3:21).⁶¹ As David Brown observes, Paul's language stresses that our future glorification is rooted in the resurrection, where the body is not discarded but redeemed.⁶² This stands in stark contrast to Hellenistic notions of disembodied immortality and the transhumanist vision of abandoning the frailties of the human body in favor of technological enhancements. The Christian doctrine of resurrection affirms the goodness of the body and its ultimate redemption through divine action, underscoring that human efforts to bypass death through technological means are futile when compared to the promise of bodily transformation in Christ.

Romans 8:23–24 complements this vision, where Paul speaks of believers "groaning inwardly" as they await the redemption of their bodies. Here, the Greek term *apolytrosis* (ἀπολύτρωσις, redemption) indicates not merely a spiritual deliverance but the full eschatological renewal of the entire person, body and soul.⁶³ This redemption is not achieved through human mastery over the natural world or technological manipulation but is the result of God's sovereign grace. As John Barclay elucidates in *Paul and the Gift*, divine grace in Pauline theology is inherently relational and transformative, operating through God's initiative rather than human effort.⁶⁴ Thus, the Christian hope for resurrection challenges the technological utopias envisioned by transhumanism, affirming that salvation lies beyond the reach of human innovation and is grounded in the finality of Christ's work.

60. Martin, *Philippians*, 169.
61. Martin, *Philippians*, 169.
62. Brown et al., *Acts–Revelation*, 435–36.
63. Brown et al., *Acts–Revelation*, 242.
64. Barclay, *Paul and the Gift*, 185.

Grace as the Foundation for Eternal Life

While transhumanism seeks to achieve eternal life through technological mastery, Christianity teaches that eternal life is the gift of divine grace. The contrast between these two visions is profound: whereas transhumanism views human life as a problem to be solved through enhancement, the Christian faith sees life as a gift, sustained and redeemed by God's grace. This grace is not a tool for self-improvement but the foundation for the believer's participation in eternal life with God.

John Barclay, in his seminal work *Paul and the Gift*, emphasizes that grace in Pauline theology is a *gift* in its fullest sense—a gift that is unmerited and transformative.[65] Grace is not simply a divine favor bestowed upon those who earn it; rather, it is the very means by which God reconciles humanity to himself, offering redemption and eternal life through the death and resurrection of Christ. This stands in stark contrast to transhumanist ideals, which treat immortality as a commodity to be acquired through technological means. While transhumanism seeks to control and extend life, Christianity teaches that eternal life is a divine gift, freely given and received through faith.

In Rom 8:23–24, Paul speaks of the "firstfruits of the Spirit," signaling the partial experience of redemption that believers have in the present as they await the full realization of their hope. The tension between the "already" and the "not yet" of salvation is central to Paul's eschatology. Douglas Moo, in his commentary on Romans, highlights that the believer's present experience of the Spirit is a foretaste of the complete redemption that will come at the resurrection.[66] This redemption is not something that believers can bring about through their own efforts; it is the work of God, who redeems not only individuals but the entire creation.

The contrast between human striving and divine grace is further illustrated in Phil 3:20–21, where Paul emphasizes that it is Christ, not human effort, who will "subdue all things" and bring about the transformation of the believer's body. As Barclay notes, the Christian life is lived in anticipation of the final act of grace, when God will complete the work he began in Christ.[67] This future-oriented hope is fundamen-

---

65. Barclay, *Paul and the Gift*, 178.

66. Douglas J. Moo, *The Epistle to the Romans*, New International Commentary on the New Testament (Grand Rapids: Eerdmans, 1996), 517.

67. Barclay, *Paul and the Gift*, 182.

tally incompatible with the transhumanist vision of salvation through technological advancement, which seeks to place humanity in control of its own destiny.

In conclusion, the Christian response to transhumanism is rooted in the finality of Christ's work and the sufficiency of divine grace. While transhumanism offers a vision of immortality based on human innovation, Christianity affirms that true redemption and eternal life are the work of God, received through grace and secured by the resurrection of Christ. As believers await the full realization of their salvation, they are called to trust in the power of Christ, who alone can transform their lowly bodies and bring about the redemption of the world.

Technology's Place in a Theological Worldview

As we draw this discussion to a close, it is essential to affirm the central theological argument that, while technology can offer tools to improve human life, it cannot provide ultimate redemption. This distinction is critical because the promises of AI and transhumanism, though ambitious in their scope, ultimately fail to address the deeper existential needs of humanity. In contrast, the Christian worldview, grounded in grace and the resurrection of Christ, asserts that true redemption and eternal life are not within human power to achieve, but are gifts of divine grace.

Theologically, the role of technology is best understood as one of enhancement and utility rather than a means of salvation. N. T. Wright, in *Surprised by Hope*, makes the critical point that while technological advances can alleviate suffering and improve conditions in this present world, they do not and cannot transcend the limitations of death, sin, and the need for divine grace.[68] Wright argues that Christian hope is firmly anchored in the resurrection, where God will renew and transform creation, including humanity. This eschatological vision contrasts sharply with the secular aspirations of transhumanism, which seeks to bypass death through technological innovation. The Christian perspective does not dismiss the benefits of technology, but places them in their proper context—as tools to aid human flourishing in this life, while recognizing that they cannot offer ultimate deliverance.

Stanley Hauerwas, in *Suffering Presence*, also critiques the modern reliance on technology to overcome suffering, noting that such efforts

---

68. Wright, *Surprised by Hope*, 120.

often stem from a deeper reluctance to engage with the realities of human frailty and dependence on God.[69] For Hauerwas, suffering and limitation are not merely problems to be solved but are opportunities for God's grace to be most fully realized. He argues that in trying to eliminate suffering through technological means, humanity risks losing sight of the redemptive possibilities that lie within suffering itself. Christian theology underscores that suffering and mortality, while painful, are not final or ultimate; they serve as the avenues for God's grace to bring about true transformation and redemption.

One of the primary critiques of transhumanism within a theological worldview is that it promotes an understanding of salvation that is rooted in human achievement and control. Transhumanism offers a vision of the future where human beings can transcend their biological limitations, overcome death, and achieve a kind of technological immortality. Yet, as we have argued throughout this chapter, this vision is inherently limited because it fails to address the relational and moral dimensions of human existence. Salvation, from a Christian perspective, is not about avoiding death or enhancing life through artificial means; it is about reconciliation with God and the restoration of the *imago Dei*—the divine image within each person—through Christ's redemptive work.

The resurrection of Jesus Christ is the cornerstone of this redemptive vision. In Phil 3:20–21, Paul writes that "our citizenship is in heaven," signaling that Christian identity and hope are not rooted in earthly achievements but in the promise of transformation through Christ.[70] The word *politeuma* (πολίτευμα, citizenship) used by Paul serves as a reminder that Christians live in this world but are ultimately citizens of a heavenly kingdom. This citizenship does not imply an escape from the world but points to a future where God will transform "the body of our humiliation" to be like Christ's glorified body. This transformation cannot be replicated or achieved through technology; it is entirely a divine act of grace that supersedes human effort.

Similarly, Rom 8:23–24 speaks to the deep longing for redemption, not only of the body but of all creation. Paul's language of "groaning" reflects the human condition—subject to decay, weakness, and suffering—but also points to the hope of bodily resurrection and the redemption that comes through Christ.[71] The Christian response to mortality

69. Hauerwas, *Suffering Presence*, 75.
70. Martin, *Philippians*, 167.
71. Barclay, *Paul and the Gift*, 204.

is not to try and escape it through technological means but to trust in the promise that God will one day redeem both body and soul in a new creation. As Douglas Moo emphasizes, the Christian hope is not found in human progress but in God's future intervention to restore and renew all things.[72]

In light of these theological affirmations, we can see that while technology has an important role to play in improving human life, it is not a substitute for the grace of God. Technology may extend life, improve health, and even alleviate some forms of suffering, but it cannot address the deeper issues of sin, brokenness, and the need for redemption. Christian theology offers a more profound vision of salvation that is relational and transformative, grounded in the work of Christ and not in human effort. This understanding provides a necessary corrective to the transhumanist narrative, reminding us that human life is more than a biological or cognitive problem to be solved. Life is a gift to be lived in relationship with God, shaped by grace, and ultimately redeemed through the resurrection.

In conclusion, the place of technology in a theological worldview is one of limited but significant value. Christians are called to embrace technological advances as tools that contribute to human flourishing, while recognizing that these advances cannot offer ultimate hope or salvation. The promises of AI, biotechnology, and transhumanism, while compelling in their scope, are ultimately inadequate when viewed through the lens of Christian theology. True salvation comes not through human ingenuity but through the grace of God, revealed in the life, death, and resurrection of Jesus Christ. It is through this grace that humanity finds its true hope, its true identity, and its true future.

CONCLUSION: SALVATION BEYOND THE SINGULARITY

As explored throughout this chapter, the promises of technological salvation offered by transhumanism and AI—whether through life extension, cognitive enhancement, or the eradication of suffering—fall short of addressing the deeper existential needs of humanity. In contrast, the Christian worldview emphasizes that true salvation, rooted in divine grace, is beyond human mastery or technological innovation. Only through Christ's redemptive work, culminating in the resurrection, can humanity

---

72. Moo, *Epistle to the Romans*, 516.

experience the ultimate transformation and restoration that transcends the limits of mortality.

By highlighting the relational and communal aspects of grace, we see that salvation is not about individual enhancement or self-perfection. Instead, it is about reconciliation with God and the fulfillment of the *imago Dei*. As Christians, we are called to embrace technological advances as tools that can improve life, while always acknowledging that they cannot offer the eternal hope found only in the grace of God.

In this, the Christian response to transhumanism becomes clear: human efforts to control life and death cannot replace the finality of Christ's redemptive work. While technology has its place, true transformation—the kind that overcomes not just death but sin and spiritual alienation—lies solely in the hands of God. As the book's broader thesis argues, salvation is not within human control but is a divine gift, bringing humanity into a future where both body and soul are redeemed through the grace of Christ.

CASE STUDY #13: AI-AUGMENTED AFTERLIFE EXPERIENCES

In 2045, EterniLife, a tech start-up, releases its flagship product: the Afterlife Experience,[73] an AI-powered program that allows users to experience a simulated afterlife based on their personal desires, memories, and beliefs. Utilizing neural interfaces, memory mapping, and AI-generated virtual realities, the program creates an idealized version of the afterlife, where users can interact with deceased loved ones, experience eternal peace, or confront unresolved emotional issues. Marketed as a "spiritual preparation tool," the product is aimed at individuals grappling with existential fears of death, offering comfort and closure before they pass away.

At first, the Afterlife Experience is celebrated as a groundbreaking innovation for palliative care and psychological support. Many individuals find solace in being able to design their afterlife according to their personal worldview. However, religious and ethical leaders quickly raise concerns. Christian theologians argue that the program distorts the

---

73. EterniLife is a fictional company and Afterlife Experience is fictional technology created for illustrative purposes within this case study. Any resemblance to real companies, technologies, places, or individuals is purely coincidental. The case study is intended to explore ethical and theological questions related to AI-augmented afterlife experiences and does not reference any actual existing entity.

biblical understanding of life after death, reducing the sacred mystery of the afterlife to a consumer product manipulated by human control. The program risks supplanting divine sovereignty over life, death, and eternity with artificial experiences engineered to satisfy individual desires.

Further criticism arises from the ethical implications of manipulating people's perceptions of death and eternal life. While the technology may provide comfort, it also encourages users to place their trust in human-made simulations rather than the Christian hope in resurrection and eternal life through Christ. As the program gains popularity, Christian leaders must confront these questions: Is it possible for technology to simulate something as profound as eternity? And does EterniLife's Afterlife Experience foster a false sense of spiritual security?

Case Study #13: Takeaway

The Afterlife Experience highlights the growing tension between technological solutions for existential fears and the Christian understanding of life, death, and resurrection. By creating virtual simulations of the afterlife, EterniLife raises critical theological and ethical concerns about the proper role of technology in addressing humanity's deepest spiritual needs. This case study challenges Christian leaders to discern how to guide believers in the face of such technological advancements that promise comfort but may distort the Christian vision of eternity.

Case Study #13: Discussion Questions

1. *Eschatology and Eternal Life:* How does the introduction of EterniLife's Afterlife Experience challenge traditional Christian eschatology, particularly the doctrines of heaven, hell, and the resurrection? Does this simulation undermine the finality and divine sovereignty of God's judgment as described in Scripture? Can AI-driven versions of the afterlife coexist with the Christian promise of eternal life, or does it create a misleading alternative to the hope of bodily resurrection?

2. *Divine Sovereignty vs. Human Control:* To what extent does the commercialization of EterniLife's simulated afterlife compromise the theological understanding of God's control over life and death? In offering a human-engineered "afterlife," does this technology risk subverting divine authority by placing ultimate matters of existence, eternity, and

spiritual destiny into human hands? How does this relate to biblical warnings against idolatry and attempts to transcend God's role in the cosmic order?

3. *The Role of Technology in Addressing Mortality:* Can technology like the Afterlife Experience ethically address humanity's existential fears about death without distorting Christian hope? How does the use of AI simulations to "alleviate" fear of death impact the way individuals relate to God's promises of eternal life and salvation? Could the increasing reliance on such technology replace faith-based understandings of mortality and immortality with superficial, human-centered solutions?

4. *Heaven, Hell, and Simulated Realities:* How might EterniLife's portrayal of a simulated afterlife affect the theological understanding of heaven and hell? Can AI ever truly replicate the reality of these eschatological realms, as described in Scripture, or does it create a false equivalence that misleads people about the true nature of judgment, grace, and the final destiny of the soul? Could such simulations trivialize the significance of eternal separation from God or eternal communion with him?

5. *AI Simulations and the Christian Hope of Resurrection:* In what ways could AI-driven simulations of the afterlife distort or diminish the Christian hope of bodily resurrection, as promised in Phil 3:20–21 and Rom 8:23–24? Does the technological "immortality" offered by EterniLife create a pseudo-eschatological hope, shifting focus from divine promises to human innovation? How might this lead to a theological confusion between spiritual renewal through Christ and artificial prolongation of consciousness?

6. *Idolatry and the Control of Eternity:* Could AI simulations of the afterlife represent a modern form of idolatry, where humanity seeks to control and manipulate spiritual realities through technology? How does this echo the biblical themes of human pride and attempts to "become like God" (Gen 3:5)? What are the implications of entrusting ultimate questions of eternity to AI, and how can Christians guard against this form of idolatry in a technologically driven culture?

CASE STUDY #14: GLOBAL GOVERNANCE

By 2050, the TheoLogos Initiative[74]—a powerful, AI-driven global governance system—is introduced as a solution to the growing challenges of international conflict, inequality, and environmental collapse. Developed through a coalition of governments, major religious leaders, and tech corporations, TheoLogos functions by creating a universal ethical framework derived from a synthesis of the world's major religions, including Christianity, Islam, Hinduism, and Buddhism. This system is heralded as the future of global peace, offering impartial governance that transcends human divisions.

As part of its governance, TheoLogos introduces a new global economic system based on cybercurrency. All transactions are processed through a universal currency, secured by an AI-driven blockchain, which requires every global citizen to have a biometric implant—either in their hand or forehead—for secure and instant identification. This implant allows individuals to access the global economic system, enabling commerce and participation in society. Proponents argue that this system eliminates fraud, inequality, and the complexities of international trade, bringing about an era of economic fairness and global stability.

However, Christian theologians and ethicists express profound concern. Many point to the book of Revelation, particularly chapters 13 and 17, where the apostle John warns against a global system that requires the "mark of the beast" for economic participation. For them, the biometric implant symbolizes a disturbing convergence between technological control and spiritual compromise. They argue that TheoLogos is not only a practical solution but also a theological challenge—diluting the uniqueness of Christian salvation, denying divine sovereignty, and creating a human-made global utopia that echoes the Tower of Babel.

As TheoLogos gains traction, many Christians are forced to confront whether they can participate in a system that promises global peace and economic equality at the cost of religious distinctiveness and free moral agency. Can they trust AI-driven governance and a unified global religion to uphold their faith, or does TheoLogos represent an insidious

---

74. TheoLogos Initiative is fictional technology created for illustrative purposes within this case study. Any resemblance to real companies, technologies, places, or individuals is purely coincidental. The case study is intended to explore ethical and theological questions related to AI-driven global governance and does not reference any actual existing entity.

attempt to replace divine authority with a human-controlled global order?

Case Study #14: Takeaway

The TheoLogos Initiative presents a vision of global peace and harmony driven by AI-powered governance and a cyber-economic system, yet it raises significant theological questions regarding divine authority, religious distinctiveness, and human autonomy. The universal use of biometric implants and a unified currency challenges Christian teachings about eschatology, particularly the warnings in Revelation about end-time systems of control. Christian leaders must grapple with the ethical and theological implications of a global governance system that not only governs the world but also risks replacing divine sovereignty with technological and human authority.

Case Study #14: Discussion Questions

1. *Revelation, Eschatology, and the "Mark of the Beast"*: How does the TheoLogos system, with its requirement for biometric implants to participate in commerce, resonate with the warnings in Rev 13:16–18 about the "mark of the beast"? Does this cybercurrency system reflect the eschatological concerns raised by John, or is it simply a technological advancement? How should Christians interpret the relationship between global governance systems and biblical prophecy?

2. *Global Governance and Religious Unity*: What theological challenges arise from the blending of Christianity with other world religions in TheoLogos's ethical framework? Does this universal religion compromise the exclusivity of Christ as the only path to salvation (John 14:6)? How might Christian eschatology view the rise of such a global religion, and in what ways does it reflect the prophetic warnings of a one-world system in Revelation?

3. *Human Agency vs. AI Control in Moral Decisions*: TheoLogos's reliance on AI to govern morality and global ethics raises significant concerns about free will and moral agency. How does the enforcement of a universal ethical framework by AI conflict with the Christian understanding of human autonomy under God's sovereignty? Could

such a system be seen as an overreach of human authority, challenging divine law and moral freedom?

4. *Theological Implications of Cybercurrency and Control:* With the requirement for a biometric implant to participate in global commerce, how does TheoLogos's economic system challenge Christian notions of stewardship, free choice, and individual dignity? Does the system reflect the warnings in Revelation about the loss of economic freedom under an end-time global regime, or is it simply a way to ensure equality and prevent corruption in modern economies?

5. *Tower of Babel and Modern Technological Idolatry:* How does the TheoLogos system mirror the ambitions of the Tower of Babel (Gen 11:1–9), where humanity sought to establish unity and control apart from God? In what ways does the merging of religion, governance, and economic control through AI reflect the same idolatrous desire to create a human utopia, and what are the theological dangers of such technological ambitions?

6. *Christian Engagement with Global Governance:* Should Christians engage with global governance systems like TheoLogos if they promise peace, equality, and environmental sustainability? What theological risks are involved in placing trust in AI-powered systems for ethical decisions, and where should the line be drawn between participating in global efforts for justice and resisting systems that appear to usurp divine authority?

CHAPTER 8

The Future of Humanity

As we stand at the intersection of unprecedented technological advancements, the task of reclaiming the biblical vision of the *imago Dei* has never been more urgent. The rise of AI, transhumanism, and other transformative technologies challenges the very essence of what it means to be human, offering promises of enhancement, immortality, and even salvation through artificial means. Yet, amid these promises, Christian theology asserts a radically different view—that humanity's dignity and purpose are not found in technological transcendence but in our divine identity as bearers of God's image. This chapter aims to offer a practical framework for Christian leaders, scholars, and students to navigate the ethical and spiritual challenges posed by these advancements, grounded in the biblical narrative of the *imago Dei* and the redemptive work of Christ.

RECLAIMING THE *IMAGO DEI*

Throughout this book, we have explored the tension between technological ambition and theological reality. AI and transhumanism promise a future where human limitations—suffering, mortality, and even sin—are overcome through innovation. However, these aspirations often obscure deeper spiritual needs, reducing human identity to a mere set of functions and capacities. Christian theology, on the other hand, teaches that human beings are more than the sum of their cognitive abilities or physical potential. We are created in the image of God, endowed with relationality, moral agency, and the capacity for communion with the divine.

The *imago Dei* cannot be reduced to technological perfection or human enhancement. As Stanley Hauerwas reminds us in *Suffering Presence*, our true identity is not found in the avoidance of suffering or the pursuit of self-perfection but in our relationship with God and with one another. The biblical account of the *imago Dei* in Gen 1:26–27 emphasizes that humanity's uniqueness lies in our calling to reflect God's character, not in our ability to manipulate or transcend our natural limitations. This vision of humanity calls us to resist the allure of technological salvation and instead embrace the grace that redeems and transforms us.

As Christian leaders and scholars, the task before us is to reclaim this theological vision in the face of modern technological narratives that offer an alternative view of human identity. We must remind ourselves and those we serve that our worth is not found in our cognitive prowess or physical strength but in the divine image we bear. This reclamation of the *imago Dei* is not a rejection of technology but a call to critically engage with it in ways that honor both human dignity and divine purpose.

ETHICAL ENGAGEMENT WITH TECHNOLOGY

The question is not whether Christians should engage with AI and transhumanism but how we should do so in a manner that reflects our theological convictions. Here, we offer a practical roadmap for ethical engagement with technology, grounded in the biblical understanding of the *imago Dei* and the eschatological hope of the resurrection.

1. *Affirming Human Dignity*: As we engage with technologies that promise to enhance human capacities, we must begin by affirming that human dignity is intrinsic, not earned. Whether through AI-driven cognitive enhancements or genetic modifications, no technology can add to the inherent dignity that comes from being created in the image of God. Christian leaders must remind their communities that our value is not determined by our abilities but by our status as God's image-bearers. This affirmation should guide our ethical evaluation of emerging technologies, particularly those that risk commodifying human life or reducing it to a set of mechanical functions.

2. *Fostering Relationality*: The *imago Dei* is fundamentally relational, reflecting God's triune nature. As such, any engagement with technology must prioritize the relational dimensions of human life over the pursuit of autonomy or self-sufficiency. Transhumanism's focus

on individual enhancement risks isolating human beings from one another, as we prioritize personal gain over communal flourishing. Christian leaders must advocate for the responsible use of technology that fosters human relationships, strengthens communities, and enhances our capacity for empathy, love, and service.

3. *Embracing Human Limitation:* Rather than viewing human limitations as obstacles to be overcome, Christian theology teaches that these limitations are part of what it means to be human. Paul's reflections on the "thorn in the flesh" (2 Cor 12:7–10) and his declaration that God's power is made perfect in weakness remind us that our frailty is not something to be eradicated but embraced as an opportunity for God's grace to work in and through us. Technological advancements should be assessed through this lens, asking whether they contribute to or undermine our dependence on God and our communal relationships with others.

4. *Resisting Technological Idolatry:* As we have seen throughout this book, the danger of idolatry lies not only in worshiping false gods but in placing ultimate trust in human creations. The Tower of Babel (Gen 11:1–9) serves as a cautionary tale for our own time, warning against the hubris of believing that technology can provide salvation. Christian leaders must encourage a posture of humility in the face of technological progress, recognizing that while technology can enhance life, it cannot offer redemption. Salvation is the work of God alone, achieved through the death and resurrection of Christ. Christian leaders must encourage a posture of humility in the face of technological progress, recognizing that while technology can enhance life, it cannot offer redemption. Salvation is the work of God alone, achieved through the death and resurrection of Christ, which ultimately restores the *imago Dei* and fulfills the eschatological hope of resurrection.

REIMAGINING HUMAN FLOURISHING

At the heart of the Christian response to AI and transhumanism is a reimagining of what it means for humanity to flourish. For transhumanists, flourishing is often equated with self-optimization, where human life is perfected through technological means. However, Christian theology offers a broader and deeper vision of flourishing that encompasses not only individual achievement but also communal well-being, relational harmony, and spiritual transformation:

1. *Flourishing as Participation in God's Mission:* True human flourishing is not achieved through self-perfection but through participation in God's redemptive work in the world. As N. T. Wright argues in *Surprised by Hope*, the Christian vision of the future is not one where we escape the limitations of our bodies or transcend the material world but one where God redeems and renews all of creation, including the human body. This eschatological hope should shape our approach to technology, reminding us that human flourishing is ultimately about participating in God's mission of restoration and renewal.

2. *The Role of Technology in Human Flourishing*: While technology cannot provide salvation, it can play a role in enhancing human flourishing when used responsibly. Christian leaders must guide their communities in discerning how technology can be harnessed to serve the common good, particularly in areas like healthcare, education, and justice. AI and other technological innovations have the potential to alleviate suffering, improve quality of life, and promote equity—goals that align with the biblical vision of justice and compassion. However, this potential must always be balanced with the recognition that technology is a tool, not a savior.

3. *Hope in the Resurrection:* The Christian hope for the future is not found in technological immortality but in the promise of the resurrection. As Paul reminds us in Phil 3:20–21, our citizenship is in heaven, and we await the transformation of our bodies through the power of Christ. This hope is not an escape from the world but a declaration that God's redemptive plan includes the renewal of all things. As we navigate the ethical challenges posed by AI and transhumanism, we must hold fast to this hope, trusting that true human flourishing is found not in transcending our humanity but in being transformed by the grace of God.

CONCLUSION: A CALL TO ACTION

As we step boldly into a future shaped by the potentials of AI and transhumanism, Christian leaders, scholars, and students have the opportunity not only to engage ethically but to inspire a vision of human flourishing that transcends the limitations of both human frailty and technological ambition. By reclaiming the biblical vision of the *imago Dei*, we are invited to reimagine a world where technology serves as a tool for justice, compassion, and creativity, all while being grounded in the eternal hope found in Christ.

Rather than seeing technology as a force to be feared or blindly embraced, we can harness its power in ways that honor human dignity, nurture relationships, and advance the common good. This is not a rejection of progress but a call to engage with it through the lens of divine grace and relational love. Together, we can craft a future where human identity is not lost in the drive for enhancement but found and fulfilled in the Creator who calls us to reflect his image in every aspect of life.

Let us then be pioneers not of technological dominion but of a faithful presence in the world—a people who navigate innovation with wisdom, humility, and a heart for redemption. As we participate in this unfolding narrative, may we remain steadfast in our hope, knowing that the ultimate renewal of humanity and creation lies not in our own hands but in the hands of the One who has already begun his transformative work, promising that all things will be made new.

A Prayer for Readers

Heavenly Father,

We come before you with hearts full of gratitude and awe for the gift of your inspiration and wisdom. You, who created the heavens and the earth, have also created us in your image—fearfully and wonderfully made. We thank you for the privilege of reflecting your divine nature, for the breath of life that sustains us, and for the grace that shapes us.

As we stand on the cusp of a new era, where technology and human advancement present both promise and peril, we ask for your guiding hand to lead us. Help us to discern the path of righteousness amid the noise of innovation. Grant us the humility to know that we are not the architects of our salvation but the stewards of your creation, called to reflect your love, justice, and mercy in a world that so desperately needs it.

Lord, for every reader of this book, I ask that you open their hearts and minds to your truth. May your Holy Spirit speak to them in ways that are clear and profound, reminding them of their sacred identity as bearers of your image. May they be empowered to engage with the challenges and opportunities of this world not with fear but with hope and confidence in your eternal plan.

We thank you for the minds that you have given us to create, to imagine, and to innovate, but we surrender our works and our lives into your hands, trusting in your perfect will. Let every step we take in the realm of technology, every question we ponder, and every decision we make be done in the light of your grace and truth.

Father, may your love fill us, your wisdom guide us, and your peace surround us. We pray for the courage to stand firm in our faith, to be agents of reconciliation, and to reflect the glory of Christ in all that we do.

In the name of Jesus Christ, who is our Redeemer, our Savior, and our Eternal Hope, we pray.

Amen.

Bibliography

Ackerman, Susan. *Under Every Green Tree: Popular Religion in Sixth-Century Judah.* Atlanta: Scholars, 1992.

Adams, Robert M. *Finite and Infinite Goods: A Framework for Ethics.* New York: Oxford University Press, 1999.

Aeschylus. *Prometheus Bound.* Translated by David Grene. Chicago: University of Chicago Press, 1991.

Agar, Nicholas. "Enhancement, Mind-Uploading, and Personal Identity." In *The Ethics of Human Enhancement: Understanding the Debate*, edited by Steve Clarke et al., 184–97. Oxford: Oxford University Press, 2016.

Agrawal, Vishakha. "Demystifying the Chinese Social Credit System: A Case Study on AI-Powered Control Systems in China." *Proceedings of the AAAI Conference on Artificial Intelligence* 36:11 (June 2022) 13124–25. https://doi.org/10.1609/aaai.v36i11.21698.

Albright, William F. *From the Stone Age to Christianity: Monotheism and the Historical Process.* Baltimore: Johns Hopkins Press, 1940.

Anders, Max. *Galatians, Ephesians, Philippians and Colossians.* Holman New Testament Commentary 8. Nashville: Broadman and Holman, 1999.

Arendt, Hannah. *The Human Condition.* Chicago: University of Chicago Press, 1958.

Aristotle. *Nicomachean Ethics.* Translated by Terence Irwin. Indianapolis: Hackett, 1999.

Augustine. *The City of God.* Translated by Henry Bettenson. London: Penguin, 1972.

———. *The City of God.* Translated by Marcus Dods. New York: Random House, 1950.

———. *De Trinitate.* Translated by Edmund Hill. New York: New City, 1991.

———. *On Free Choice of the Will.* Translated by Anna Benjamin and L. H. Hackstaff. New York: Bobbs-Merrill, 1964.

———. *On the Trinity.* Translated by Stephen McKenna. Washington, DC: Catholic University of America, 1963.

Balthasar, Hans Urs von. *Theo-Drama: Theological Dramatic Theory.* Vol. 2, *The Dramatis Personae: Man in God.* Translated by Graham Harrison. San Francisco: Ignatius, 1990.

Barclay, John M. G. *Paul and the Gift.* Grand Rapids: Eerdmans, 2015.

Barth, Karl. *Church Dogmatics.* Vol. 3/1, *The Doctrine of Creation.* Edited by G. W. Bromiley and T. F. Torrance. Translated by J. W. Edwards et al. London: T&T Clark, 2010.

———. *Church Dogmatics*. Vol. 3/2, *The Doctrine of Creation*. Edited by G. W. Bromiley and T. F. Torrance. Translated by Harold Knight et al. Edinburgh: T&T Clark, 1960.

———. *Church Dogmatics*. Vol. 3/4, *The Doctrine of Creation*. Edited by G. W. Bromiley and T. F. Torrance. Translated by A. T. Mackay et al. Edinburgh: T&T Clark, 1961.

Barth, Markus. *Ephesians: Introduction, Translation, and Commentary on Chapters 1–3*. Anchor Yale Bible 34. New Haven: Yale University Press, 2008.

Başer, Turgut. "Artificial Intelligence and Social Credit System in China." Term project, Middle East Technical University, 2021. https://open.metu.edu.tr/bitstream/handle/11511/101891/Artificial%20Intelligence%20and%20Social%20Credit%20System%20in%20China%20-%20Turgut%20BASER%20-%202013605.pdf.

Bauckham, Richard. *Bible and Mission: Christian Witness in a Postmodern World*. Grand Rapids: Baker Academic, 2003.

———. *Jesus and the God of Israel: God Crucified and Other Studies on the New Testament's Christology of Divine Identity*. Grand Rapids: Eerdmans, 2008.

———. *The Jewish World Around the New Testament*. Grand Rapids: Baker Academic, 2010.

Baylis, Françoise. *Altered Inheritance: CRISPR and the Ethics of Human Genome Editing*. Cambridge, MA: Harvard University Press, 2019.

Beale, G. K. *We Become What We Worship: A Biblical Theology of Idolatry*. Downers Grove, IL: InterVarsity, 2008.

Benjamin, Ruha. *Race After Technology: Abolitionist Tools for the New Jim Code*. Cambridge: Polity, 2019.

Black, Jeremy A., and Anthony Green. *Gods, Demons, and Symbols of Ancient Mesopotamia: An Illustrated Dictionary*. Austin: University of Texas Press, 1992.

Boff, Leonardo. *Cry of the Earth, Cry of the Poor*. Translated by Philip Berryman. Maryknoll, NY: Orbis, 1997.

Bonhoeffer, Dietrich. *The Cost of Discipleship*. New York: Macmillan, 1959.

———. *Creation and Fall: A Theological Exposition of Genesis 1–3*. Minneapolis: Fortress, 1997.

———. *Ethics*. Translated by Neville Horton Smith. New York: Simon and Schuster, 1995.

———. *Life Together*. Translated by John W. Doberstein. New York: Harper and Row, 1954.

Bonner, Gerald. *St. Augustine of Hippo: Life and Controversies*. Norfolk, UK: Canterbury, 1986.

BostonDynamics. "Atlas and Beyond: The World's Most Dynamic Robots." BostonDynamics. https://bostondynamics.com/atlas.

Bostrom, Nick. *Superintelligence: Paths, Dangers, Strategies*. Oxford: Oxford University Press, 2014.

———. "Transhumanist Values." In *Ethical Issues for the Twenty-First Century*, edited by Frederick Adams, 3–14. Charlottesville, VA: Philosophy Documentation Center, 2005.

Bostrom, Nick, and Anders Sandberg. *Whole Brain Emulation: A Roadmap*. Oxford: Future of Humanity Institute, 2008. https://www.fhi.ox.ac.uk/Reports/2008-3.pdf.

Bottéro, Jean. *Religion in Ancient Mesopotamia*. Chicago: University of Chicago Press, 2001.

Brown, David, et al. *A Commentary, Critical, Experimental, and Practical, on the Old and New Testaments*. Vol. 6, *Acts–Revelation*. London: Collins, n.d.
Brown, William P. *Seeing the Psalms: A Theology of Metaphor*. Louisville: Westminster John Knox, 2002.
Brueggemann, Walter. *The Message of the Psalms*. Minneapolis: Augsburg Fortress, 1984.
———. *The Prophetic Imagination*. Philadelphia: Fortress, 1978.
———. *The Ten Commandments: A Humanist's Reflection*. Louisville: Westminster John Knox, 2012.
———. *Theology of the Old Testament: Testimony, Dispute, Advocacy*. Minneapolis: Fortress, 1997.
Byrne, Niall. "Human Brain Cells in a Dish Learn to Play Pong." Neuroscience News, Oct. 12, 2022. https://neurosciencenews.com/organoid-pong-21625.
Calvin, John. *Institutes of the Christian Religion*. Translated by Ford Lewis Battles. Philadelphia: Westminster, 1960.
———. *Institutes of the Christian Religion*. Translated by Henry Beveridge. Grand Rapids: Eerdmans, 2001.
Caplan, Arthur L. "No Time to Waste—The Ethical Challenges Created by CRISPR." *EMBO Reports* 17:10 (2016) 1401–6.
Cassuto, Umberto. *A Commentary on the Book of Exodus*. Jerusalem: Magnes, 1967.
Cellan-Jones, Rory. "Stephen Hawking Warns Artificial Intelligence Could End Mankind." BBC News, Dec. 2, 2014. https://www.bbc.com/news/technology-30290540.
Char, Danton S., et al. "Implementing Machine Learning in Health Care—Addressing Ethical Challenges." *New England Journal of Medicine* 378:11 (2018) 981–83. https://doi.org/10.1056/NEJMp1714229.
Chavalas, Mark W., ed. *The Ancient Near East: Historical Sources in Translation*. Malden, MA: Blackwell, 2006.
———. "Hittite Rituals and Religious Beliefs in Mursili's Plague Prayers." In *The Context of Scripture: Canonical Compositions from the Biblical World*, vol. 1, edited by William W. Hallo, 160–64. Leiden: Brill, 2003.
Chopra, Deepak. *The Future of God: A Practical Approach to Spirituality for Our Times*. New York: Harmony, 2014.
Clements, R. E. *Amos: A Commentary*. Philadelphia: Westminster, 1989.
Clifford, Richard J. *The Cosmic Mountain in Canaan and the Old Testament*. Cambridge, MA: Harvard University Press, 1972.
Coogan, Michael D. *The Old Testament: A Historical and Literary Introduction to the Hebrew Scriptures*. New York: Oxford University Press, 2017.
Cranfield, C. E. B. *Romans: A Shorter Commentary*. Grand Rapids: Eerdmans, 1985.
Crouch, Andy. *Culture Making: Recovering Our Creative Calling*. Downers Grove, IL: InterVarsity, 2008.
Dalley, Stephanie. *Myths from Mesopotamia: Creation, the Flood, Gilgamesh, and Others*. Oxford: Oxford University Press, 2000.
Davis, Ellen F. *Scripture, Culture, and Agriculture: An Agrarian Reading of the Bible*. Cambridge: Cambridge University Press, 2009.
Day, John. *Yahweh and the Gods and Goddesses of Canaan*. Sheffield: Sheffield Academic, 2000.

Diodorus, Siculus. *Library of History*. Vol. 12, *Fragments of Books 33–40*. Translated by Francis R. Walton. Loeb Classical Library 423. Cambridge, MA: Harvard University Press, 1967.

Doudna, Jennifer A., and Samuel H. Sternberg. *A Crack in Creation: Gene Editing and the Unthinkable Power to Control Evolution*. Boston: Houghton Mifflin Harcourt, 2017.

Dunn, James D. G. *The Theology of Paul the Apostle*. Grand Rapids: Eerdmans, 1998.

Ellul, Jacques. *The Technological Society*. Translated by John Wilkinson. New York: Vintage Books, 1964.

Epictetus. *The Discourses*. Translated by Robert Dobbin. London: Penguin, 2008.

Epicurus. "Letter to Menoeceus." In *The Essential Epicurus: Letters, Principal Doctrines, Vatican Sayings, and Fragments*, translated by Eugene O'Connor, 51–54. Buffalo, NY: Prometheus, 1993.

Fee, Gordon D. *The First Epistle to the Corinthians*. Grand Rapids: Eerdmans, 1987.

Fitzmyer, Joseph A. *Romans: A New Translation with Introduction and Commentary*. Anchor Yale Bible 33. New Haven: Yale University Press, 2008.

Fretheim, Terence E. *Exodus*. Louisville: Westminster John Knox, 1991.

Galton, Francis. "Vox Populi." *Nature* 75 (Mar. 1907) 450–51.

George, Andrew R. *The Epic of Gilgamesh*. London: Penguin, 2003.

Gibbs, Samuel. "Elon Musk: Artificial Intelligence Is Our Biggest Existential Threat." *Guardian*, Oct. 27, 2014. https://www.theguardian.com/technology/2014/oct/27/elon-musk-artificial-intelligence-ai-biggest-existential-threat.

Goldingay, John. *Old Testament Theology: Israel's Faith*. Downers Grove, IL: InterVarsity, 2006.

Gómez-González, Emilio, et al. "Artificial Intelligence in Medicine and Healthcare: A Review and Classification of Current and Near-Future Applications and Their Ethical and Social Impact." Preprint, last revised Feb. 6, 2020. https://arxiv.org/abs/2001.09778.

Gorman, Michael J. *Becoming the Gospel: Paul, Participation, and Mission*. Grand Rapids: Eerdmans, 2015.

Gregory, of Nyssa. *On the Making of Man*. Translated by Philip Schaff. Edinburgh: T&T Clark, 1888.

Grenz, Stanley J. *The Social God and the Relational Self: A Trinitarian Theology of the Imago Dei*. Matrix of Christian Theology. Louisville: Westminster John Knox, 2001.

Hamilton, Victor P. *The Book of Genesis: Chapters 1–17*. New International Commentary on the Old Testament. Grand Rapids: Eerdmans, 1990.

———. *Handbook on the Pentateuch*. 2nd ed. Grand Rapids: Baker Academic, 2005.

Hanson Robotics. "Humanizing AI." Hanson Robotics. https://www.hansonrobotics.com/humanizing-ai.

———. "Sophia." Hanson Robotics. https://www.hansonrobotics.com/sophia.

Hart, David Bentley. *The Beauty of the Infinite: The Aesthetics of Christian Truth*. Grand Rapids: Eerdmans, 2003.

Hauerwas, Stanley. *God, Medicine, and Suffering*. Grand Rapids: Eerdmans, 1990.

———. *The Peaceable Kingdom: A Primer in Christian Ethics*. Notre Dame: University of Notre Dame Press, 1983.

———. *Suffering Presence: Theological Reflections on Medicine, the Mentally Handicapped, and the Church*. Notre Dame: University of Notre Dame Press, 1986.

Hays, Richard B. *The Faith of Jesus Christ: The Narrative Substructure of Galatians 3:1–4:11*. 2nd ed. Grand Rapids: Eerdmans, 2002.

———. *The Moral Vision of the New Testament: Community, Cross, New Creation; A Contemporary Introduction to New Testament Ethics*. New York: HarperCollins, 1996.

Herzfeld, Noreen. *In Our Image: Artificial Intelligence and the Human Spirit*. Minneapolis: Fortress, 2002.

Hornung, Erik. *The Ancient Egyptian Books of the Afterlife*. Ithaca, NY: Cornell University Press, 1999.

Hunter, Ron. "The Ethics of AI: Navigating the Moral Maze of Artificial Intelligence." *D6 Family Ministry* (blog), 2024. https://d6family.com/the-ethics-of-ai-navigating-the-moral-maze-of-artificial-intelligence.

Irenaeus. *Against Heresies*. Translated by Alexander Roberts and William Rambaut. Edinburgh: T&T Clark, 1868.

Jackson, Joshua Conrad, and Kai Chi Yam. "The In-Credible Robot Priest and the Limits of Robot Workers." *Scientific American*, July 25, 2023. https://www.scientificamerican.com/article/the-in-credible-robot-priest-and-the-limits-of-robot-workers.

Jamieson, Robert, et al. *A Commentary, Critical, Experimental, and Practical, on the Old and New Testaments*. Vol. 1, *Genesis–Deuteronomy*. London: Collins, n.d.

Jonas, Hans. *The Imperative of Responsibility: In Search of an Ethics for the Technological Age*. Chicago: University of Chicago Press, 1984.

Jónsson, Gunnlaugur A. *The Image of God: Genesis 1:26–28 in a Century of Old Testament Research*. Translated by Lorraine Svedsen. Stockholm: Almqvist and Wiksell, 1988.

Kant, Immanuel. *Groundwork of the Metaphysics of Morals*. Translated by Mary Gregor. Cambridge: Cambridge University Press, 1998.

Keel, Othmar. *The Symbolism of the Biblical World: Ancient Near Eastern Iconography and the Book of Psalms*. Winona Lake, IN: Eisenbrauns, 1997.

Keel, Othmar, and Christoph Uehlinger. *Gods, Goddesses, and Images of God in Ancient Israel*. Minneapolis: Fortress, 1998.

Kelsey, David. *Eccentric Existence: A Theological Anthropology*. Louisville: Westminster John Knox, 2009.

Kilner, John F. *Dignity and Destiny: Humanity in the Image of God*. Grand Rapids: Eerdmans, 2015.

———. *Dignity and the* Imago Dei: *Theological Anthropology and Ethics*. London: Routledge, 2019.

Klotzko, Arlene Judith. *The Ethics of Cloning*. London: Routledge, 2004.

Kruse, Colin G. *2 Corinthians: An Introduction and Commentary*. 2nd ed. Tyndale New Testament Commentaries 8. Nottingham, England: InterVarsity, 2015.

Kurzweil, Ray. *The Singularity Is Near: When Humans Transcend Biology*. New York: Penguin, 2005.

Lange, Christian Lous. *Technology and Human Progress*. New York: Harper and Row, 1936.

Lanier, Jaron. *Ten Arguments for Deleting Your Social Media Accounts Right Now*. New York: Henry Holt, 2018.

———. *Who Owns the Future?* New York: Simon and Schuster, 2013.

———. *You Are Not a Gadget: A Manifesto*. New York: Knopf, 2010.

Leick, Gwendolyn. *The Babylonians: An Introduction*. London: Routledge, 2003.
Lewis, C. S. *The Abolition of Man*. New York: HarperOne, 2001.
Liao, S. Matthew. "Designing Humans: A Human Rights Approach." *Bioethics* 33:1 (2019) 98–104.
Lindsell, Harold. *The Battle for the Bible*. Grand Rapids: Zondervan, 1976.
Lints, Richard. *Identity and Idolatry: The Image of God and Its Inversion*. Downers Grove, IL: InterVarsity, 2015.
Locke, John. *An Essay Concerning Human Understanding*. Edited by Peter H. Nidditch. Oxford: Clarendon, 1979.
MacIntyre, Alasdair. *After Virtue: A Study in Moral Theory*. 3rd ed. Notre Dame: University of Notre Dame Press, 2007.
Martin, Ralph P. *Philippians: An Introduction and Commentary*. Tyndale New Testament Commentaries 11. Downers Grove, IL: InterVarsity, 1987.
Mathews, Kenneth A. *Genesis 1–11:26*. New American Commentary 1A. Nashville: Broadman and Holman, 1996.
Mays, James L. *Psalms*. Interpretation: A Bible Commentary for Teaching and Preaching. Louisville: Westminster John Knox, 1994.
McKinsey & Company. *Transforming Healthcare with AI*. McKinsey & Company, Mar. 2020. https://www.mckinsey.com/~/media/McKinsey/Industries/Healthcare%20Systems%20and%20Services/Our%20Insights/Transforming%20healthcare%20with%20AI/Transforming-healthcare-with-AI.ashx.
Michaelis, Johann David. *Commentaries on the Laws of Moses*. Vol. 1. Translated by Alexander Smith. London: Rivington, 1814.
Michaelis, Wilfried. "Idolatry in the Old Testament." In *Theological Dictionary of the Old Testament*, vol. 3, edited by G. Johannes Botterweck and Helmer Ringgren, 145–65. Grand Rapids: Eerdmans, 1978.
Moltmann, Jürgen. *The Ethics of Hope*. Translated by Margaret Kohl. Minneapolis: Fortress, 2012.
———. *The Spirit of Life: A Universal Affirmation*. Minneapolis: Fortress, 1992.
———. *Theology of Hope: On the Ground and the Implications of a Christian Eschatology*. Translated by James W. Leitch. Minneapolis: Fortress, 1993.
Moo, Douglas J. *The Epistle to the Romans*. New International Commentary on the New Testament. Grand Rapids: Eerdmans, 1996.
Morris, Leon. *1 Corinthians: An Introduction and Commentary*. Tyndale New Testament Commentaries 7. Downers Grove, IL: InterVarsity, 1985.
Moule, C. F. D. *The Origin of Christology*. Cambridge: Cambridge University Press, 1977.
Muller, Richard. *The Unaccommodated Calvin: Studies in the Foundation of a Theological Tradition*. Grand Rapids: Baker Academic, 2000.
Mullin, Emily. "China Has a Controversial Plan for Brain-Computer Interfaces." *Wired*, Apr. 30, 2024. https://www.wired.com/story/china-brain-computer-interfaces-neuralink-neucyber-neurotech.
Neuralink. "PRIME Study Progress Update." *Neuralink* (blog), Apr. 12, 2024. https://neuralink.com/blog/prime-study-progress-update.
Niebuhr, Reinhold. *The Children of Light and the Children of Darkness*. Chicago: University of Chicago Press, 1944.
———. *Moral Man and Immoral Society*. New York: Scribner's Sons, 1932.
———. *The Nature and Destiny of Man*. New York: Scribner's Sons, 1941.

Niskanen, Paul. "The Poetics of Adam." *Journal of Biblical Literature* 128:3 (2009) 417–36.

Noble, David. *The Religion of Technology: The Divinity of Man and the Spirit of Invention*. New York: Knopf, 1997.

O'Donovan, Oliver. *Resurrection and Moral Order: An Outline for Evangelical Ethics*. 2nd ed. Grand Rapids: Eerdmans, 1994.

Olson, Roger E. *Arminian Theology: Myths and Realities*. Downers Grove, IL: InterVarsity, 2006.

O'Neill, Kate. *Tech Humanist: How You Can Make Technology Better for Business and Better for Humans*. New York: Kogan Page, 2018.

Peterson, Jordan B. *12 Rules for Life: An Antidote to Chaos*. Toronto: Random House Canada, 2018.

———. "Biblical Series 2: Genesis 1—Chaos and Order." May 27, 2017. YouTube video. https://www.youtube.com/watch?v=hdrLQ7DpiWs.

Plato. *Phaedo*. Translated by David Gallop. Oxford: Oxford University Press, 1993.

———. *Phaedrus*. Translated by Robin Waterfield. Oxford: Oxford University Press, 2002.

———. *Republic*. Translated by G. M. A. Grube. Indianapolis: Hackett, 1992.

Plotinus. *The Enneads*. Translated by Stephen MacKenna. London: Penguin, 1991.

Porter, Stanley E. *The Apostle Paul: His Life, Thought, and Letters*. Grand Rapids: Eerdmans, 2016.

Pratt, Richard L., Jr. *I and II Corinthians*. Holman New Testament Commentary 7. Nashville: Broadman and Holman, 2000.

Rad, Gerhard von. *Genesis: A Commentary*. Translated by John H. Marks. Old Testament Library. London: SCM, 1972.

———. *Old Testament Theology*. Vol. 1. Translated by D. M. G. Stalker. London: Harper and Row, 1962.

Richardson, Rashida, et al. "Dirty Data, Bad Predictions: How Civil Rights Violations Impact Police Data, Predictive Policing Systems, and Justice." *New York University Law Review* 94:2 (2019) 192–98.

Rist, John M. *Plato and the Christian Thought*. Cambridge: Cambridge University Press, 1968.

Sailhamer, John H. *Genesis Unbound: A New Reading of the Early Chapters of Genesis*. Colorado Springs: Multnomah, 1996.

———. *The Pentateuch as Narrative: A Biblical-Theological Commentary*. Library of Biblical Interpretation. Grand Rapids: Zondervan, 1992.

Sarna, Nahum M. *Exploring Exodus: The Heritage of Biblical Israel*. New York: Schocken, 1986.

———. *Genesis: The Traditional Hebrew Text with New JPS Translation*. JPS Torah Commentary. Philadelphia: Jewish Publication Society of America, 1989.

Savulescu, Julian. "Procreative Beneficence: Why We Should Select the Best Children." *Bioethics* 15:5–6 (2011) 413–26.

Schreiner, Thomas R. *1 Corinthians: An Introduction and Commentary*. Tyndale New Testament Commentaries 7. London: InterVarsity, 2018.

Seneca. *Letters from a Stoic*. Translated by Robin Campbell. London: Penguin, 2004.

Stager, Lawrence E., and Samuel R. Wolff. "Child Sacrifice at Carthage—Religious Rite or Population Control?" *Biblical Archaeology Review* 10:1 (1984) 31–51.

Surowiecki, James. *The Wisdom of Crowds*. New York: Anchor, 2005.

Sutherland, Dawn Lewis. "God's Narrative of Redemption: Creation, *Imago Dei*, and Water Imagery." PhD diss., Liberty University, Apr. 2024. https://digitalcommons.liberty.edu/doctoral/5352.

Taylor, Charles. *Sources of the Self: The Making of the Modern Identity*. Cambridge, MA: Harvard University Press, 1989.

Thiselton, Anthony C. *The First Epistle to the Corinthians*. New International Greek Testament Commentary. Grand Rapids: Eerdmans, 2000.

Thomas Aquinas. *Summa Theologiae*. Translated by Fathers of the English Dominican Province. New York: Benziger Brothers, 1947.

Tillich, Paul. *The Courage to Be*. New Haven: Yale University Press, 1952.

Tipler, Frank J. *The Physics of Immortality: Modern Cosmology, God, and the Resurrection of the Dead*. New York: Doubleday, 1994.

Torrance, Andrew. "Artificial Intelligence and the Crisis of Human Agency." *Journal of Theological Ethics* 45:2 (2021) 156.

Torrell, Jean-Pierre. *Aquinas's Summa: Background, Structure, and Reception*. Washington, DC: Catholic University of America Press, 2005.

Turkle, Sherry. *Alone Together: Why We Expect More from Technology and Less from Each Other*. New York: Basic Books, 2011.

———. *The Second Self: Computers and the Human Spirit*. New York: Simon and Schuster, 1984.

Walsh, Catherine. "AI and the Temptation of Transhumanism." *Journal of Theological Ethics* 23:1 (2020) 33–45.

Waltke, Bruce K. *Genesis: A Commentary*. Grand Rapids: Zondervan, 2001.

Walton, John H. *Ancient Near Eastern Thought and the Old Testament: Introducing the Conceptual World of the Hebrew Bible*. Grand Rapids: Baker Academic, 2006.

———. *Genesis*. NIV Application Commentary. Grand Rapids: Zondervan, 2001.

———. *The Lost World of Genesis One: Ancient Cosmology and the Origins Debate*. Downers Grove, IL: InterVarsity, 2009.

———, ed. *Zondervan Illustrated Bible Backgrounds Commentary: Old Testament*. Vol. 1, *Genesis, Exodus, Leviticus, Numbers, Deuteronomy*. Grand Rapids: Zondervan, 2009.

Wang, Irene, and Rocky Swift. "Say Cheese: Japanese Scientists Make Robot Face 'Smile' with Living Skin." Reuters, July 18, 2024. https://www.reuters.com/science/say-cheese-japanese-scientists-make-robot-face-smile-with-living-skin-2024-07-18.

Waters, Brent. *Christian Moral Theology in the Emerging Technoculture*. 2nd ed. Farnham, Surrey, UK: Ashgate, 2014.

———. *From Human to Posthuman: Christian Theology and Technology in a Postmodern World*. Burlington, VT: Ashgate, 2006.

Wells, Samuel. *Improvisation: The Drama of Christian Ethics*. Grand Rapids: Brazos, 2004.

Wenham, Gordon J. *Genesis 1–15*. Word Biblical Commentary 1. Waco, TX: Word, 1987.

Westermann, Claus. *Genesis*. Darmstadt: Wissenschaftliche Buchgesellschaft, 2016.

Wilkinson, Richard H. *The Complete Gods and Goddesses of Ancient Egypt*. London: Thames and Hudson, 2003.

Wippel, John F. *The Metaphysical Thought of Thomas Aquinas*. Washington, DC: Catholic University of America Press, 2000.

Witherington, Ben, III. *Paul's Narrative Thought World*. Louisville: Westminster John Knox, 1994.

Wooldridge, Michael. *A Brief History of Artificial Intelligence*. New York: Flatiron, 2021.

Wright, Christopher J. H. *Old Testament Ethics for the People of God*. Downers Grove, IL: InterVarsity, 2004.

Wright, N. T. *Colossians and Philemon: An Introduction and Commentary*. Tyndale New Testament Commentaries 12. Downers Grove, IL: InterVarsity, 1986.

———. *Paul and the Faithfulness of God*. Minneapolis: Fortress, 2013.

———. *Paul for Everyone: Romans, Part 1; Chapters 1–8*. Louisville: Westminster John Knox, 2004.

———. *The Resurrection of the Son of God*. Minneapolis: Fortress, 2003.

———. *Surprised by Hope: Rethinking Heaven, the Resurrection, and the Mission of the Church*. New York: HarperOne, 2008.

Yang, Zeyi. "China Just Announced a New Social Credit Law: Here's What It Means." *MIT Technology Review*, Nov. 22, 2022. https://www.technologyreview.com/2022/11/22/1063605/china-announced-a-new-social-credit-law-what-does-it-mean.

Zuboff, Shoshana. *The Age of Surveillance Capitalism: The Fight for a Human Future at the New Frontier of Power*. New York: PublicAffairs, 2019.

www.ingramcontent.com/pod-product-compliance
Lightning Source LLC
Chambersburg PA
CBHW070245230426
43664CB00014B/2412